WINNIE
&
GEORGE

WINNIE

&

GEORGE

An Unlikely Union

Allison Murphy

MERCIER PRESS

IRISH PUBLISHER – IRISH STORY

For my husband, Rowland, who has followed his parents'
example and made the world a much finer place.

MERCIER PRESS
Cork
www.mercierpress.ie

© Allison Murphy, 2017

ISBN: 978 1 78117 470 8

10 9 8 7 6 5 4 3 2 1

A CIP record for this title is available from the British Library

Printed and bound in the EU.

CONTENTS

ACKNOWLEDGEMENTS

I am indebted to many people for their support, encouragement and assistance during all the years I have been researching and writing this book. So many have helped in small ways and I apologise in advance if any are omitted.

My thanks must go to the Public Record Office of Northern Ireland, the National Library of Ireland, the Somme Heritage Centre and the Belfast Central Library for allowing me to access the wealth of material their archives contain. In particular, I would like to thank Matthew Gamble of the Somme Heritage Centre, Gerry Kavanagh of the National Library of Ireland and Stephen McFarland of the Belfast Central Library for assistance far exceeding the remit of their positions.

I would like to thank Michael Lyons of Redhead Conference and Exhibitions, Sam Reilly, Una Reilly, Elaine Roddy, Vivienne Foster and Alex Robinson for their assistance and advice. My thanks must go to Julie McDonald and Irene Lowry for their encouragement, to Noel Brennan and James Elliott for instant technical support, and to Professor John Wilson Foster for his valuable critical comments and suggestions.

Ann Hope, past president and secretary of the Belfast and District Trades Union Council, has given me incredible support and information. I am also grateful to Ian Boyle, Billy Nelson and Philip Kelly for providing me with images from their personal collections and to Nigel Henderson of History Hub Ulster for the information from the Great War Ulster Newspaper Archive. His willingness to share his extensive knowledge has ensured accuracy in details relating to George McBride's war service.

I would also like to thank Mary Feehan of Mercier Press for her support and encouragement, and Noel O'Regan and Wendy Logue, outstanding and inspirational editors, whose every suggestion improved my work.

Finally, I must also thank my family, who have patiently given me the time and space in which to tell Winnie and George's story.

INTRODUCTION

On a significant birthday in June 1998, my in-laws, Rita and Roly Murphy, presented me with a handsome wooden Victorian writing box profusely inlaid with sparkling marquetry. I had admired it greatly on the only time I had ever been in their bedroom, where it was kept. On that occasion, my mother-in-law said that it had been a gift from her favourite old gentleman in the retirement home where she worked as a nurse. She told me that he treasured it because it had belonged to his late, beloved wife. I was moved by such a beautiful present and tried to protest, but Rita said that she knew I would value it as I had recently found the company of old people so rewarding.

She was referring to the fact that, a few years before, I had completed a dissertation for which I gathered the memories of more than a dozen people, one of whom was her own eldest sister, Ena McKenna. The dissertation was about the realities of growing up in the north of Ireland in the decade before partition. At the time of my birthday I was using these memories to write a book, published two years later, called *When Dublin was the Capital: Northern Life Remembered.*

I was struggling with the book because the memories of all those I had recorded were strangely out of line with many historical interpretations I had read of the period. It seemed that much of what I believed was based solely on the major events in history – in other words, it was history 'from above' – whereas my elderly informants were giving me history 'from below' in the day-to-day happenings of what constituted ordinary life. Moreover, the two sets of accounts could be contradictory and presented two different pictures of the same decade. From above, Belfast was a city utterly divided by sectarianism, politics and religion, yet my interviewees – male and female, Catholic and Protestant, rich and poor – recalled a society in which most people were educated, worked and spent their leisure time side by side, irrespective of religion. When I asked them about the divisions of the time one Catholic lady told me that there was only a bit of bother around the 'Twelfth of July' and one Protestant gentleman said that the only trouble was from 'them republicans, not ordinary Catholics'.

As the World Wide Web was in its infancy as a global information system, all I could do was spend weeks studying original documents to ascertain the veracity of the personal memories that my interviewees had shared with me. Nowadays, I can simply look up the census online to discover that in 1911 Protestants and Catholics lived physically cheek-by-jowl in the little streets surrounding the shipyard where *Titanic* was built, or examine Forces War Records to discover unionists and nationalists fighting on the same side and in the same regiments. In 1998 I had to rely on the veracity of the memories of men and women in their eighties and nineties. Almost twenty years later, after further research, I can only say that their memories were accurate.

When I opened the writing box that warm June evening, I found two pieces of paper inside. One was a brown envelope on which was written in shaky cursive script: *George McBride, 3 Whitewell Parade, Whitewell Road, Belfast.*

My mother-in-law explained that it was her favourite old gentleman's address. He had lived there for over fifty years and spent the happiest fifteen years of his life in that house with his wife. He had wanted my mother-in-law to have a record of where the box came from.

The second piece of paper was a cutting from an unidentifiable newspaper that had the headline, 'UVF pioneer and Somme veteran dies'. The opening paragraph stated: 'Somme veteran, George McBride, a member of the old UVF, who married James Connolly's secretary, has died in the UVF Hospital, Belfast, aged 92.' While I was struck by the incongruity of a UVF soldier marrying Connolly's secretary, my mother-in-law was horrified that her friend's age was incorrectly reported. 'He was only ninety!' was her response as I read aloud.

I should point out that my mother-in-law had no knowledge of history and, in fact, studiously avoided discussing anything related to the past. I was sure she had never heard of James Connolly and the fact that the article stated that George's wife had been Connolly's secretary would have been of no relevance to her. The obituary continued by describing Mr McBride's war record and his wife's role in the Easter Rising of 1916. It included the following paragraph: 'Speaking from Dublin, Mr McBride's niece, Mrs Mabel Farrell, said the marriage was a strange alliance for the time and although they argued politics incessantly, they loved each other very much.'

My mother-in-law asked me if, when I had the time, I would try to write about George's life. She wanted him to be remembered by more than an address on an old brown envelope. She knew only that he loved his wife very much, although he told her that many thought it was an unusual marriage. She was emphatic that the story should be told for the general public – people like her – to read.

I spent the next ten years gathering and researching everything I could about Winifred Carney and George McBride and their backgrounds, and amassed hundreds of pages of historical notes about the Ireland they inhabited and the historical events in which they were involved. I asked my mother-in-law to tell me everything she knew about George and what they had talked about. When she told me about his being interviewed for a journal, I was able to track down the article which had resulted. I discovered that his memories had been recorded by the Somme Association and I was able to obtain a transcription. With Winnie, I found small pieces written about her in many books and, thanks to Helga Woggon's excellent book, *Silent Radical: Winifred Carney, 1887–1943*, I was able to find letters that Winnie had written. James Connolly's letters to Winnie provided evidence of her intellect and the breadth of topics she was capable of discussing.

When I began to write the story of George and his beloved wife, Winnie, I was acutely aware of my mother-in-law's wish that it should be told for people like her to read and therefore must flow and not simply be a collection of facts. The book starts by setting the scene for their lives, describing their backgrounds and the Belfast in which they both lived, so that the scale of their decisions and the strength of their love can be understood.

This is a story in which all the people are real and all the major episodes happened. The events of World War I have been researched using war records and diaries and the Easter Rising and subsequent events have been reconstructed with reference to the Bureau of Military History witness statements. However, in the midst of actual occurrences, based on my research, it has been necessary to create some scenes and dialogue, partly in deference to my mother-in-law's request for readability. All historical dialogue has been referenced; the rest I have imagined. I hope my mother-in-law, and Winnie and George themselves, would have approved.

PROLOGUE

Wednesday, 16 March 1988

George McBride resided in the Ulster Volunteer Force retirement hospital in east Belfast. As a survivor of the 36th Ulster Division, which had distinguished itself at the Somme, Messines, Ypres and St Quentin, George had been happy to come and live among other old soldiers.

Every morning he shaved carefully with hands that shook more than he cared to admit. His favourite nurse, Rita Murphy, always ensured that he had a good supply of razor blades. After shaving, he dressed in a suit, slowly tying the knot on his tie. He had no time for morning or daytime television – days were for reading – but the evening news was a necessity. Therefore, after he had enjoyed his evening tea of scrambled eggs and toast, he walked slowly to the dayroom, sat down in his favourite chair and waited for the BBC news to begin. George prided himself on keeping up-to-date with world and local political news. Being ninety was no excuse for being ignorant.

Every evening Big Ben chimed across the room and George listened attentively. Then one evening the newsreader reported:

Three mourners were killed at Milltown Cemetery in Belfast today during an attack at the funerals of the Gibraltar bombers. The attacker, identified as loyalist Michael Stone, threw grenades and shot indiscriminately at mourners, killing three and injuring more than fifty. Security forces had stayed away from the funerals in an attempt to keep tension at a minimum. As the bodies were being lowered into the grave, Stone began shooting and throwing grenades at mourners. Holding the crowd back with an automatic pistol, Stone threw more grenades before running towards the nearby motorway. He was caught and beaten by the crowd before police arrived and intervened to save his life.

George froze as he watched the television images of a long-haired scruffy man running over graves in the cemetery. He clenched his fists and leapt up with the agility of a much younger man, shouting in response to the images on the television screen: 'You go near my Winnie and I swear I'll kill you! Loyalist! Loyalist! Scum like you don't know the meaning of the word. One footprint on her grave and I'll show you what a soldier is.'

Tears flowing down his cheeks, George slumped to his knees in front of the television set. Rita scurried to his side and eased him to his feet. Although past sixty years of age, she was tall and strong and bore his weight without difficulty. 'George, George, don't distress yourself so,' she said. 'It'll not be good for you. Come on, sit in your chair and tell me all about it. Nothing could be this bad.'

George gazed up at the kind, concerned face. His chest heaved as he tried to speak. 'Oh Rita, it is. He's running over the graves in Milltown cemetery where my beloved Winnie lies. And worst of all, he would have the ignorance to believe he's on the same side as me.'

I

BELFAST:
THE RISE TO SUCCESS

In 1912 almost 4,500,000 people lived in Ireland, which was then an integral part of the United Kingdom of Great Britain and Ireland. George V was king and Herbert H. Asquith, the leader of the Liberal Party, was prime minister, with Winston Churchill as his home secretary. The people of Ireland were represented in Westminster by the Irish Parliamentary Party, led by John Redmond, and the Irish Unionist Party, led by Edward Carson.

Fourteen-year-old George McBride's parents strongly supported the Irish Unionists because of the threat of Home Rule. The Home Rule question had dominated politics since 1885 and was the name given to the process of allowing Ireland more say in how it was governed. If passed, Home Rule would give power in Ireland to a government in Dublin. Irish nationalists were in favour of this, while Irish unionists were opposed. Although the first and second Irish Home Rule Bills had been defeated in Westminster, the general election of 1910 had seen the Liberals lose their majority. In order to stay in power they were dependent on the support of John Redmond's Irish Parliamentary Party. This meant that any Third Home Rule Bill was almost guaranteed to be successful.

Ireland was, in many respects, a modern country. Women were graduating from universities; trade unions were growing in strength in Belfast and Dublin; the Irish Women's Suffrage Federation had been running for a year, and Emmeline Pankhurst, the famous suffragette, had been to speak in the Ulster Hall in Belfast.

Belfast was the capital of Ulster, Ireland's northernmost province. By 1912 almost 400,000 people lived in this bustling city. The city was the third port in the United Kingdom in terms of custom revenue, and Belfast's workforce enjoyed the highest wages in Ireland.

The growth of the city had been phenomenal. By the late eighteenth century the seeds of industrialisation in the north-east of Ireland had been planted with the establishment of foundries, sugar refining, vitriol factories and linen manufacturing. As the century ended, there was an increase in imports and exports from England as a result of the Industrial Revolution. Belfast became a thriving trading city and its population grew from 8,500 in 1757 to 20,000 as the nineteenth century began.

The boom in cotton appears to have pushed Belfast into the factory age and made it accountable for a quarter of total Irish imports of cotton, wool and yarn. That figure was to double in the following twenty years. At this time mechanical spinning was invented and when Thomas Mulholland's cotton mill in Belfast was burnt down in 1828, he decided, either brilliantly or fortuitously, to rebuild his mill for spinning flax, the plant from which linen is made. A mechanised linen industry rapidly began to flourish, although weaving was still a handloom, cottage industry. Other mill-owners followed Mulholland's example and by the 1860s, when steam power was applied to the weaving of linen, there were thirty-two flax-spinning mills in Belfast and the surrounding area, and linen exports were higher than ever.

Such levels of exports required a large port. As a result, for the first quarter of the nineteenth century, the harbour in Belfast was continuously deepened, using the sand for ballast for outgoing vessels. By 1835 it had become the first port in Ireland in value of trade. As this trade continued to expand, the far-seeing Harbour Commissioners – formerly known as the Ballast Board – planned to dredge Belfast Lough and thereby create three artificial islands with the material excavated. Once the work was complete, the largest of these islands, Dargan's Island, was perfect for shipbuilding.

Shipbuilding had been known in Belfast since 1791, when William Ritchie had arrived from Saltcoats in Scotland to establish his wooden shipbuilding company. In 1853 the Harbour Commissioners financed the first iron-building shipyard on Dargan's Island, which had been renamed 'Queen's Island' following a visit from Queen Victoria in 1849. The man who benefited from the financing was a boilermaker called Robert Hickson. It is debatable whether shipbuilding would ever have become such a major success story in Belfast had it not been for Hickson's inspired choice for his general manager, Edward J. Harland, who had learned his trade in the engineering works on the rivers Tyne and Clyde. Harland's design skills and financial contacts, as well as the invaluable assistance of his personal assistant Gustav Wolff, saw Hickson's yard grow rapidly, from 120 employees on Harland's appointment in 1854 to 2,400 by 1870. Hickson sold the company to Harland for £5,000 in 1857 and in 1862 the shipbuilding company of Harland and Wolff was formed when Harland went into partnership with Wolff. Aided by the brilliant William Pirrie, they specialised in ocean-going liners and made their shipyard the largest in the world.

Two other shipbuilding firms were established in the 1860s in Belfast and one of them, Workman Clark, became one of the top six shipbuilding firms in the world. Although they never competed with the 'Big Yard', as Harland and Wolff's was known, they contributed to the creation of a wide variety of ancillary industries. These included marine engineering, ropeworks, heating and ventilation machinery, roadworks and armaments.

Shipbuilding and its associated industries required a large workforce and this led to a rapidly expanding population, which, in turn, required service industries and the products of food and drink companies. Success bred success and Belfast became the success story of Ireland – an industrial powerhouse with flourishing linen, shipbuilding and engineering trades. It had become the largest city in Ireland, with a port that gave employment directly and indirectly to tens of thousands of men and women.

There was a large working class, an expanded middle class and a wealthy new entrepreneurial upper class. Middle-class suburbs were built and a new electrified tramway system made outer areas of the city accessible. The new City Hall, completed in 1906, was built of Portland stone at the huge cost of £360,000. It was, like all the buildings of the time, a reflection of Belfast's success.

By the start of 1912 the city could boast of having the largest dry dock in the world – the Thompson Graving Dock, which was designed by William Redfern Kelly, the harbour engineer. The world's largest and most luxurious ships were being built in this dock. *Olympic* had already been launched and the final preparations to her sister ship, *Titanic*, were under way in Harland and Wolff.

It was in this great shipyard that George McBride's father worked and the boy never tired of hearing his father talk about the technological achievements that were present in the shipyard and allowed them to build the biggest ships in the world. His father told great tales about workers flooding into Belfast in search of work and high wages. He said they came from all parts of Ireland, England and Scotland, and the yard was awash with different accents – there were even some men who spoke only Irish.

Belfast had an abundance of manpower and craftsmanship, and what it lacked in raw materials it made up for with its incredible workforce. By 1912 the city was a world leader at the very forefront of technology. All this made Belfast prosperous, and it was filled with elegant buildings, hospitals, theatres, music halls, cinemas, international sporting events, restaurants, pubs and famous fish and chip shops. There were even many Italian ice-cream parlours with bright lights and gramophone music. A skilled worker earned £2 (40 shillings) a week, while a labourer earned 16–19 shillings. They were able to use this money to enjoy what free time they had after a hard week's work. Furthermore the fact that the electric trams had been introduced in 1905 meant that people could travel around the city at a low cost. Theatres and music halls were extremely popular and for 6d (2½p) people in Belfast could go to the Alhambra, the Alexandra Music Hall, the Empire Theatre of Varieties or the Theatre Royal.

The establishment of national schools in Ireland in 1831 had led to almost ninety per cent of the population becoming literate. The vast majority of the working-class population attended school, although in Belfast only part-time schooling was possible for those whose labour was sought in the linen mills. Academic institutions had been built all over Belfast to address the needs of wealthier Catholic and Protestant families. These included the Belfast

Royal Academy, founded in 1785; Royal Belfast Academical Institution, founded in 1810; St Malachy's College, founded in 1833; Belfast High School, founded in 1854; St Mary's Grammar School, founded in 1866; Methodist College, founded in 1868; and Campbell College, founded in 1890. Only one child in sixty passed from national to secondary school so, with few scholarships on offer, secondary school was the preserve of those who could afford it.

The education of girls from the upper classes was also included and in some instances catered for exclusively. In 1859 Margaret Morrow, the daughter of the flax mill owner Andrew Morrow of Windsor Hall, Rathfriland, opened her own school in Belfast after the death of her husband. The girls were taught current affairs and dancing, as well as subjects like French and needlework. It became Victoria College in the year 1887, when the fifty-year anniversary of Queen Victoria's reign was celebrated.

The Belfast College of Technology was built at the start of the twentieth century. This meant that education, if you were not wealthy, did not have to end with the leaving of school and many continued their education in evening classes. Secretarial colleges such as Hughes' Academy opened and flourished because young women, unlike their mothers, wanted careers.

All this made Belfast a regional industrial city much like those in the north of England, but it differed in that it was, at times, polarised by politics and religion. While Belfast prospered, sectarian tensions simmered below the surface and, at times, erupted into bloody conflict. Workers had flocked into the city during the prosperous times, changing the demographics and leading to Catholics becoming one-third of the population. At the same time, the political scene was changing, as unionism, once led by landed southern Irish unionists, came to be dominated by the industrial leaders and workers of the Ulster region. When it became clear that Home Rule may become a reality, such unionists directed their energies into keeping Ireland in the union with Great Britain and ensuring that power over the industrialised north remained with Westminster. In the same period, nationalism in Ireland was also becoming more uncompromising, and movements to strengthen cultural nationalism were growing.

In March 1912, on the eve of the introduction of the Third Home Rule Bill to parliament, the Protestant-dominated Belfast Corporation was emphasising the link between prosperity and the union with Great Britain. Religious and political apartheid were being encouraged by the development and divisive influence of the Orange Order and the growing nationalism of Irish politics. Despite economic vitality and industrial prowess, these ominous political developments led to an increasing anxiety pervading the streets of the city.

2

WINNIE AND GEORGE:
THE EARLY YEARS

Maria Winifred Carney was born twelve miles outside Belfast, in Bangor, County Down, on 4 December 1887. Known as 'Winnie', she was the youngest child of Alfred and Sarah Carney. The latter was a staunch supporter of John Redmond's nationalist Irish Parliamentary Party and hoped to see Home Rule and maybe more in Ireland one day.

As a young man Alfred Carney lived on the Old Lodge Road in north Belfast. His father, Robert, had been a tailor. On 25 February 1873, at the age of twenty-five, Alfred married Sarah Cassidy of 28 Denmark Street, located just around the corner from his home. She was twenty-two and the daughter of Patrick Cassidy, a commercial traveller. The ceremony took place in St Patrick's Church on Donegall Street, only the second Roman Catholic church built in Belfast since the Reformation. Rev. H. Magorian officiated and Patrick Henry and Maria McIldoon were witnesses. Both Alfred and Sarah's denominations are listed as Roman Catholic on the church marriage record.

Alfred and Sarah had seven children, six of whom survived. They were called Ernest, Louie, Alfred, Maud, Mabel and Winifred. At some point before Winnie's birth the family moved to Bangor, and Winnie was baptised on 13 December 1887 in St Patrick's Roman Catholic Church in Newtownards, a small town six miles away.

Alfred changed jobs often and his occupation, as a commercial traveller and occasional antique dealer, necessitated him travelling to England. In April 1881 he was a boarder in the Trevelyan Hotel, Godwin Street in Bradford, Yorkshire. Some time before 1891 the whole family moved to England and, according to the census, lived at 28 Fulham Road, London, where Alfred Senior worked as a commission agent. Alfred Junior was fourteen, Ernest was ten, Louie was eight, Maud was six, Mabel was five and Winnie was three.

In later life Winnie's three older brothers seem to have inherited their father's wandering nature. Ernest and Louie both emigrated to the United States and Alfred Junior embarked on a career as a ship's steward before settling down as a waiter in Belfast.

Sometime before 1901 Sarah and Alfred's marriage broke down and the family, without Alfred Senior, moved to 13 Perth Street in the Court Ward electoral district of west Belfast. It was a small terraced house that opened onto the street and had three front windows. There was a living room and kitchen downstairs and two bedrooms upstairs. The kitchen contained the house's only sink and the toilet was in the back yard. Perth Street contained 276 residents, all crowded into similar living conditions. There were ninety-six residents who described themselves as Presbyterian, eighty-two as Church of Ireland, twenty-nine as Methodists, twenty-five as Jews and five as Catholic.

The 1901 Census of Ireland records Winnie's mother, Sarah, aged fifty, as a housekeeper and head of the family. Living at home were her daughters Maud, aged seventeen, a shop assistant; Mabel, aged fifteen, a printer's assistant; and Winnie, aged thirteen, a scholar. Winnie was attending the Christian Brothers' school in Donegall Street in Belfast. This school was attached to the church in which her parents had been married. All the family could read and write.

Shortly afterwards the family moved to 1 Carlisle Circus, next door to where Sarah Carney ran a small sweet shop in which Maud worked as a shop assistant. The census of 1911 lists the occupants as Maud, aged twenty-seven, Mabel, aged twenty-five, and Winnie, aged twenty-three, all still unmarried and living with their mother. No occupations are listed for Mabel and Winnie, although the latter had worked as a junior teacher in her former school and also qualified as one of the first shorthand typists from Hughes' Academy. Alfred Junior's son, Jack Carney, aged eleven, is also listed as living in the house.

Records show that 1 Carlisle Circus was a private dwelling containing six rooms. The sweet shop was at 2 Carlisle Circus and Robert McKnight, a pharmaceutical chemist from County Cavan, had a shop at 3 Carlisle Circus. Only eleven people lived in Carlisle Circus; six were members of the Church of Ireland and five were Roman Catholic.

George McBride was born in Crimea Street, Belfast, on 10 February 1898. The second child of George and Marjory McBride, he was baptised on 23 March in St Stephen's Church in Millfield. His parents, both members of the Church of Ireland, had married on 22 June 1892 in Trinity Church in the Shankill parish of Belfast, but later joined Millfield as it was the first free church where parishioners did not have to pay to sit on pews. By 1901

George Senior and Marjory had moved to 10 Rusholme Street in the Shankill area of Belfast with their three children: Isabella, aged seven; George, aged three, and Marjory, aged two. George McBride Senior served his time as a fitter in a company called Combe Barbour, which made large machinery, and then gained employment as an engine fitter in the shipyard of Harland and Wolff. Both he and his wife were able to read and write.

Rusholme Street consisted of small four-roomed terraced houses with only one sink each and toilets in the back yards. The majority of people who lived on the street were of the Presbyterian or Church of Ireland denominations and, according to the census of 1901, no Catholics lived in the street.

By 1911 George Senior and his wife, who now was known as Madge, had moved to Glenwood Street in the Woodvale area of west Belfast. Madge had given birth to nine children, six of whom survived. They are listed in the 1911 census as: Bella, a flax spinner, aged seventeen; George, aged thirteen; Madge, aged eleven; Agnes, aged nine; John, aged six; and Mary, aged one. All the children except John and Mary could read and write.

Glenwood Street was filled with small, terraced houses, many of which contained large families. There were 715 residents living in the one street and almost all were Protestant: 296 were Church of Ireland like George's family, 294 were Presbyterian and ninety-four were Methodist. Many of the men and women in the street worked in the shipyards, mills and other manufacturing industries that abounded in Belfast.

Like most of their neighbours, the McBrides were vehemently opposed to Home Rule in Ireland and were supporters of Edward Carson's fight to defeat it. They believed that it would weaken the union with Great Britain and were told that it would lead to the Church of Rome having more influence over Irish politics. George McBride Senior was also a prominent supporter of trade unions, which were growing in strength, advocating reforms to minimum wages and working conditions in industrialised cities.

Young George attended two local primary schools, Argyle Street National School and St Saviour's. He completed his education by the age of twelve and found a job as a message boy with a local newspaper, the *Belfast Telegraph*. He found the work boring and unchallenging, however, so his father arranged for him to begin an apprenticeship as a fitter in James Mackie & Sons, one of the leading manufacturers of textile machinery in the world. He would remain in Mackie's for many years.

3

2 April 1912

By ten o'clock on the morning of 2 April 1912 thousands of people had lined the shores of Belfast Lough to see the world's largest ship, the new Royal Mail triple-screw steamer named *Titanic*, leave the deepwater wharf in the shipyard of Harland and Wolff. Some had walked for hours, while others travelled by tramcar to gain a good vantage point on both sides of the lough. The *Titanic* was due to cross the Irish Sea to Southampton ahead of its maiden voyage to New York.

The usual scenes of bustle and animation that attended the departure of a great liner were witnessed from an early hour. Excitement rose until the moment when the thick cable ropes, known as hawsers, were cast off and the huge vessel, the world's greatest man-made moving object, floated proudly on the water.

At Greencastle, on the northern shore of the lough, a young George McBride waited with his father for what seemed like hours until the sirens sounded and the great *Titanic* headed up Belfast Lough towards them. At fourteen, in his first pair of long trousers, George tried to contain his excitement – he was almost a man, after all – while, around him, thousands of others jostled for a better view and children jumped up and down with undisguised glee. The ship looked nearly as big as the lough itself as he strained his eyes to see the names on what looked like a dozen tugboats that were needed to pull the ship up the lough. His father said that some of the tugboats had to travel from Liverpool to assist the great White Star liner and, as they drew closer, George could make out the names on a few of them – *Herculaneum*, *Haskisson*, *Herald* and *Wallasey*.

The crowds cheered when the mammoth vessel was towed into the channel. As the sun shone down, *Titanic* presented a picturesque spectacle, perfect from keel to truck.

'Do you know, George,' said his father in a voice loud enough to be heard by many nearby, 'there are eight steel decks amidships and an extra deck at each end? And there are three million rivets holding that ship together. Can you imagine what three million rivets would look like?'

He held out his big, work-callused hands to demonstrate the size of just one, ensuring that those around were aware that this man knew what he was talking about.

'The rudder's so big it had to be made in six pieces – it's as big as a house! That ship is nearly 900 feet long and as tall as an eleven-storey building. Have you ever seen an eleven-storey building or even a picture of one?'

Before George could reply he was almost deafened by the sound of the enormous propeller blades beginning to churn up the sea at the mouth of the lough in front of them. Smoke belched from three of the four huge funnels and he imagined the engineers feverishly stoking the boilers. All around, people cheered, women waved their handkerchiefs and men threw their caps up in the air. The pride of Belfast, *Titanic*, was off across the sea.

Everyone seemed reluctant to move and instead stared after the ship, talking about its proportions and how great the city was that had workmen capable of building the most luxurious ship in the world.

'It's not just the ships that we're great at,' said his father to those around him. 'Sure that ship was built in the world's biggest dry dock. And we've the largest ropeworks in the world and linen spinning mill and tea machinery works!'

'That's right,' said a man nearby with obvious pride. 'And don't forget we've the world's biggest tobacco factory and aerated water factory. You've only to look at our new City Hall to see what a great city Belfast has become.'

Murmurs of agreement sounded. Then a dour-faced man standing nearby began talking loudly to a group of young women by his side. He had a harsh Scottish accent.

'Och aye, a great city! Listen to them all. Waving off a ship with bathrooms for the rich when they have only a toilet at the bottom of their own yards! Working twelve hours a day to install a swimming pool on a ship when the only time they see a pool is in the Falls Road baths when they go for their weekly ablutions! I heard there's even a Jacobean dining saloon with a rose carpet. Put there by men who, if they're lucky, set their feet on cold linoleum each morning at half past five. A ship for the rich, that's what they've built. A ship with leaded glass in the lounge, a squash court, a gymnasium, bedrooms bigger than their whole houses where they're rearing eight and nine children. Pawns of Pirrie and Ismay and the English! They'll make thousands while the men who built that great ship will still have to put their only suits in the pawn to buy food on a Monday.'

Such was the intense feeling behind the man's words that people around him stopped to listen. Many nodded their heads, even George's father, who had been praising the city such a short time ago. This heavy-built man with dark hair and piercing light-blue eyes reminded him of his hero, James Larkin, the founder of the Irish Transport and General Workers' Union (ITGWU).

'You've a point there,' he said. 'But what can we do about it? They're the lords and masters and we're the workers. We need the work and they know it.'

'That's why everyone should join the Irish Transport and General Workers' Union,' the Scottish man said. 'Why should Belfast workers not follow the lead of the rest of Ireland and the world? That's what all men, and women come to that, can do. If the workers of Ireland unite they could break them. The low dock workers won by striking last year! Take a lead from the women – they're rushing to join the Irish Textile Workers' Union because they are exploited. Look at that ship. It's magnificent. Who built that ship? The workers did! There's no coal in this country, no oil, no steel. You have the biggest shipyard in the world and what makes it so great? The workers do. That's what your masters have got. No natural resources, their wealth is in their workers.

'And who's going to make all the profit from *Titanic*'s millionaire passengers? Not the people of Belfast who built her, you can be sure of that. Think about it, boys. And when you do, come and see me at the Union Branch at 122 Corporation Street.'

George had never heard anyone speak so vehemently in public before and he was amazed at the agreement so quickly won from all the people who had been able to hear the man's powerful voice. As the middle-aged man walked away, George's eyes were drawn to one young woman who stepped daintily behind him. Her long skirt skimmed the top of her laced button boots and the matching jacket nipped into her tiny waist. He was captivated by the red ribbon that swung jauntily from her dark hair, piled precariously on top of her head. He could not decide whether to watch her or the great *Titanic*, fast disappearing out into the Irish Sea.

4

WINNIE:
AUGUST 1912

Born to Irish parents in 1868 in Edinburgh, Scotland, James Connolly had been a socialist and union activist since 1895 when he became the secretary of the Scottish Socialist Federation. A former printer, soldier and deserter, he left for Dublin in 1896 to take up employment as the paid organiser of the Dublin Socialist Club. Shortly after that he founded the Irish Socialist Republican Party (ISRP) and for the next six years his writings and public lecture tours made him a well-known figure throughout the two islands.

In 1902, on behalf of the Socialist Labor Party, he toured the United States of America and such was the power of his oratory that he was in great demand. Unhappy with internal disputes in the ISRP, he decided to move himself, his Dublin-born wife, Lillie, and his family to New York to live and work. By day he had a variety of jobs, and when not working he continued his links with the Socialist Labor Party. He co-founded the Irish Socialist Federation in 1907 and published *The Harp* journal with his daughter, Nora, as the manager. In 1908 he was appointed organiser of the Industrial Workers of the World.

James Connolly arrived back in Ireland on 26 July 1910. He recognised that Irish trade unions were generally rather inactive and set out to change that, becoming the Ulster organiser of the ITGWU during a strike of seamen in ports that included Belfast.

His successful leading of that strike, and the vigour with which he set about gathering new members, gave him and the union a prominent position in the labour movement in the northern city. This was in spite of the religious and political disturbances that prevailed in Belfast, the city which now became his home.

Connolly despaired of the working conditions that he found, conditions that meant that women were working in sweatshops or mills or their own homes for a pittance. He longed for the day when a socialist movement would guide and direct the efforts of labour in Ireland. A day when Catholic and Protestant workers would unite and realise that it was within their power to remove the causes of poverty.

Under his leadership the union, with its headquarters in Corporation Street in the centre of Belfast, was an active force in the political labour movement, as well as in trade unionism. In nearby York Street he established the Irish Textile Workers' Union for the women workers in the linen mills. He instituted open-air meetings and even tried to introduce social activity with Irish and ballroom dancing. He was also an ardent supporter of the militant sections of the suffragette campaigners.

All this he explained to the young woman, Winnie Carney, seated in front of him in the little office on York Street in August 1912. His secretary, Marie Johnson, had taken ill and left very suddenly. As he needed a replacement immediately, Mrs Johnson had recommended this young friend of hers who had accompanied them to the launch of *Titanic*. 'You must understand what our movement is all about,' he emphasised. 'You cannot work here unless you sympathise with our aims. That's why you need to know all about me and what I believe in. We in the union believe that workers should unite and, as Karl Marx stated, that no nation is good enough or wise enough to rule another. When all the socialists in Ireland recognise this principle, and unite with us, they will have cause to wonder at the readiness with which the workers of Ireland will respond to the socialist appeal. Until they do, however, we will be compelled to see Irish Tory employers hiding their sweatshops behind orange flags, and Irish Home Rule landlords using the green sunburst of Erin to cloak their rackrenting in the festering slums of our Irish towns. Do you understand?'

Winnie, who had been listening to this tirade made in a tone that lacked any geniality, was about to reply when Connolly spoke again. 'It's vital that you understand and are at one with us. Your predecessor, taken ill so suddenly, was in total agreement. She lived for the labour movement at work and at home. Of course her husband is himself a great labour man, Thomas Johnson. Destined for great things! Do you have a labour background, Miss Carney? Maybe you should tell me more about yourself. It's a grand evening and I'm tired of this office chair. Let's jump on a tramcar and take a stroll in the grounds of the City Hall. You can tell me all about yourself there.'

Winifred Carney lifted her coat and followed Connolly out of the cramped office, realising that she had barely uttered a word in the last hour.

James Connolly's monologue continued on the double-ended tramcar after they had seated themselves on the open-topped deck. He told her how, at James Larkin's request, he arrived in Belfast the previous year just at the time 600 workers at the low docks came out in support of a general seaman's strike over the exploitation of dockers.

'Do you know what exploitation those dockers who unloaded the grain were suffering? A daily average of a hundred tons was considered to be a normal load. If the dockers succeeded in unloading 120 tons they got a bonus of sixpence! That meant they did a fifth of a day's work for sixpence! But we won, Miss Carney. We won. It was my first strike in Belfast and we succeeded in raising the general wage from five shillings to six shillings a day and reducing the workload by over fifty per cent. Wasn't that an achievement? No wonder we decided to stay. My daughter Nora and I found a grand wee house at Glenalina Terrace on the Falls Road and set up our home there. We'd another victory soon after when we succeeded in abolishing the old system where stevedores paid workers when, where and how they pleased. Wasn't that great work too?'

'It was, Mr Connolly, it was,' Winnie demurely replied as the driver rang the gong with his left foot to let the people on the roadside know that the tramcar was coming.

'You know, last year,' he continued, stroking his thick moustache, 'all the mill women workers turned to us for support and advice when they went on strike in October. Nora was with them. She was horrified at the deplorable conditions at the factory. She said the desolate surroundings and inhumane treatments under which the women worked were more severe than anything she had witnessed in American mills. That's when Mrs Johnson and I formed the Textile Workers' Union and, with our support, that strike too ended in success. The most oppressed workers in this city come to our offices. Have you the background to deal with those people, Miss Carney?'

These last words he addressed to her as he helped her down

from the tramcar at Castle Junction, the centre of the tramcar system in Belfast. As Winnie considered her response, they strolled past the fashionable shops in Donegall Place on that warm summer's evening and, like many others, gazed into the windows of Robinson & Cleaver, a huge store with electric lights and an elevator just like those in America. At last they reached the grounds of the white stone City Hall. Dusting off a seat, James Connolly sat and waited for her to answer the many questions he had posed along their route.

Winnie took a deep breath and began. 'Well, Mr Connolly, I've no experience of strikes, but I do learn quickly and I do have great sympathy with the workers here. My family travelled around a lot in search of work and I saw first-hand the living conditions of people in England. I've spent many years in Carlisle Circus where my mother runs a sweetshop but actually I was born at Fisherhill in Bangor, County Down. I'm the youngest of six children but two of my brothers are in America, the other is married, and my two sisters are leaving soon to become nuns. We still live with our mother. I had a good Catholic education from the Christian Brothers in Belfast at St Patrick's School in Donegall Place and I taught there as a junior teacher. Then I went to Hughes' Commercial Academy where I qualified as one of the first lady secretaries, so my shorthand and typing are good. I was a clerk at a solicitor's in Dungannon for a short time. I'm sure Marie told you that – she and Thomas are great friends of mine. Marie and I both love literature and art and I like to sing and play the piano.'

'Good skills, Miss Carney, but what do you feel? What do you feel about the plight of women in our country?'

Here was a question that, even though she was only twenty-four, Winnie felt she could answer honestly. 'I feel women need to become more politically active, Mr Connolly. We can't wait for men to do it all for us. That's why I joined the Irish Women's Suffrage Society last year, but that hasn't changed things yet. How much I agreed with Mrs Pankhurst when I heard her speak in the Ulster Hall! Women need the vote. With the right to vote, a woman's right to an independent life would at least partly be recognised. Those mill rules that they tried to impose last year were draconian. Imagine forbidding human beings from singing or speaking to each other while they worked. As if the working conditions weren't bad enough.

'I was so pleased when your actions helped win that battle. But more battles lie ahead. There are families living in single, squalid rooms and people working seventy hours a week. Women are being paid one-third of what men receive and they are doing equal work. That can't be right, Mr Connolly! Being a solicitor's secretary was pleasant enough but I wasn't going to help win the vote for women or improve working conditions or even help Ireland achieve Home Rule while I was working in a solicitor's office.'

As she spoke Winifred Carney, usually rather reticent, became alive and animated. Her cheeks flushed pink, her dark eyes shone and she spoke with undisguised passion. James Connolly nodded but, for once, remained silent. She worried that she might have been too outspoken.

'Well, Miss Carney,' he said after a few minutes during which she hardly dared breathe, 'Mrs Johnson recommended you without reservation. I can't offer you much money, probably no more than five shillings a week. In fact, for the first few weeks there may be nothing at all. The union's finances are in a very bad state at the moment. The Johnsons tell me that you speak some Irish, have studied the history of Ireland and are greatly interested in the Gaelic Revival. I can't offer much money to such a learned young lady but you'd be doing a grand job for the workers of Ireland if you were to take over Mrs Johnson's job and run our office at 50 York Street. Miss Gordon will work with you. The National Health Insurance Scheme has just been introduced and it's vitally important to get all the benefits sorted out for our members. I can't do that by myself. I can't do that while I'm walking the streets of Belfast encouraging men to fight for better working conditions, can I, Miss Carney? What do you say, Miss Carney, would you consider taking the position?'

'It would be an honour, Mr Connolly,' she said, smiling. 'But I would prefer it, sir, if you would call me Winnie. My friends call me Winnie.'

'I prefer "Miss Carney", it is more business-like,' he replied brusquely. 'Consider yourself, forthwith, Miss Carney, the secretary of the Irish Textile Workers' Union. As well as being the secretary, you will help me with the insurance work for both men and women. I will pay your wages and you can give your whole time to the work of organising. I trust that you find this arrangement suitable?'

His reprimand about using her Christian name had stung but nonetheless Winnie nodded. Something told her that it would be an honour to work for this man. From childhood her mother had instilled a love of Ireland in her heart and Mr Connolly really seemed to care about the working people of her country. She felt that she had truly found her vocation.

5

GEORGE:
FEBRUARY–SEPTEMBER 1912

Political tension was rife in Ireland. Opposing views regarding Home Rule were creating greater tension, and outbursts of sectarian or political violence, which had often been a fact of life in certain parts of Belfast, increased.

Most unionists loathed the prospect of being placed under a Dublin government and were considering the mobilisation of a citizen army. At first, the government in London dismissed such moves as unthreatening, but their attitude began to change when, in February 1912, Winston Churchill was invited to speak at the Ulster Hall on behalf of the Home Rule cause. A hostile crowd prevented him reaching the venue and he was forced to speak in Celtic Park with Royal Irish Constabulary (RIC) protection. On his way to the new venue, an angry crowd of men jostled and threatened to overturn his vehicle. Luckily, one burly shipyard worker shouted, 'Stop boys, there's a woman inside', and the men desisted.

In April Andrew Bonar Law, leader of the Conservative Party, watched a three-hour march of 100,000 loyalist demonstrators at the Balmoral Showgrounds on the outskirts of Belfast. Seventy trains were needed to bring in the provincial demonstrators and the city's tramcar service was stopped from half past eight in the morning until six o'clock in the evening. Those present included contingents from the Orange Order and Unionist Clubs who had marched from the city centre. Bonar Law and Sir Edward Carson addressed the demonstration.

This demonstration became known as the Balmoral Review. It gave rise to the idea of a pledge that all those opposed to Home Rule should sign. Thomas Sinclair, a leading Belfast businessman, accepted the task of drafting the pledge and took his title from the 1643 Scottish Solemn League and Covenant. The text was sent to Sir Edward Carson who said that he considered it excellent. The Ulster Unionist Council also gave its approval and designated 28 September as 'Ulster Day' on which the signing was to take place.

On 10 September the inaugural meeting of the Young Citizen Volunteers (YCV) of Ireland took place in Belfast's City Hall. Some 2,000 young men turned up to join this group, of which the president was the Lord Mayor of Belfast, Robert James McMordie. George McBride and his friends, Hugh Scott and Samuel Cunningham, discussed going down to join but, although they were tall for their fourteen years, they feared that they might face the embarrassment of being recognised as underage and subsequently turned away.

Their friend Billy White was able to join even though he was only sixteen and excitedly told them about it the next day. 'There were hundreds and thousands of us at the City Hall and a big piper in a highland uniform played the bagpipes. The lord mayor was there and he told us that men had to carry guns in difficult times and between the growing German threat in Europe and Home Rule we were in difficult times. We must all show great discipline, he said, and we will achieve that through drills. We'll have uniforms and guns and everything and the government is going to support us.'

Two weeks later George and his three friends spent Friday night at the Alhambra picture-house where they paid 2d each to watch *The Triumph of Strength*. At nine o'clock they walked home up the Shankill Road and debated whether to go to the Distillery versus Celtic football match the next day. When they reached George's home they still had not decided.

George's father came out of the scullery and listened to their conversation. 'Don't be going at all boys,' said Mr McBride. 'There's sure to be trouble at that match. You know that Distillery is a Protestant team and Celtic's a Catholic one and they'll all be in favour of Home Rule. Tomorrow is Ulster Day and, now that the bill has been introduced, us men are going to sign the Covenant. Home Rule will not be good for this country. We've prospered too well under the union and we'll not fare as well under native government.'

Billy nodded his head; he had heard all about the Covenant at the YCVs.

'What's the Covenant, Mr McBride?' asked Hugh.

'It's the Solemn League and Covenant which hundreds and thousands of Ulstermen are going to sign. The women will even have their own version to sign though, of course, they'll not have to promise to defend our position if needs be,' replied Mr McBride. 'Here, I'll read you what it says in the paper.'

Mr McBride lifted a copy of *The Belfast News-Letter* and read it aloud. '"The Solemn League and Covenant is a pledge to stand by one another and use all means necessary to defeat the present conspiracy to set up a Home Rule parliament in Ireland." It says here that there could be half a million people going to sign tomorrow. There'll be services in meeting halls, churches and even the Ulster Hall. Then we'll follow bands from every Protestant area of Belfast to the City Hall. It'll not be the day for a football match, boys, especially with a Catholic club playing. I don't know how true it is but folks are saying that Catholics are all nationalists now.'

George was used to listening to his father's outbursts. He was a shipyard fitter, a strong supporter of trade unions and had been very active during the strike in 1907. George could still remember pictures of the founder of the ITGWU, James Larkin, hanging in the house at the time. His father had heard Larkin speak on the Shankill Road and someone said that it was Larkin's magnificent physique that gave him mastery. He said people thought Larkin was like the Arc de Triomphe on the march and looked as though he could crush the capitalist system in his grip. Usually his father didn't talk about Protestants and Catholics – they were all workers to him – but this Home Rule business had stirred something up in him.

When George lay in bed that night, in the room he shared with his two younger brothers and three younger sisters, he wondered sleepily if men like his father could crush the capitalist system while marching behind bands to the City Hall.

The next day all work in the great industries of Belfast ceased as those who supported the union with Great Britain gathered to sign the Covenant. At eleven o'clock, congregations met in over a hundred churches and in the Assembly Buildings and the Ulster Hall.

It was in the Ulster Hall that Edward Carson and the unionist leadership pledged never to accept Home Rule. After the services ended, Carson and the unionist leaders, with a smart guard of bowler-hatted men commanded by Major Fred Crawford, walked from the Ulster Hall in Bedford Street to the City Hall. Crowds and bands from every area of Belfast had converged on the City Hall to witness the event and solemnly watched as the leaders of Home Rule resistance made their way in to begin the signing.

The unionist leaders were welcomed by Lord Mayor McMordie and the fifty-two unionist members of Belfast Corporation. Sir Douglas Savory witnessed the event:

> The first sheet of the Covenant was spread out on a large table covered with a Union Jack. Carson took up the silver pen that had been presented to him for the occasion. Through the open door of the City Hall I could see a large crowd, each one of whom was waiting to take part in this historic ceremony. I saw Carson signing the Covenant and then handing the pen to Lord Londonderry who followed him. Then the Moderator of the General Assembly, the Bishop of Down, and the President of the Methodist Conference, as well as Lord Castlereagh, joined one another in signing the document. Lines of desks had been placed all around so that 500 persons could sign the Covenant simultaneously.[1]

The Covenant had been signed by 471,414 people (237,368 men and 234,046 women) by the end of the day in venues all over Ulster, and in some English and Scottish cities. All agreed to resist any attempt to implement Home Rule. George McBride senior was one of them. The document read:

BEING CONVINCED in our consciences that Home Rule would be disastrous to the material well-being of Ulster as well as of the whole of Ireland, subversive of our civil and religious freedom, destructive of our citizenship, and perilous to the unity of the Empire, we, whose names are underwritten, men of Ulster, loyal subjects of His Gracious Majesty King George V, humbly relying on the God whom our fathers in days of stress and trial confidently trusted, do hereby pledge ourselves in solemn Covenant, throughout this our time of threatened calamity, to stand by one another in defending, for ourselves and our children, our cherished position of equal citizenship in the United Kingdom, and in using all means which may be found necessary to defeat the present conspiracy to set up a Home Rule Parliament in Ireland. And in the event of such a Parliament being forced upon us, we further solemnly and mutually pledge ourselves to refuse to recognise its authority. In sure confidence that God will defend the right, we hereto subscribe our names. And further, we individually declare that we have not already signed this Covenant.[2]

Women signed a separate document called the Declaration for Women, which read:

We, whose names are underwritten, women of Ulster, and loyal subjects of our gracious King, being firmly persuaded that Home Rule would be disastrous to our Country, desire to associate ourselves with the men of Ulster in their uncompromising opposition to the Home Rule Bill now before Parliament, whereby it is proposed to drive Ulster out of her cherished place in the Constitution of the United Kingdom, and to place her under the domination and control of a Parliament in Ireland. Praying that from this calamity God will save Ireland, we hereto subscribe our names.[3]

There were some Protestants who opposed the Covenant. The rector of St Nicholas' in Carrickfergus, John Frederick MacNeice, father of the poet Louis, declined to sign on religious grounds. Reverend J. B. Armour, a Liberal Home Ruler, was opposed to the politics of Carson and Craig, and dismissed Ulster Day as 'Protestant Fools' Day' and Edward Carson as 'a sheer mountebank and the greatest enemy of Protestantism in my opinion existing'.[4] He produced a counter-Covenant, which repudiated Carson's claim to represent united Protestant opinion:

> We desire to live upon terms of friendship and equality with our Roman Catholic fellow-countrymen and, in the event of Home Rule becoming law, we are prepared to take our turn with them in working for the good of our common country.[5]

Meanwhile, for many people in Belfast, Ulster Day was just another day. In fact, newspapers reported that there had been exemplary sobriety when the number of men involved was considered. When George's father came home he described the long, orderly queues to sign in halls all over Belfast. 'Everybody lined up and took their turn and every signature had a witness. I heard tell that there were even some who signed in blood but I didn't see any. It was all very peaceful. Mind you, I'm glad I told you not to go to watch Distillery and Belfast Celtic because I heard tell there was some unpleasantness after the game. Sure there's always a bit of bother when those two play!'

6

WINNIE:
FEBRUARY 1913

'Take a dictation quickly,' bellowed James Connolly as he strode into the cramped little office. Winnie snatched her pencil and notepad. She knew that he would not linger long before launching into one of his tirades, which would later become a speech or an article.

Connolly was a believer in an Irish Workers' Republic and he despised what he saw as Tory lawyers, with huge resources of finance and propaganda, playing on the emotions and prejudices in Belfast to destroy the promise of a united labour movement. A month earlier, as the year began, he had contested a local election and polled 900 votes in the Labour interest in the electoral constituency of Dock Ward. Winnie had typed his letter to the electors at the time, a letter which had echoed all her own feelings and given her great pleasure to type, once she had overcome the difficulty of deciphering his scrawling handwriting:

January 1913
To the Electors:

Ladies and Gentlemen,
In view of the fact that the National Health Insurance Act comes into working operation on January 13, and that one of

the governing bodies to administer that Act will be an Insurance Commission partly elected by the City Council, it is felt, because of the well-known hostility to labour of our present representatives, that some steps should be taken to have a labour representative on the Council in order to try and prevent enemies of the working class being sent from that Council to the Insurance Commission.

For this reason a General Meeting of the Irish Transport and General Workers' Union, very largely composed of residents in this Ward, unanimously decided to ask me to contest Dock Ward in the labour interest. The Belfast Trades and Labour Council also unanimously passed a resolution approving of this contest and recommending the labour candidate to the electors. As the Irish Trades Congress at its recent meeting in Clonmel also declared in favour of organised labour in Ireland taking steps to secure independent labour representation, I feel compelled to accept this duty, and therefore I ask your hearty support in our resolve to capture this seat, and thus let the voice of labour be heard in the City Council, in spite of the stupid, intolerant, and labour-hating gang who rule there.

I desire to be returned in order to advocate, among other things, that the Act for the feeding of children at school at present in force in Great Britain, be applied to Ireland. We have a right to demand equal treatment for Irish and British workers, and as the British workers have secured that their children must be fed before being educated (because it is impossible to educate hungry children), we also claim that when the poverty, or neglect, of the parents is such that the children are suffering, that the Local Authorities should be empowered to make provision for the supply of at least one good meal per day to each child. To those who object that this would 'pauperise' the children, I answer that the children of the working class have as much right to be maintained thus as have the children of royalty. If it does not pauperise the one it cannot pauperise the other.

The Corporation of Dublin and many other Public Boards in Ireland have declared for this measure; it is time Belfast City Council was interesting itself more about such matters and less about the perpetuation of the religious discords that make Belfast a byword among civilised nations.

My general attitude, if elected, will be to insist upon the importance of the interests of labour being studied; that wherever possible all Corporation work be done by direct employment of labour; that the trade union clause be enforced in all Corporation contracts; that a minimum wage of at least 6d. per hour be established for all Corporation employees; that membership in a trade union be made compulsory for all wage-earners in Corporation employment; and that the Tramways Committee and its manager be compelled to supply covered cars for workers, morning and evening.

As every citizen in Belfast is interested in the proper administration of the Harbour, I favour the abolition of the present undemocratic and unrepresentative Board and the establishment in its place of a Harbour Board elected on the same franchise and at the same time as the Aldermen of the city. If elected, I will move that the City Council promote a bill on these lines.

I stand as a labour candidate, totally independent of any political party. But as the personal views of a candidate cannot be ignored – and as mine are likely to be misrepresented – I judge it well to state mine here that I may at least be heard in my own defence.

Believing that the present system of society is based upon the robbery of the working class, and that capitalist property cannot exist without the plundering of labour, I desire to see capitalism abolished, and a democratic system of common or public ownership erected in its stead. This democratic system, which is called socialism, will, I believe, come as a result of the continuous increase of power of the working class. Only by this means can we secure the abolition of destitution, and all the misery, crime, and immorality which flow from that unnecessary evil. All the reform legislation of the present day is moving in that direction even now, but working class action on above lines will secure that direct, voluntary, conscious, and orderly cooperation by all for the good of all, will more quickly replace the blundering and often reluctant legislation of capitalist governments.

As a lifelong advocate of national independence for Ireland, I am in favour of Home Rule, and believe that Ireland should be ruled, governed, and owned by the people of Ireland.

I believe that men and women, having to face the battle of life together, could face it better were all enjoying the same political rights.

Fellow workers: I leave my case in your hands. As a trade union official, I stand for the class to which I belong. If you are content to be represented by men belonging to some section of the master class, then do not vote for me, but if you want your cause represented from Dock Ward by one of your own class, who will battle for your rights, who is the determined enemy of the domination of class over class, of nation over nation, of sex over sex, who will at all times stand for the cause of the lowly paid and oppressed, then vote for

Yours fraternally,
James Connolly[1]

Now, in the office, Winnie was filled with admiration for Connolly's seemingly limitless energy. The pencil in her hand flew as he proceeded with more words and sentiments that she wished she had the ability to form:

> In these industrial parts of the North of Ireland the yoke of capitalism lies heavy upon the lives of the people. The squalor and listless wretchedness of some other parts is, indeed, absent, but in its stead there exists grinding toil for old and young – toil to which the child is given up whilst its limbs and brain are still immature and undeveloped, and toil continued until, a broken and enfeebled wreck, the toiler sinks into a too early grave. In this part of Ireland the child is old before it knows what it is to be young …
>
> In their wisdom our lords and masters often leave full-grown men to be unemployed, but they can always find a use for the bodies and limbs of our children. A strange comment upon the absurdities of the capitalist system, illustrating its idiotic wasteful-ness of human possibilities; that the intellect and strength of men should be left to rot for want of work, whilst children are by pre-mature work deprived of the possibilities of developing fully their minds and their bodies.[2]

'Do you not agree, Miss Carney?'

'There's not one word to which I would take exception,' she replied without hesitation.

Once clear that Connolly had finished, she returned to the huge pile of paperwork before her. The volume of work in the little office had increased dramatically as membership had grown, and Nellie Gordon and she had struggled to cope. Nellie had started at the same time as Winnie and had formerly been a doffing mistress at the Owen O'Cork spinning mill in east Belfast. She had taken a cut in pay to work for the union, but believed firmly in its objectives. Winnie and she became firm friends and they often accompanied Connolly to factory gates. Like him, Nellie was an impressive speaker and she always received tremendous applause from the mill girls, who knew she was one of their own.

Other events had also helped make the last eight months busy ones for Winnie. Nellie and she had tried to raise the morale of the workers by organising socials and dances at the Mill Girls' Room on the Falls Road and at Danny McDevitt's Tailors Rooms in 5 Rosemary Street in the centre of Belfast. They persuaded John and James Flanagan, two brothers who were organisers of the dockworkers, to bring some young men along to make events livelier.

The workload associated with the increase in membership often kept them busy long past their supposed finishing time of six o'clock, and Connolly's election campaign in January had added to their duties. The insurance section became an invaluable part of their trade union work although some viewed it as dry, unrewarding and thankless. In this section Winnie oversaw the accounts of the collection of union dues, payments for those on strike or in need, and gave assistance to all members who struggled with the completion of official forms for national health insurance. She thought it was vitally important because so many of their members were helpless when confronted with the official red tape, and she performed her tasks with interest, care and patience. In addition, she typed all official letters and pamphlets and Connolly's frequent articles for the Scottish labour journal, *Forward*.

Sometimes there was humour to ease the tedium and, uncharac-teristically for Winnie when at work, she laughed aloud on the day that one nervous young father came into the office and requested 'an eternity form' instead of a maternity form. Connolly dryly remarked, 'Try the Salvation Army!'[3]

On other occasions, when he was feeling low, Connolly would grab his coat at a quarter to six and tell them to leave it all for now. Then he would hustle them onto the Falls Road tramcar and, with his spirits steadily reviving, suggest that they all go to the dog-racing at Celtic Park and have some fun.

Connolly's daughter, Nora, often came to help them in the office. When they stopped for a cup of tea, Winnie and Nellie would sit and chat with her. At first, the young women would discuss men they had met at the dances and laugh about who had offered to walk them home. Nellie was stepping out with some-one and couldn't understand why Winnie didn't seem interested in the many possible suitors they had met. Nora could be very serious and, after indulging in their chatter for a while, she always brought the young women's conversation around to the struggle of the working class for independence and the need for women to play an equal part in that struggle.

'My father founded the Irish Socialist Republican Party. He believes the working class must have economic independence and freedom. He says women should take part in the struggle too. When we lived in America, I worked at a milliner's but I also at-tended outdoor labour meetings with Papa and heard him talk. We met John Devoy and the whole American branch of the Irish Republican Brotherhood [IRB] there and they felt the same way – well, maybe not about the women, but Mr Devoy talked to us about peasant ownership and protection for poor tenants. That's why my father set up the Irish Socialist Federation – he discovered that all the aims for independence in Ireland were eventually the same.'

'Does James Larkin think the same way?' asked Winnie.

'Of course,' replied Nora vehemently. 'Father says he is a man of genius, of splendid vitality, great in his conceptions, magnificent in his courage, a great Irishman.'

'He's not actually Irish, is he?' interjected Nellie. 'Wasn't he born in Liverpool?'

'He might have been born there,' answered Nora, 'but, as Wellington said, being born in a stable doesn't make you a horse! Larkin's parents were Irish, so he was too. He was raised in poverty and had no formal education. Like thousands of others he was forced into casual labour as a child. No wonder he hates exploitation. He rose to be the organiser of the National Union of Dock Labourers in Liverpool and, when he came to Belfast in 1907, he was the first person ever to try to organise the unskilled labour force. He established his own union in Dublin and look at it now. It's Ireland's largest and most militant union. Father admires him more than any other person I know.'

'Like I must admire your father,' said Nellie, with a giggle. 'I must, because after I met him in this very office last July I gave up a position earning fifteen shillings a week and took on this one with the marvellous salary of five shillings. My young man, James, thinks I am quite mad.' She laughed again.

'You admire your father very much, don't you, Nora?' asked Winnie in a serious tone. She had heard the fervour in Nora's voice and didn't want her to think that Nellie and she were being frivolous.

'Indeed I do,' she answered. 'Like him, I have a love for all things Irish and desire equality for all. I would do anything he asked of me.'

Winnie and Nellie nodded. Both knew that they would too.

7

WINNIE:
THE GAELIC REVIVAL

There had been a resurgence of interest in all things Gaelic towards the end of the nineteenth century and this led to a cultural, political and social revival in Ireland. The Gaelic Athletic Association, for example, was set up in 1884 to promote and preserve native sports. In Ulster, new clubs were set up, county boards were formed in all counties between 1901 and 1905, and the Ulster Council was founded in 1903. The GAA grew rapidly in size, and Gaelic games became the chief sporting interest of nationalists in rural areas and many in the towns and cities too.

Due to the fact that Sunday was the only day agricultural labourers had free, it became the main day of play. Consequently few Protestants played, as the majority held the view that the Sabbath day should be kept holy and work and sports should not be undertaken. Indeed Sunday play remained the most consistent unionist objection to Gaelic games; even the Belfast Corporation, the only local authority that provided a pitch for Gaelic games (at Falls Park), did not allow Sunday games. The Great Northern Railway Company, meanwhile, refused to run special trains for Gaelic games, lest they attract 'loutish' crowds and this limited the size of crowds at Ulster matches.

In 1893 the foundation meeting of the Gaelic League had been held. Winnie's mother, Sarah, was an avid supporter of the

Gaelic League and had frequently told her all about it. The non-political, non-sectarian organisation was aimed at involving people of different religions and political loyalties in a common cultural effort. Its objective was the revival of the Irish language and the preservation of Irish literature, music and traditional culture. By 1905 there were 550 branches throughout the country. Each branch organised Irish classes, lectures, concerts and dances, and Sarah encouraged her three daughters to embrace the aims and attend everything they could. Winnie was the most passionate about all aspects.

From 1899 onwards the Gaelic League published *An Claidheamh Soluis*, an Irish-language weekly newspaper. It staged an annual cultural festival, the Oireachtas, and had Saint Patrick's Day designated a national holiday. It also succeeded in having Irish made compulsory for matriculation at the National University of Ireland. While the Gaelic League was strictly non-political and the membership included some unionists, the majority of members were nationalists. Over a generation the Gaelic League accomplished significant cultural change in the nationalist population. John Redmond, the leader of Ireland's nationalists, never wavered in his support of the Gaelic League.

Women were encouraged to become a part of this Gaelic Revival. Inghinidhe na hÉireann (daughters of Ireland) was formed in 1900 by a group of nationalist women whose aim was the complete independence of Ireland, the popularisation of goods of Irish manufacture, the revival of the Irish language and the restoration of Irish customs, games, music and dancing.

An Irish literary renaissance was also inspired by the nationalistic pride of the Gaelic Revival. The early leaders of the renaissance wrote rich and passionate verse, filled with the grandeur of Ireland's past and the music and mysticism of Gaelic poetry. They were mainly members of the privileged class and extolled the simple dignity of the Irish peasant and the natural beauty of Ireland. The movement developed into a vigorous literary force centred on the poet and playwright William Butler Yeats. His chief colleague was Lady Isabella Augusta Gregory, who took a leading part in the Abbey Theatre's management and wrote many plays, such as *Spreading the News*. The Irish Literary Theatre, established in 1898, also excelled in the production of peasant plays. The greatest dramatist of the movement was John Millington Synge, who wrote plays of great beauty and power in a peasant dialect, such as *The Playboy of the Western World*.

Winnie learned all of this at the many meetings she attended in the Belfast Central Library, one of her favourite places. She spent most of her free time in the public reading room. Her great interest was in art and she was spellbound at a lecture given in the library by Mr William Laird on local art, past and present. Her sister accompanied her and in return she went with Mabel, who was interested in all things spiritual, to hear Rabbi J. Rosenzweig give a lecture on 'Women in Temple and Synagogue'. These evenings were all free, but so popular that a ticket had to be obtained beforehand. One of the finest evenings had taken place on 19 November 1912 when they attended a lecture on ancient Irish music given by Carl G. Hardebeck, the well-known musician and composer. The evening also included vocal examples, where singers gave renditions of ancient tunes.

Winnie's knowledge was supplemented by reading journals and papers such as *Bean na hEireann*, *Irish Freedom* and *The Irish*

Citizen. The latter was produced by the Irish Women's Franchise League and reinforced Winnie's admiration for the work of the suffragettes. She had always been an avid reader and her studious disposition meant that she absorbed and retained all the information she gleaned.

Winnie tried never to miss any meetings at which women were the speakers. Miss Florence F. Hobson gave one speech on the subject of town planning and its relation to public health. Women had come to play a significant role in the fields of science and literature in Ireland, and Winnie was very proud to see a woman taking the lead in such matters.

Another meeting was addressed by Alice Milligan, born in 1866, who was a prolific writer and one of the main organisers of the Gaelic League in Ulster. In 1891 Milligan had founded a series of cultural, feminist, commemorative and political organisations that put the north on the map of the Irish Revival. Born into a Northern Irish Protestant unionist family, Alice was educated at Belfast's Methodist College and later King's College London. She then went to Dublin to learn Irish and was a member of Inghinidhe na hÉireann and Sinn Féin. Alice was to become a lifelong friend of Winnie, as well as of James Connolly, W. B. Yeats and Arthur Griffith.

Winnie also became a member of Na Fianna Éireann, an Irish nationalist youth organisation founded in 1909 by Bulmer Hobson and Constance Markievicz. Originally it was a version of the Boy Scouts, but Winnie's friends, Nora Connolly and her sister Ina, had formed the first female branch in Ireland in Belfast in 1911, and she really enjoyed accompanying them to the Tuesday night meetings in Berry Street. There were nearly fifty members and they took part in Irish language classes, route marches, drill parades and first aid. Being the only girls' branch was a great source of pride, although Winnie was rather alarmed at the controversy caused when they attended the national Na Fianna Ard-Fheis in 1913. However, it did not deter her from joining Nora and Ina when they formed the Young Republican Party in order to organise more public meetings and recruit members for Na Fianna. Winnie could be relied upon to offer assistance at any event and was often seen helping to carry the box with collapsible legs that they used as a platform for outdoor public meetings. She was not keen on public speaking, but was filled with admiration for those who were. Carrying boxes, taking dictation, recording minutes and typing manifestos were her strengths and she would use them to support those people in whom she recognised leadership qualities.

8

GEORGE:
APRIL 1913

It was a year since *Titanic* had foundered in the Atlantic Ocean on her maiden voyage from Southampton to New York. A year in which inquiries had sought to find the cause of the sinking that led to the loss of over 1,500 lives. A pall of gloom still hung over Belfast and added to the unease with which the whole city seemed to be gripped.

This unease was primarily due to the growth of volunteer armies in the city. The inaugural meeting of the YCV of Ireland had taken place in Belfast's City Hall on 10 September 1912. The constitution of the YCV, as proposed by Fred T. Geddes, a prominent member of the Belfast's Citizens' Association, stated that members should not take part in any political meeting or demonstration. Membership was open to young men between the ages of eighteen and thirty-five who were over five feet in height and could present credentials of good character. The organisation was stated as being non-sectarian and non-political, but the membership was overwhelmingly Protestant. Furthermore, the high joining fee of two shillings and sixpence meant that only young professionals or those from well-off families could afford to join. A further sixpence was to be paid each month.

One of the objectives, drawn up by a committee of many middle- and upper-class members, including Mayor McMordie and Gustav Wolff, was 'to develop the spirit of responsible citizenship and municipal patriotism by means of lectures and discussions' and a further one was 'to cultivate a manly physique, with habits of self-control, self-respect and chivalry'. Members were to attend weekly drills and also pledged to assist, when called upon, the civil power in the maintenance of peace. *The Belfast News-Letter* of 10 September noted that 'the large banqueting hall was well occupied by fine specimens of the young manhood of the city'.

While the initial plan had been to extend the membership further afield, the YCV rapidly became a Belfast-based militia. Membership had expanded as winter set in and young men were busy trying to find the money with which to pay off their uniforms by instalments.

In December George McBride attended one of the YCV meetings with his friend Billy and was enthralled by the words of the speaker, Francis Forth, principal of the Municipal Technical Institute of Belfast. One section of his speech especially struck a chord with the young son of a shipyard man:

> Young men, above all else you need discipline. The well-ordered and intelligent discipline that expands the mind, exalts the faculties, refines the tastes and cultivates a spirit of patriotism. Let the old Roman submission to authority be cultivated by all young men as a virtue at once most characteristically social, and most becoming in unripe years. Obedience is the link that ties everyone to their immediate superior in the pyramid of society, and sound discipline will be achieved not merely through self-discipline but through drills.
>
> Consider the recent loss of the great ship *Titanic*. That has been a great blow to Belfast's confidence. But has the city's grief

not been softened by the knowledge that many on board showed great discipline in time of peril? The Young Citizen Volunteers must do the same. You must show self-sacrifice and courage in these difficult times.[1]

Fifteen-year-old George could hardly wait to become a member, and a few months later, in April 1913, he joined the North Belfast Battalion with his friends. No one asked his age when he arrived at the headquarters in Yarrow Street off the Crumlin Road. Every week he attended the training that took place on the property of the commanding officer, Captain Slack, at Ardoyne on the edge of Belfast.

Just as in his workplace, Mackie's, George listened to endless debates about the horrors Home Rule would bring and the need for Ulstermen to be able to rise up in opposition. At YCV meetings some young men talked angrily about the growth of nationalist and republican organisations and about how the city of Belfast was changing. They blamed the influx of Roman Catholics into the city and debates developed into quarrels more bitter than George had ever heard.

Some of George's friends left the YCV to join the Ulster Volunteer Force (UVF), a recently established force that had largely grown out of the Orange lodges and unionist clubs. Members of these groups had started to drill as a force to counter the threat of Home Rule in March 1912. By January 1913 the Ulster Unionist Council decided that these volunteers should be united into a single body called the UVF. Recruitment was to be limited to 100,000 men, aged between seventeen and sixty-five, who had signed the Solemn League and Covenant. It was a Protestant force and the required number of men proved eager to join.

With the arrival of Lieutenant General Sir George Richardson as commanding officer of the UVF in June 1913, a regimental system was established. The general was a retired officer of the British Indian Army and a veteran of the second Anglo-Afghan War and the Boxer Rebellion. He decided that each county was to provide a UVF regiment. Initially, there was little by way of a uniform – simply a belt, bandoliers and a haversack. Suppliers were soon sought for puttees, gaiters, water bottles, army boots, rifle slings, waterproof greatcoats and groundsheets.[2]

In Belfast, each parliamentary constituency (North, South, East and West) provided a regiment. Drilling took place in lots of venues, including Orange Halls and picture-houses. Dummy wooden rifles were used, made by an enterprising Belfast firm, Gregg and Company, and sold to UVF units at one shilling and sixpence in spruce and one shilling and eight pence in pitch pine. But the lack of real arms became a major problem and source of discontent, and George listened at home and in work as talk about acquiring weapons spread like wildfire.

9

WINNIE:
MARCH–DECEMBER 1913

Throughout the spring and early summer of 1913 James Connolly, Winnie and Nellie worked tirelessly on ITGWU business in Belfast. Their attempt to enlarge the membership of the Irish Textile Workers' Union was also time-consuming. In an appeal to female workers, the three of them wrote and published a manifesto, 'To the Linen Slaves of Belfast'. Winnie and Nellie both signed the document, as Winifred Carney, Secretary, and Ellen Gordon, Delegate.

Fellow-workers,

Your condition, and the condition of the sweated women of all classes of labour in Belfast, has recently become the subject of discussion on all the political platforms of England, and of long articles in all the most widely read newspapers and magazines of both countries. Almost unanimously, they agree in condemning the conditions under which you work, your miserable wages, the abominable system of fining which prevails, and the slaughtering speed at which you are driven. It is pointed out that the conditions of your toil are unnecessarily hard, that your low wages do not enable you to procure sufficiently nourishing food for yourselves or your children, and that as a result of your hard work, combined with low wages, you are the easy victims of disease, and that your children never get a decent chance in life, but are handicapped in the race of life before they are born.

All this is today admitted by every right-thinking man and woman in these Islands. Many Belfast Mills are slaughterhouses for the women and penitentiaries for the children. But while all the world is deploring your conditions, they also unite in deploring your slavish and servile nature in submitting to them; they unite in wondering of what material these Belfast women are made, who refuse to unite together and fight to better their conditions.

Irish men have proven themselves to be heroes in fighting to abolish the tyranny of landlordism. Irish women fought heroically in the same cause. Are the Irish working women of Belfast not of the same race? Can they not unite to fight the slavery of capitalism as courageously as their sisters on the farms of Ireland united to fight the slavery of Irish landlordism? Public opinion in these islands is anxious to help you, but public opinion cannot help you unless you are ready to help yourselves.

Especially do we appeal to the spinners, piecers, layers, and doffers. The slavery of the Spinning-room is the worst and least excusable of all. Spinning is a skilled trade, requiring a long apprenticeship, alert brains, and nimble fingers. Yet for all this skill, for all those weary years of learning, for all this toil in a super-heated atmosphere, with clothes drenched with water, and hands torn and lacerated as a consequence of the speeding up of the machinery, a qualified spinner in Belfast receives a wage less than some of our pious millowners would spend weekly upon a dog. And yet the Spinning-room is the key to the whole industry. A general stoppage in the Spinning-rooms of Belfast would stop all the linen industry, factories and warerooms alike. Reelers and spinners united control the situation. Disorganised as they are today, they are the helpless slaves of soulless employers. United as they might be, as they ought to be, as we are determined they shall be, they could lift themselves into the enjoyment of prosperity and well-paid healthful labour. As a first step to that end, we wish to propose a programme of industrial reform to be realised in the near future, and we invite all our toiling sisters to enrol in our Society – the Irish Textile Workers' Union – whose Belfast headquarters is at 50, York Street, in order that we may unitedly, and at a given moment, fight for its success.

We demand that the entire Linen Industry be put under the Sweated Industries Act, which gives power to a Trades Board, on which employees and employers are represented, to fix the minimum wages for the whole.

Under that Act the wages of women in the Clothing Operatives Trade has been already fixed at a minimum wage of 3d. per hour. Until the extension to the Linen Industry of that Act, we demand and pledge ourselves as a Union to fight for a minimum wage of 3d. per hour for all qualified spinners, proportionate increases for all lower grades in the Spinning-room, and increases in the piece rates for the Reeling-room and all departments in piece work; abolition of fines for lost time; all stoppages to be at the same rates as the daily pay per hour.

We also demand from Government the appointment of a competent Woman Inspector for the Belfast District exclusively, in order that the inspection of our mills, factories, and warerooms may be a constant reality, instead of the occasional farce it is today.

United action can secure every point on this modest programme within less than a year. It depends upon you, the working women of Belfast. If you have courage enough, faith enough in yourselves and in each other, you can win. Most of this programme can be won by direct industrial action, by a General Strike for it if need be; the rest will be conceded by Government as soon as you show yourselves in earnest in your demands for it.

To make easy the work of organising, we are prepared to

establish an office or Women's Club-room in each district, if the request for the same is made by a sufficient number of members. Take advantage of this offer, give in your name to us at this office, or to any of your collectors, and we will welcome you as sisters, and enroll you as comrades in the coming battle for juster conditions.

Should this manifesto come into the hand of any not themselves sufferers, but willing to help in the coming battle, if they communicate with us we shall be prepared to enroll them as auxiliaries, and welcome their help.

Sisters and Fellow-workers, talk this matter over, do not be frightened by the timid counsels and fears of weaklings. Be brave. Have confidence in yourselves. Talk about success, and you will achieve success.[1]

Winnie and Nellie were both honoured to contribute to such a worthy manifesto.

To add to the women's workload, in June they were dealing with simultaneous strikes in the brickworks in Belfast and Larne. The work was further complicated by the fact that a rival union, the Belfast Transport Workers' Union, had been set up in the docks. Connolly viewed this as a divisive move, orchestrated by the Orange Order in an attempt to divide unions along Protestant and Catholic lines.[2] In July he wrote to James Larkin in Dublin to ask for more money to pay arrears in wages and insurance benefits. He told Larkin that he felt insulted and undervalued and that Larkin would need to come to Belfast. Until he did so Connolly would be absent from the office and Miss Carney and James Flanagan would be in charge of all the books.[3]

By August, however, all this was seemingly forgotten when Connolly was called to Dublin, where the right to unionise was causing dispute. Workers in the Dublin United Tramway Company, owned by William Martin Murphy, had been asked to sign declarations that they would not join a union or else they would be dismissed. Thousands refused. Larkin, who had founded the now 10,000 member strong union, called the tramway-men in his union out on strike and other sympathetic strikes ensued. Murphy, who was one of the city's most wealthy and powerful industrialists, persuaded the Dublin employers to lock out all employees who belonged to the ITGWU. Within weeks at least 20,000 workers were locked out and dependent on the union food fund. With their dependants also affected, one-third of the population of Dublin found themselves destitute and facing starvation.

Connolly threw himself into the fight with speeches and newspaper articles in defence of the workers. He wrote to Winnie on 30 August to tell her that his next letter might come from Mountjoy Gaol and it would have, had he been allowed to write letters from the prison. He was arrested and sentenced to three months for taking part in a banned protest meeting. He was refused bail and promptly went on hunger strike on 6 September. No attempt was made to force-feed him but he was no longer allowed visitors, newspapers or letters.

Violent clashes between workers and police were common throughout August and September. The strike caused most of Dublin to come to an economic standstill and was marked by vicious rioting between the strikers and the Dublin Metropolitan Police, particularly at a rally on Sackville Street on 31 August, in which two men were beaten to death and about 500 more were injured. Larkin too was arrested. Both Connolly and Larkin were heard, at the time, to state that they wished they had followed

Carson's example and established a volunteer movement, as had been advocated in the IRB's monthly paper, *Irish Freedom*, in 1912.

When Connolly was released from prison in September, a release prompted by his hunger strike, he travelled directly to Belfast. Knowing of his impending arrival, Winnie organised dozens of mill girls to accompany her to meet him at the Great Northern Railway station in order to give him a rousing reception and escort him home. News of his impending arrival spread to dockworkers and Connolly was overwhelmed on his arrival to see hundreds of men and women waiting for him. At the front stood Winnie and his wife, Lillie, who had left their daughter Nora at home in charge of the children. He was delighted to see them both. Outside the station, Connolly was put in a sidecar and, with loud cheers, the whole crowd followed him as he travelled past the City Hall, down Royal Avenue and York Street, into Dock Street to the union headquarters. The crowd refused to disperse until he had addressed them all. Winnie felt that she might burst with pride.

The Irish Citizen Army (ICA) was born out of the Dublin workers' struggle. In November 1913 it was formed as a workers' defence corps for the protection of workers at strike meetings. The proposer of the workers' militia was Jack White from County Antrim, the son of Field Marshal Sir George White, VC, who had famously defended Ladysmith in Natal against the Boers during the South African War of 1899 to 1902. Although surrounded and massively outnumbered, and instructed to surrender, he held the British garrison at Ladysmith for four months before being relieved. Jack

White had fought against the Boers himself but came to associate the Unionist Party with sectarianism.

Larkin and Connolly were co-founders of the ICA. Connolly urged the men to train as they were doing in Ulster. Another founder was Countess Constance Markievicz, who had an Anglo-Irish ascendancy background. Her grandfather, Sir Robert Gore-Booth, had been an MP in the House of Commons.

According to the constitution of the ICA, its members were supposed to work for an Irish Republic and for the emancipation of labour. The ICA was the first Irish army to admit women and Winnie felt a great sense of pride and achievement in this fact and that James Connolly was her friend as well as her employer. He had not forgotten their many discussions and letters in support of equal rights for all women, just as she had been inspired by his great speeches about women's liberation and colonial revolutions.

The Irish Volunteer Force was formed a few weeks after the ICA, on 25 November 1913. It was set up on the initiative of nationalists who had also been impressed by the successful organisation and political impact of the UVF. They were influenced by one of the founders of the Gaelic League, Eoin MacNeill, who had been born in Glenarm, County Antrim and educated in Belfast at St Malachy's College and Queen's College, Belfast. Having founded the Gaelic League with Douglas Hyde, he became the editor of its newspaper, *Gaelic Journal*. In 1908 MacNeill was appointed professor of early Irish history at University College Dublin. On 1 November 1913, in the Irish nationalist newspaper *An Claidheamh Soluis*, MacNeill published an article entitled 'The North Began'. In this he advocated the formation of an Irish national volunteer force, with the purpose of safeguarding Home Rule, structured along the same lines as the UVF. MacNeill was approached by Bulmer Hobson – a member of the IRB from a County Down Quaker family – and asked if he would take the lead in forming the Irish Volunteers. After a series of meetings, the organisation was launched in Dublin on 25 November, and MacNeill was appointed commander-in-chief.

Membership was open to people of all classes, from supporters of the IRB to followers of John Redmond's Irish Parliamentary Party. The Volunteers were organised nationwide and members were supplied with uniforms free of charge. Recruitment to the Volunteers grew quickly, but relations with the ICA were strained. Members of the ICA were resentful because some members of the Volunteers were employers who had locked them out, or supporters of employers, like Sinn Féin leader Arthur Griffith.

As 1913 drew to a close Ireland had four volunteer armies. Winnie Carney fervently supported the ICA because of its links to Connolly, as well as its support for women's suffrage and republicanism. However, she also found herself agreeing with some of the ideas of the Irish Volunteer Force and its commitment to Home Rule. George McBride was still a dedicated member of the YCV and supported the idea pervading the organisation that perhaps – to prevent Home Rule – they should join with the UVF.

The four armies had one thing in common. To be effective they all needed real guns.

10

Gun-running 1914

Members of the UVF encamped in every park in Ulster for training during Easter Week in 1914. Although many of the men owned guns, a shortage of rifles and ammunition was apparent. On Easter Tuesday James Craig, Edward Carson and their committee sat dining in the comfortable surroundings of Craig's home, Craigavon, to discuss the matter and try to find solutions. They had already set one plan in motion, but in recent days this had looked doomed.

Their meeting was interrupted by the arrival of a haggard little man with wild reddish hair. He was Major Frederick Crawford, the great-grandson of a United Irishman. A native of Belfast, Fred Crawford had been a premium apprentice in the shipbuilding yard of Harland and Wolff. He served as an engineer for the White Star Line before settling down to work in his father's engineering business in Belfast. Fiercely loyalist, Crawford had formed a secret society called Young Ulster in 1892, which had an oath of loyalty to the crown and the aim of fighting the imposition of Home Rule. One condition of membership was that you had to own a revolver or a rifle or a cavalry Winchester carbine. Many young men joined.

When a Liberal government was returned to Westminster in 1905, Crawford believed that Home Rule was becoming a danger once again and so set about making preparations for acquiring arms. He advertised for '10,000 rifles and 1,000,000 rounds of small arms ammunition' in the French, Belgian, Italian, German and Austrian newspapers. Responses to the advertisement provided him with knowledge of the system for trafficking arms in Europe, particularly through the free port of Hamburg. By the time the UVF was organised in 1912 he had been an officer in the British Army's Mid-Ulster Artillery and the Donegal Artillery for nearly twenty years and so was an obvious choice for the position of Director of Ordnance in the headquarters staff of the UVF.

In February 1914, with the backing of Edward Carson and £70,000 of the UVF's money, Crawford set off for Hamburg to pick up 30,000 rifles and 3,000,000 rounds of ammunition for which he had already negotiated. Helped by a friend, Captain Andrew Agnew, he sourced and purchased a steamer, the *Fanny*, and Agnew brought her to a rendezvous between the Danish islands of Langeland and Funen. Crawford had all his 'packages' tugged down the Elbe and transferred onto the *Fanny* on 30 March.

Without papers, and with the newspapers becoming aware of the gun-running, the *Fanny* spent many days dodging around the North Sea. Then, painted and rechristened as the *Doreen*, she had crossed to Yarmouth by 7 April. By this time the committee had read the newspaper reports, thought the whole scheme damned and sent a telegram to Crawford telling him not to bring the cargo to Ireland but to cruise in the Baltic for three months. Outraged, Crawford left the ship and set out for Belfast, arriving at Craigavon in the middle of the very dinner where the committee was discussing the lack of arms.

Crawford informed them of all that he had done and insisted that he be allowed to complete the task. Although the overall feeling of the meeting was against him, both Carson and Craig were in support and persuaded the others. It was decided that the shipment would be transferred into the collier, the *Clyde Valley*, which was in Glasgow and had a cargo of coal set for Belfast.

As the committee made all the necessary preparations, asking Sam Kelly, a coal merchant, to purchase the boat, and changing its destination on Crawford's recommendation to Larne, Crawford travelled to Wales. The *Clyde Valley* picked him up on the sands of Llandudno on 17 April and they then travelled out to sea to reconnoitre with the *Fanny*. All the guns and ammunition were moved between the two boats while moored together in the Irish Sea. The *Fanny* steamed off to the Baltic and the *Clyde Valley*, now renamed the *Mountjoy*, headed for Ireland.

The *Belfast Evening Telegraph* of 25 April 1914 reported the details of the *Mountjoy's* arrival:

On Friday night there were landed at Larne within a few hours 40,000 rifles and nearly three and a half million rounds of ammunition. It was accomplished with celerity, yet without fuss or splutter, because it was done in pursuance of a well-formed plan … All the arms were landed at Larne Harbour, and a vast transport of hundreds of motor cars, lorries, and waggons drawn from their various centres came to the town. It was an amazing sight to see this huge procession of cars nearly three miles in length descending upon the town with all their headlights ablaze …

By eight o'clock, right from Belfast to Larne, the whole coast road was under close patrol by strong bodies of pickets. In Belfast itself and in all the neighbouring towns every battalion of every regiment mobilised in like fashion …

At nine o'clock the throb of an approaching steamer's engines could be heard coming up the Lough … In a few minutes she was alongside the landing stage and made fast to her moorings.

The mystery ship bore on her bows the name 'Mountjoy' ... Hardly had the hatches been removed before bands of great sturdy fellows, stripped to their shirts and pants, plunged into the vitals of the ship to join the crew in getting her cargo ashore.

The rifles had been carefully packed, five to each case, with ammunition and bayonets to suit ... and as fast as packages were checked they were seized by strong hands and dumped into cars. As each car received its complement ... it slipped away in a cloud of smoke.

Another ship crept into the circle of the harbour lights and took up position alongside the floating arsenal. The cranes whirred and buzzed as they swung thousands of rifles over the side to the newcomer, which later on slipped swiftly and silently to her destination.

The race against time prospered and just as the first faint streaks of the coming dawn crept over the horizon the last band of tired, but well-pleased 'stevedores' came ashore leaving the 'Mountjoy' empty ... in ten minutes she had passed into the melting shadows.

It was an amazing piece of work, perfectly executed. The frank boldness of it leaves one almost breathless.

With her pencil poised for dictation, Winnie sat with James Connolly in their little office several days later while he perused all the newspaper reports. His mood was one of outraged indignation. He had already begun an article about the Liberals and Ulster and the fact that Winston Churchill had not been permitted to speak in the Ulster Hall. Now he planned to complete it.

'Write this, Miss Carney, we will publish this,' he said when he calmed down:

Next in importance to the abandonment of the right of public meeting came the tacit permission given to the Ulster Volunteers to arm themselves with the avowed object of resisting the law.

For two years this arming went on, accompanied by drilling and organising upon a military basis, and no effort was made to stop the drilling or to prevent the free importation of arms until the example of the Ulster Volunteers began to be followed through the rest of Ireland. The writer of these notes established a Citizen Army at Dublin in connection with the Irish Transport & General Workers' Union, and this was followed by the establishment of Irish Volunteer corps all through Nationalist Ireland. Hardly had the first of these corps been organised, and the desirability of having them armed been mooted, than the Liberal Government rushed out a proclamation forbidding the importation of arms into Ireland. What had been freely allowed whilst Orangemen alone were arming was immediately made illegal when Labour men and Nationalists thought of obtaining the same weapons. Then having allowed the Unionists to drill and arm, the Government made the fact of their military preparations an excuse for proposing the dismemberment of Ireland as a sop to those whom it had allowed to arm against it. Ulster, where democracy had suffered most because of religious ascendancy, was to be handed over to those whose religious ascendancy principles and practices had made democracy suffer.

Then we had the revolt, or mutiny, at the Curragh.[1] Some regiments were ordered North, and the Liberal Minister humbly inquired of the officers if these gentlemen would kindly consent to go. The Orange leaders, their ladies and the royal family itself, had, it is believed, been usually engaged for two years in seducing these officers from all sense of duty – in teaching them to believe that they should refuse to act against the poor dupes who were being humbugged by the brothers, uncles, fathers, cousins and other relatives of those officers. And hence, as the ties of class are stronger than the ties of governments, the officers very quickly told your backboneless Liberal War Minister that they would not proceed against their fellow landlords and capitalists in the North, nor against the poor wretches who had surrendered their political initiative to them. And the Liberal War Minister, instead of promptly cashiering those officers, or ordering them to be tried by court-martial, humbly crawled to them, asked their pardon, so to speak, for daring to suggest such a thing, and gave them a guarantee that their services would not be called for against the Orange leaders. The guarantee was afterwards repudiated, but the rebellious officers are still in high favour with royalty, and still in command of their regiments. And the Liberal Government itself allowed the men who had corrupted the army to put it upon the defensive, and stand it in the dock, pitifully denying that it did the very thing that it is not fit to hold office if it fears to do, viz., to use its armed forces to make an ascendancy clique beaten at the polls recognise the machinery of the law from which it derived its powers in the past.

A final consummation to all this pitiful compromise and treachery to a people's hopes is the gun-running of the past few weeks. A ship sails into Larne Harbour one fine Friday evening, and immediately the Ulster Volunteers take possession of that town and seaport, the Royal Irish Constabulary are imprisoned in their barracks, the roads are held up by armed guards, the railway stations of Park Road, Belfast, of Larne, Bangor and Donaghadee are seized by the Ulster Volunteers and thousands of stands of rifles are landed together with a million rounds of ammunition. Along with the landing at Larne, vessels are used to tranship arms and ammunition from the original gun-running steamer and land the cargo so transhipped at Bangor and Donaghadee. Some hundreds of motor cars were used to convey the arms and ammunition to safe places, that night, and the same motor cars worked all day on Saturday conveying them from temporary resting places to more secure and handy depots throughout Ulster.

In a few days afterwards the affair came up for discussion in the House of Commons. The Liberals stormed and raved, and the Tories laughed. Why should they not? All the laugh was on their side. Then up rose again the hero of the Ulster Hall – Winston Churchill. He screeched and shouted and perorated and declaimed about law and order until one might have thought that, at last, a wrathful government was about to put forth its mighty powers to crush its unscrupulous enemy. And then, having attained to almost Olympic heights, Mr Churchill ended by cooing more gently than a sucking dove and blandly assured the Orange law breakers that he had not yet reached the limits of concession – he was willing to betray the Irish some more. If they would only let him know how much degradation of the mere Irish would satisfy them, he would try and work it for them. And Parliament adjourned, wondering what it all meant.

Now let me put the situation regarding the gun-running to any unprejudiced reader. Can anyone believe that the gun-ship, the *Fanny*, which had been reported at Hamburg a month before its appearance at Larne and the nature of its cargo known, could keep hovering around these coasts for a month without the Government having it under close supervision?

Can anyone believe that if this gun-running feat had been attempted at Tralee, Waterford, Skibbereen or Bantry and Nationalists had attempted to imprison armed Royal Irish Constabularymen in their barracks that no shots would have been fired and no lives lost?

Can anyone believe that if railway stations were seized, roads held up, coastguards imprisoned and telegraph systems interfered with by Nationalists or Labour men, that at least 1,000 arrests would not have been made the next morning? Evidence is difficult to get, they say. Evidence be hanged! If Nationalists or Labour men were the culprits, the Liberal Government would have made the arrests first and looked for evidence afterwards. And been in no hurry about it either.

My firm conviction is that the Liberal Government wish to betray the Home Rulers, that they connive at these illegalities that they might have an excuse for their betrayal, and that the Home Rule party through its timidity and partly through its hatred of Labour in Ireland is incapable of putting the least pressure upon its Liberal allies and must now dance to the piping of its treacherous allies.

Who can forecast what will come out of such a welter of absurdities, betrayals and crimes?[2]

Winnie's hand ached, her neat shorthand covering many pages. She would have liked to talk to him about the gun-running, which made her feel terribly afraid, but without saying another word, Connolly grabbed his coat and hurried out of the cramped office. In some ways Winnie was relieved; now she could type up his words in peace.

The success of the Larne gun-running reverberated throughout Ireland and generated mixed responses. For members of the UVF it filled them with pride and meant that serious training could begin. To sixteen-year-old George McBride it had all the elements of an adventure story and Fred Crawford became his hero for a time. All the apprentices in Mackie's talked of little else. George's father said that he hoped the guns would never be used but that there were those in the shipyard who were spoiling for a fight.

Members of the Irish Volunteers felt alarmed but envious. One of their senior men, Patrick Pearse, stated that the only thing more ridiculous than an Ulsterman with a rifle was a nationalist without one.[3] There was a vigorous demand throughout the ranks to redress the balance by obtaining arms.

Connolly was often away from the Belfast office on other business but when he returned he kept Winnie informed of developments. There were rumours that an armament sub-committee of the Irish Volunteer Executive had been set up in the spring and was actively pursuing the quest for arms. Some thousands of Italian rifles had previously been acquired and distributed but, as there was no ammunition, they were mainly for show on public parades.

An attempt was made to organise fundraising in London for the purchase of arms from the continent. Sir Roger Casement, an Irish-born retired British diplomat who fervently supported Home Rule and had helped form the Irish Volunteers, had gone there himself and a special committee had been established. Alice Stopford Greene, a wealthy Protestant nationalist, gave the use of her house in Grosvenor Square for meetings and the group was extremely successful in raising money. At the request of the group, Casement went to Germany in May as an agent of the committee. He managed to source 1,500 vintage 1871 Mauser rifles in Germany and, once collected, plans were set in place to bring them to Ireland.

Other members of the committee included Erskine and Molly Childers. The Childers offered their yacht, the *Asgard*, to run the guns into Ireland. The German-sourced arms consisted of single-shot rifles and 29,000 rounds of ammunition. They completely filled the *Asgard*'s cabin.

The decision was made to land the arms at Howth on Sunday 26 July. Over 1,200 Irish Volunteers assembled in Father Mathew Park and marched out of Dublin towards Howth. A small detachment of Fianna nationalist boy scouts accompanied them with an ambulance cart. Most had no idea of the purpose of the march but once at the pier in Howth they took possession of the shipment.

With the help of two sailors, the Childers, Mary Spring Rice and Conor O'Brien sailed the white yacht through severe storms and an entire fleet of the British Navy from the coast of Belgium. In broad daylight the yacht sailed into the harbour and tied up at the pier held by the Volunteers. A group of leading Volunteers, as well as Douglas Hyde, Countess Markievicz and members of Cumann na mBan and Na Fianna, greeted the yacht. They all cheered.

The coastguard fired off rockets to warn the authorities. With the use of handcarts and wheelbarrows the arms were rapidly unloaded and distributed among the Volunteers, who then formed ranks and marched back to Dublin. Some motor cars also appeared and the remainder of the rifles and ammunition were whisked away.

Since the authorities had turned a blind eye to the UVF's gun-running in Larne, it had been presumed that they would do the same in Dublin. However, the police had been anticipating an arms shipment and troops of the King's Own Scottish Borderers had been sent to Howth in an attempt to stop the landing. As they made their way back into the city, having failed in their mission, the troops were jeered and stoned by a thousand-strong crowd on Bachelor's Walk made up mostly of young men. The soldiers, in retaliation, opened fire, killing three people and injuring over thirty more.

Winnie listened as Connolly related all this to her and she wondered if he had heard it from Nora, who was in Dublin, or Constance Markievicz, about whom he often talked. He was delighted at the success of the mission and that arms had finally arrived, but horrified that three people had died. These deaths were confirmation of all that he had written about in May. Unionists were allowed to arm but nationalists were not. This unequal treatment filled Winnie with anger and the loss of three people suddenly made the events real. Even though Connolly had often chided her about her naivety in believing that change could be achieved without deaths, she had fervently hoped that no blood would be shed.

11

WINNIE:
AUGUST 1914

As the summer progressed, life became more hectic than ever for Winnie. As well as continuing her duties as secretary to the Belfast branch of the ITGWU, she now undertook all the clerical work for both the trade union and insurance sections of the union, as well as of the Women's Trade Union. For this her salary had grown to one pound a week; however, she was frequently not paid as the union was operating with a large deficit. She was continually transferring money between funds which should have been quite separate. In addition, she increasingly became James Connolly's personal secretary and confidante. He told her that he was fed up with all the financial difficulties and confided that the only reason he remained at his post was that he did not want the Orange element to think they had driven him out of Belfast.[1]

With Connolly's support and encouragement, Winnie became a member of the militant Women's Social and Political Union, founded by Emmeline Pankhurst, who had been responsible for establishing the Women's Franchise League. Mrs Pankhurst advocated the tactics of smashing, arson and hunger strikes. Between March and August 1914 many violent attacks took place around Belfast as women became increasingly frustrated at the lack of progress in their attempts to achieve suffrage. Although Winnie did not take part, she understood their frustration and their reasons for targeting places of male entertainment. Abbeylands House, where UVF troops drilled, was burned to the ground, as was Cavehill Bowling and Tennis Club. Fortwilliam Golf Club and Knock Golf Club had either their clubhouses set on fire or their greens damaged. Other incidents took place in Antrim, Bangor, Derry and Lisburn.

Winnie had also been quick to join a new women's organisation, Cumann na mBan, of which a Belfast branch had been formed. Cumann na mBan, the 'League of Women', had been launched in Dublin in April 1914 as an auxiliary corps to complement the Irish Volunteers. Its recruits were from diverse backgrounds, mainly white-collar workers and professional women, but with a significant proportion also from the working class. Although it was an independent organisation, its executive was subordinate to that of the Volunteers. Its goals were to advance the cause of Irish liberty, to organise Irish women in furtherance of this goal, to assist in arming and equipping a body of Irishmen for the defence of Ireland and to form a fund to be called the Defence of Ireland fund.

Many of Winnie's friends joined with her, including Nellie, Connolly's daughters Nora and Ina, sisters Eilish and Nell Corr, Kathleen Murphy and Mary McNabb. Although they had no central premises, the women met all over Belfast where rooms were available. At first numbers were small, but by July 1914 there were over thirty members. Their activities were organising fundraising functions, such as dances and concerts, and making house-to-house collections, with all funds going to the Volunteers. There were training sessions and lectures in first aid. Lessons in rifle and revolver shooting also took place, and Winnie was surprised to discover just what a good shot she was.

Her attitude towards the possibility of using guns had changed since April, when she believed the UVF had been allowed to act with impunity. She now applauded the July gun-running at Howth, made all the more exciting by the fact that Nora had been able to give her a first-hand account. Winnie had been too busy to attend the Fianna's annual Ard-Fheis in Dublin, but Nora and Ina had gone by boat with a large crowd of boys and girls. They had camped out for a week at Constance Markievicz's cottage during the Ard-Fheis and were present on the Sunday of the gun-running. Nora and Ina helped move some of the guns to Dublin and were rewarded by being given two rifles to bring back to Belfast. Their father was immensely proud of them.

Winnie often accompanied Nora to her home in Glenalina Terrace, where the Connollys had lived since arriving in Belfast in 1911. It was a happy home where James Connolly frequently discussed the content of his writings with them all.

On the evening of 6 August they listened attentively as he outlined to them the reasons why tensions had built up all over Europe. He explained that the First Balkan War had been started by an alliance made up of Bulgaria, Greece, Serbia and Montenegro, and was waged against the Ottoman Empire. The war ended with the Treaty of London in 1913, where the territory captured in the war was divided between the allies. None of the countries were content with their allotted share, however, and the Second Balkan War began when Serbia, Greece and Romania quarrelled with Bulgaria over the division of their joint conquests. The Bulgarians were defeated but the political consequences of the wars were considerable.

Out of this turmoil, came the spark that ignited the Great War.

Archduke Franz Ferdinand, heir to the Austro-Hungarian throne, was assassinated in Sarajevo at the end of June 1914 by a secret Serbian nationalist society named the Black Hand. Following this, Germany promised Austria-Hungary support if they took action against Serbia and so, at the end of July, Austria-Hungary declared war on the Serbian nation. In a hostile turn of events, Germany then threatened to breach Belgium's neutrality in their attempt to spring a surprise attack on Paris. Russia, in turn, ordered a partial mobilisation and when Germany warned Russia to stop, the Russians ordered a full mobilisation. For that reason, Germany declared war on Russia. Great Britain and France then ordered a general mobilisation. At the start of August, Germany attacked Luxembourg. They then declared war on France and invaded Belgium. In response, Great Britain declared war on Germany. With Britain's entry into the war, her colonies and dominions abroad, including Australia, Canada, India, New Zealand and the Union of South Africa, offered military and financial assistance. The Great War had commenced.

Winnie struggled to keep all these names and facts in order, and marvelled that Connolly seemed to have no difficulty and explained all this without reference to a single note. She needed to know how this would affect Ireland. Connolly explained that the impact would be huge as men might be expected to join the British Army. There might even be conscription.

The Amending Bill regarding Home Rule, which would have temporarily excluded Ulster, was supposed to have been passed in Westminster by the end of July. However, the second reading of this amendment and the enactment of Home Rule itself were both postponed until after the war. It was claimed that this was done in order not to advertise the country's divisions at so grave a time. Connolly was sceptical of this. He did not know when, or if, the matter would ever be settled. He told Nora and Winnie of one thing of which he was sure: if ever there was a time to fight for the freedom of their country, that time was now. England could not fight the rest of Europe and keep control of Ireland. When the young women started to clear the tea dishes, he lifted that day's copy of the *Irish News* and said he was off to read about the war events that were developing so rapidly.

The mood lightened while Nora and Winnie washed the cups. Nora chatted to her about romances that had started while camping at Three Rock Mountain during the Fianna's Ard-Fheis, and about who was sweet on whom. Minutes later, Connolly stomped into the scullery, his face contorted with rage.

'The fools,' he hissed. 'Listen to this, girls. Listen to this poem the paper has published today.' He almost spat the words as he read them:

> Bless the good fortune which brings us together,
> Rich men and poor men, short men and tall.
> Some from the seaside and some from the heather,
> Townsmen and countrymen, Irishmen all;
> Ulstermen, Munstermen, Connachtmen, Leinstermen,
> Faithful to Erin, we answer her call.

'Can you believe that was composed jointly by a member of the Ulster Volunteer Force from Belfast and an Irish Volunteer from the Glens of Antrim? The fools, utter fools!'

12

GEORGE:
SEPTEMBER 1914–MAY 1915

Reaction to the outbreak of war was swift in Belfast. Edward Carson, leader of Ireland's unionists, declared that a large body of Ulster Volunteers would be willing to give their services for home defence and many were ready to serve anywhere they were required. In the same month, John Redmond, leader of Ireland's nationalists, called for members of the Irish Volunteers to enlist in an intended Irish army corps for the British Army. He promised that they would also defend the coasts of the country in comradeship with their brethren in the north. Joe Devlin, the popular and charismatic Member of Parliament for West Belfast, assured his constituents that the war was Ireland's war as much as Great Britain's or any other part of the Empire. However it might have been in the past, he believed that Britain was now fighting the battle of Ireland's liberty. So great was the response in North Belfast that, many weeks before there was organised enlistment, the doors of Crumlin Road recruiting office had to be closed and opened only to admit a few men at a time from the huge crowd outside.

George McBride, aged sixteen, had completed two years of his apprenticeship in Mackie's when the war started. Like most of his friends he was keen to join the army and defeat the enemy. The YCV, of which he was a member, had now amalgamated with the

UVF and tales of how Germany had violated the neutrality of little Belgium made him decide that he must go and fight.

At home and in work the only talk was about the war and how Lord Kitchener, the Secretary of State for War, needed a new army of a million men. George listened to the talk about expeditionary forces leaving from Cork, Dublin and Belfast and how men had already left for Gallipoli. Everyone was humming the tune of 'It's a Long Way to Tipperary', which the Connaught Rangers – an Irish infantry regiment of the British Army – sang as they marched out of Boulogne. People were surprised that John Redmond had pledged the Irish Volunteers for war service. They said around 180,000 were behind Redmond and this force was renamed the 'National Volunteers'. Only about 13,000 opposed him, and they had split from the main body and retained the name the Irish Volunteers.

Newspapers were full of news about the war and George avidly devoured each piece. They also contained recruiting advertisements appealing to men to join up and fight. Every day George travelled by tram to work in Mackie's and posters along the way seemed to have Kitchener looking directly at him, saying 'Kitchener needs you'. The poster that moved him most was of a sad and dark-haired girl who seemed to beckon to him.

On 3 September Sir Edward Carson announced the formation of the 36th Ulster Division from the UVF. He said that recruitment would begin immediately and thirteen battalions were raised for three Irish regiments based in Ulster: the Royal Inniskilling Fusiliers, the Royal Irish Fusiliers and the Royal Irish Rifles.

Early the next morning, George shook his father's hand and hugged his mother who was weeping inconsolably. Carrying a small case, he left the house and made his way on the tram into the centre of Belfast. The case contained a change of clothes and some food items, which volunteers in the UVF had been told always to have ready and carry with them. George had a tin of sardines, tea and some chocolate. There was no recruiting station near where he lived, but the Old Town Hall in Victoria Street was thronged with other young men, excited about the prospect of going off to war. Kitchener had introduced a new form of 'short service', which meant that they could sign up for three years or the duration of the war, whichever was longer.

Many of them, like George, were under age, but he was tall, much taller than the regulation five feet three inches, and simply told the recruiting sergeant that he was nineteen. In less than an hour he had signed the short service form, been assigned the regimental number of 15/12019 and emerged as a member of His Majesty's Armed Forces. Technically volunteers were allowed to choose which regiment they joined, but George was not assigned to his local battalion – the 9th Royal Irish Rifles, West Belfast Volunteers. Instead he was posted to the 15th Battalion, the North Belfast Volunteers. He was happy enough to be in the 15th, however, as they were part of the 107th Brigade of the newly formed 36th Ulster Division. The 107th was known as the Belfast Brigade because it contained the four Belfast battalions of the Rifles: the 8th, 9th, 10th and 15th. Therefore, he would still see all of his friends and workmates, who were in these battalions, all of which were due to go to the army camp at Ballykinler in County Down to begin their training. Other battalions would train at similar, large Ulster camps at Clandeboye in Newtownards, County Down, and Finner in County Donegal. He was disappointed not to be leaving right away and knew there would be another emotional farewell with his family.

The next day, 5 September, George and the other excited lads who had joined the day before, reported for duty. They made their way from Victoria Street to the Belfast and County Down railway terminus to take the train southwards to their first army billet. They were cheered all the way through the city streets, and, amid emotional scenes at the railway station, the Ligoniel Brass and Reed band played 'Lead Kindly Light' and 'God Be With You Till We Meet Again'. George felt as though he were already a soldier because his UVF weekly training had included squad drills, battalion drills, lectures on field defences and targeting in rifle fire. He believed he would only need to be at Ballykinler for a very short time.

He had read glowing reports in *The Belfast News-Letter* about the beauties of Ballykinler, whose 'camp is situated in the centre of picturesque country, with the mountains of Mourne forming an imposing background. On the edge of the camping ground, and within easy walking distance of the tents, is an arm of Dundrum Bay, and here the men will have swimming and bathing drills. Within sight of the camp is the beautifully situated demesne of Tyrella.'[1] The reality was that the camp was not prepared for several thousand men and initially many had to stay under hastily erected canvas, eight men in each candlelit tent. They had to make drains to clear the rainwater before they could commence the building of huts. By December 1914 the entire Belfast Brigade of the Ulster Division was assembled in the newly built Ballykinler 'tin camp', made up of sturdy huts faced with corrugated iron and heated by smoky coal and log burners.

With Belfast less than thirty miles away it was not uncommon for men to absent themselves for 'weekend leave'. Officers imposed severe punishments. The men had to learn that this was not a holiday camp but a training ground for war. By bleak December George realised how true this was, especially when he heard that he must steel his heart and mind and be callous of life and death because that was the reality of war.

As 1915 began, training in Ballykinler stepped up and a rigorous regime was introduced. The digging of trenches was a daily occurrence. Among the other exercises which the men from Belfast had to carry out was a march across Dundrum Bay, on a ford visible at low tide, to the grounds of Murlough House, where they performed nocturnal manoeuvres to prepare them for the probable night-time warfare on the Western Front in France. Bayonet fighting in the camp was coupled with propaganda about German atrocities and there was also plenty of martial music – the band of each of the four battalions could be heard practising their military marches on the fife, pipe and drum. For the regular bayonet practice a row of replica figures was made out of sacking which had been stuffed with straw. These figures were hung up from a sort of gallows and the NCOs yelled commands to attack. Such attacks were accompanied by bloodcurdling screams from the men and this was greatly encouraged in an attempt to create bloodlust. Target practice with automatic pistols was another regular occurrence and this took place in the rabbit-filled sandhills bordering the sea. Their route marches were routinely of twenty or twenty-five miles and the men were healthy, fit and ready for war.

George and his mates found much to occupy themselves in their leisure time. A Soldiers' Home, which had been in existence since 1901 and had been formed by a Miss Sandes, was close to the camp. They would go there to play chess and draughts, both games that George had enjoyed playing with his family at home. On other occasions, he would walk into Newcastle with his friends and get tea in Aunt Maggie's Café. As spring arrived they would go on rambles along the sand dunes and the beach at Dundrum. Some of the soldiers made a stage at Ballykinler and held concerts. A makeshift picture-house was built and silent films were a source of great enjoyment. Sports days were held regularly and the young men enjoyed the obstacle and sack races, tug-of-war and wrestling on horseback.

Behaviour among men confined in close quarters wasn't always up to expected standards and some of the soldiers had to act as military policemen. Warning tales were told of how miscreants were dealt with. For example, one story that went around was about a tough guy called Chuck Patton. His fights and escapades were out of control and, as there was no prison at Ballykinler, he was fastened to a pole in the marquee. Some non-commissioned officers showed him to some visiting friends one Sunday but he reared up and nearly pulled the tent down. He escaped once and – still in handcuffs – managed to get a horse and cart and steer as far as Clough before they caught him.

The men of the 15th were from North Belfast; their officers, however, were not. John Stewart-Moore was an officer from near Dervock in northern County Antrim. He had been about to train as a clergyman when the war broke out, but now found himself as a young and inexperienced officer in charge of a squad of men from the back streets of Belfast. He had a room to himself in one of the 'tin huts' and he bought himself a deckchair for greater comfort and also installed his gramophone, which possessed a large horn. George often stood outside just to listen to the choral music he played.

For their evening meal together, the officers in the 15th Battalion sometimes wore stiff white collars instead of khaki and endeavoured to create a pleasant and cultivated atmosphere, despite the Spartan surroundings. Officers also were able to enjoy legitimate and regular outings. Stewart-Moore, during his stay at Ballykinler, managed to attend the theatre in Belfast and, on one occasion, spent a weekend in Dublin where he attended a Gilbert and Sullivan operetta at the Gaiety Theatre.

George was impatient to be sent to the 'Front' but the War Office had plans to ship the Ulster Division to England for the final part of their training. Before that, however, the whole division was due to be inspected and paraded in full military ceremony through the streets of central Belfast on 8 May 1915.

On the morning of 7 May, George and the men of the 15th Royal Irish Rifles set out from Ballykinler by road and marched the eleven miles to Ballynahinch. Having stopped on the way for sandwiches and water from their water-bottles, they reached their destination by late afternoon. The men camped out under the stars. They rose early the next morning and reached Malone, on the outskirts of Belfast, before midday. At half past twelve all 17,000 men of the Ulster Division were brought to attention by a bugle-call and the inspection by Major-General Sir Hugh McCalmont took place. Then, at a quarter past one, in formation, they marched the remaining few miles to City Hall in Belfast's city centre. It was a fine day and the city was bedecked with bunting.

At half past two Sir Edward Carson, Mayor Crawford

McCullagh and other dignitaries arrived at City Hall. Fifteen minutes later, General Powell and his headquarters staff rode past at the head of the division. The cheering almost drowned out the scores of bands that were playing. Shops and workplaces had closed for the day, and even schools had been given time off so that their pupils could attend. It seemed as though the whole of Belfast was present. Special trains had brought other enthusiastic spectators from all over the province.

George felt immensely proud, especially as his brigade, the 107th, was the first to appear at City Hall. Then came the cavalry, the Inniskilling Dragoons, followed by the Cyclists Company, wheeling their bicycles. The Army Service Corps completed the procession with over a hundred horse-drawn transport wagons and the Royal Medical Corps with its field ambulances and equipment. In all, the procession took one hour and forty minutes and, at the end, the crowd lustily sang 'God Save the King.'

George and the men of the Ulster Division were ready for war.

13

WINNIE:
1914–1915

At the outbreak of war, over ninety per cent of the Irish Volunteers chose to follow the urgings of John Redmond and support the war effort. Many joined the 10th and 16th (Irish) Divisions of the British Army. This left just over 13,000 members in the Irish Volunteers in Ireland. In October 1914 the Volunteers adopted a new constitution and elected a new executive. Eoin MacNeill, the scholar and eminent figure in the Gaelic League, was chief of staff. Michael O'Rahilly, a founding member of the Volunteers, better known as 'The O'Rahilly', became director of arms. Thomas MacDonagh, a poet, playwright and educationalist, would be the director of training and Patrick Pearse, a barrister and writer, would be the director of military organisation. Bulmer Hobson, a Belfast member of the IRB, was assigned the role of quartermaster and Joseph Plunkett, a journalist and poet, was to be the director of military operations. There would be a general council of fifty members that would hold monthly meetings.

James Connolly was furious that Redmond, having pushed for a Home Rule Bill, now accepted that it could not come into being until the war was over. His anger grew when, in February 1915, *The Workers' Republic* journal was banned by the authorities in Dublin Castle. His militancy rapidly increased. By April he could not contain his fury and Winnie became used to his daily rants. Even when he was travelling in his role with the union he wrote to her of his sense of betrayal. He could not understand why the workers of Ireland were so steadfast in their support of Irishmen fighting with the British Army.

This support was demonstrated in April 1915 when a successful and well-attended review and parade were organised by the National Volunteers in Phoenix Park in Dublin. Around 27,000 men from the four provinces of Ireland came to have their columns inspected by John Redmond and be praised for their response to the call to war. At least 200,000 spectators assembled to watch and cheer as they marched through the city, accompanied by marching bands.

Support for the war grew even greater after the sinking of the *Lusitania* off the coast of Queenstown (Cobh) in Cork. The *Lusitania* had left New York bound for Liverpool on 1 May 1915. A number of British merchant ships had already been sunk by German submarines and the *New York Tribune* had published warnings from the German authorities on that very day. On 7 May the Cunard liner, with almost 2,000 people on board, came within sight of the Irish coast. The ship's captain, William Thomas Turner, was concerned that he could see no protective naval ships or indeed any other ship. A submarine lurking nearby, U-20, under the command of Kapitänleutnant Walther Schwieger, fired a single torpedo at the *Lusitania*, which penetrated the hull just below the waterline. The initial explosion set off a violent secondary blast and the ship sank in eighteen minutes. The speed and the angle of sinking made it almost impossible to launch the lifeboats. The liner was about sixteen kilometres (ten miles) off the Old Head of Kinsale. A flotilla of rescue boats was launched and they managed to save 761 people. The survivors were ferried to Queenstown where they were accommodated in local hospitals, lodging houses and private homes. The bodies of the majority of the passengers who lost their lives were never recovered. Nearly three days after the sinking 150 victims were buried in mass graves in the Old Church cemetery, a mile north of Queenstown. Eighty of them were never identified. The sense of loss was palpable in the town and ripples spread all over Ireland.

Connolly did not share in the sense of loss. At his behest his daughter Nora had recently met with German officials in New York. He explained to Winnie that the *Lusitania* had been carrying thousands of cases of small arms ammunition. He said that Germany was a progressive nation and that by carrying contraband ammunition the *Lusitania* was therefore a legitimate target for the German U-boat fleet in the Atlantic.

Winnie was not convinced that the passengers, especially the Irish ones, were legitimate targets, but as usual she did not question his opinions. She knew that Roger Casement, a great supporter of Irish nationalism, had been in some type of negotiations with the Germans to support the idea of an insurrection and she wondered if this was more important to Connolly than all the lost lives.

In Belfast, Winnie, Nellie and Nora were giving all their free time to nationalist activities by helping with republican meetings and anti-recruiting drives. First aid classes and rifle drills continued for Cumann na mBan members, who felt so confident about their abilities that they challenged the local Volunteers to a handicapped shooting competition. Amidst friendly rivalry Winnie came first in this competition. When Connolly asked Nora how she had got on, Winnie heard her reply that she had scored thirty-seven out of fifty but that Miss Carney had scored forty-nine. Winnie blushed with pride at his smile.

In Dublin there was a sense of growing militancy in Liberty Hall where the *Workers' Republic* was secretly published. At regular intervals Connolly paraded units of the ICA around the town. At the Gaelic League annual conference in July 1915, the IRB, led by Patrick Pearse, took over the executive and forced a change in the constitution so that it now supported a complete separation from Britain by stating that a free Ireland be included in its aims. Founding member and president Douglas Hyde resigned in protest.

By August Winnie could feel that something monumental was about to happen. Connolly had brought her a copy of the oration that had been made by Patrick Pearse at the graveside of the Republican, Jeremiah O'Donovan Rossa, who had died in hospital in America at the age of eighty-three. He had been a prominent figure in the Irish nationalist movement in Ireland and America and, from childhood, her mother had always described him as the greatest Irish Fenian leader. Winnie read the oration dozens of times and one paragraph in particular fired her imagination.

Deliberately here we avow ourselves, as he avowed himself in the dock, Irishmen of one allegiance only. We of the Irish Volunteers, and you others who are associated with us in today's task and duty, are bound together, and must stand together henceforth in brotherly union for the achievement of the freedom of Ireland. And we know only one definition of freedom: it is Tone's definition, it is Mitchel's definition, it is Rossa's definition. Let no one blaspheme the cause that the dead generations of Ireland served by giving it any other name and definition than their name and their definition.[1]

As 1915 progressed Connolly was absent from the office more often. Sometimes Winnie accompanied him to Dublin with her typewriter close by. When he went alone he wrote to her every few days, ensuring that she was fully up-to-date with all his activities. Her workload increased when Nellie married her young man, James Grimley, in September and no longer worked in the office. James was a great supporter of trade unions and Nellie and he always came along to public demonstrations. He was proud of the fact that his wife had been a representative for the Belfast Branch of the Irish Women's Workers' Union at congresses in Cork and Dublin. James also took pride in Nellie's impressive speeches at factory gates and knew that one newspaper had said of her that she didn't give a damn. Because of this, when Winnie, Nellie and James, together with fellow worker, Cathal O'Shannon, attended socialist gatherings, they were referred to as the 'Don't give a damn league!'

By December Connolly was writing to Winnie almost every day and sending her copies of publications he was contributing to in Dublin. He described to her, in detail, meetings he had attended, and gave critiques of the speakers at such meetings. At one meeting in the Mansion House, attended by over 2,000 people, he said that Eoin MacNeill was as garrulous as ever and that all other speakers, with the exception of Bulmer Hobson, rose to the occasion. He had thought that Pearse's speech was beautiful, though not up to his usual standard. Winnie was used to Connolly's writings and, reading between the lines, she could sense that the momentum for action was growing.

In return, Winnie wrote to him most days and told him about events that she had attended. She considered herself Connolly's informant for all Belfast matters. He was quick to give her advice and exhorted her not to take at face value all the assurances about activities that she was receiving in Belfast. He kept her up-to-date with happenings in Dublin and at Liberty Hall, but also on battles taking place in the war. On other matters, he told her that they would talk them over in person, as it was hard to notice the inflection in a young lady's voice when in writing.

Before Christmas Connolly ended one letter by saying that he should be home on Friday on the usual train. Winnie rushed around trying to complete her Christmas shopping as she knew he would send for her as soon as he returned. She wanted to buy gifts for her family, as well as small tokens for Nora and Nellie. Between her work and meetings she had little time for herself and an afternoon browsing in Belfast's grandest department store, Robinson & Cleaver, raised her spirits. As she walked up the beautiful central staircase, she enjoyed the atmospheric Christmas decorations and managed to forget all about politics for a while. She even bought herself a large tortoiseshell comb with which to keep her thick hair piled up in the current pompadour fashion.

On Friday Connolly came straight to the office and presented her with a parcel wrapped in brown paper and tied with thin string. He watched with pleasure as she opened it to reveal a copy of Matthew Arnold's *Tristan and Iseult*, an epic romantic tale that he knew she had read and enjoyed. She thanked him profusely but wondered if he was aware of the tragic ending.

Winnie sat in the wooden chair, hand poised to transcribe his latest dictation. As he spoke she realised that a violent insurrection was on the horizon. A few weeks previously he had written, 'We believe in constitutional action in normal times; we believe in revolutionary action in exceptional times. These are exceptional times.'[2] This Christmas article for the *Workers' Republic* was even stronger and towards the end he said, 'The Kingdom of Heaven (Freedom) is within you. The Kingdom of Heaven can only be taken by violence.'[3]

After Christmas, Connolly returned to Dublin and they resumed their correspondence. If he did not receive a daily letter from her, he still wrote in the hope that one would arrive in the night post. She was kept informed about German submarines in Dublin Bay that had held up all the shipping. He sent her a copy of the magazine *Honesty*, which was the companion print to *The Spark*, a revolutionary periodical of the time, so that she could read the views of those who supported the Irish Volunteers and their hopes for separation from England. These publications often contained pro-German propaganda and were edited by the socialist republican and journalist, James W. Upton, who also wrote and edited for the Gaelic Press. Winnie also learned from Connolly about his meetings with Eoin MacNeill and others to finalise plans for a provisional government of Ireland. Although he was displeased by MacNeill's objection to the word 'provisional', Connolly agreed to meet the leadership of the IRB and the Irish Volunteers early in January on behalf of the ICA. He informed Winnie that they would discuss the establishment of a national government on 17 March.

Connolly ended his letter on a very dismal note, saying that they had told him his co-operation was indispensable. He feared that the scheme would fail if that were the truth, as it should not be dependent on any one man. Winnie feared this was a bad omen with which to usher in 1916.

14

GEORGE'S WAR

1915

Early in July 1915 the soldiers of the Ulster Division were told to send all their personal belongings home. It was time for them to complete their preparations and training for war in England.

The four Belfast battalions marched from Ballykinler to Newcastle, where they caught the train to Dublin. From there they boarded the Holyhead boat and arrived in Wales at midnight. Crowded together on the pier, they tried to get some sleep before the train arrived at dawn to take them on the rest of their journey. After a stop at Crewe, where a breakfast of bacon and eggs was provided, they reached Seaford in Sussex.

George found Seaford a most pleasant place to be stationed. The men were treated well by local inhabitants and, for the most part, behaved in an exemplary fashion. He had never travelled before so it was delightful, when off duty, to visit and explore the nearby seaside towns of Brighton and Eastbourne. On one occasion he and five pals were able to visit London and see sights they had only ever read about: Buckingham Palace, Westminster and the Tower of London. On very warm days they could bathe in the English Channel and even listen to minstrels performing on the beach. George, who, apart from his time at Ballykinler, had never been out of the industrialised city of Belfast, could for the first time watch shepherds using sheepdogs to herd their sheep and could take Sunday afternoon walks over the hills after he had attended church with his fellow soldiers. He was not particularly religious although his parents had always ensured he attended Sunday school and church.

Even manoeuvres were less onerous than before because they took place on the open expanse of the South Downs and the weather was dry. Tactical exercises occurred daily and soon the downs were criss-crossed with white chalk trenches. Food rations were good too, as were the huts in which they were billeted. The biggest problem came from an infestation of ants in the foundations of the huts and George spent many nights trying to kill or redirect the unstoppable little army from climbing his wooden bed frame.

The sound of gunfire in France travelled across the English Channel during the day and for the first time the war became a reality to George. Each morning he looked out over Beachy Head to where a dirigible airship was positioned and gazed up to catch a glimpse of the aeroplanes that regularly passed overhead.

The 12 July annual celebrations were not forgotten and several parades took place. George had never been a member of the Orange Order, which organised the parades at home, but he had always watched with his family or friends as the lodges marched through Belfast. He loved the music of the silver and brass bands and enjoyed the camaraderie around the bonfires lit on the night before the parade. On the day the men marched around the parade ground with a soldier representing King William at their head. In the afternoon they paraded around the town with bands playing and that night they marched to the local YMCA recreation rooms in Arundel Road where a speaker from the London branch of the Orange Order addressed them. The whole day passed off with good humour.

At the end of July, after a twenty-mile march to Sussex, Lord Kitchener inspected the entire division. He had been told that the Ulster Division deserved a higher ranking than it occupied on his hierarchical list of troops that were prepared for action at the Front. Sir Edward Carson and his wife accompanied him. Afterwards the men were told that Kitchener had said that the 36th was the finest division of the new army that he had yet seen and he was relieved to find that he had one division that was ready for the Front at a moment's notice. They were filled with a surging pride.

When Kitchener became aware that the men had not completed their official musketry and machine-gun courses and were not equipped for the Front, he gave orders for this to be rectified. On 2 September the entire division moved to Bordon and Bramshott to improve their musketry skills and undertake machine-gun training. Every morning George's battalion rose early to march into Bramshott to catch the train for Aldershot. They then marched along a track to the firing range where they spent the rest of the day. Although the ammunition was of poor quality, they all knew that these skills would be necessary when they reached France in the very near future.

On 29 September the division was informed that their final inspection was to take place the next day and that General Powell had been replaced by Major-General Nugent, who had already commanded a brigade in France. This time it would not just be Kitchener who would review them, but King George V himself.

The King arrived by motor car on 30 September to review both the 36th Ulster Division and the 1st London Territorial Artillery. Sir George Richardson and Major-General Nugent stood by his side. George McBride thought that each battalion must have looked splendid as they marched past, column after column. When it was finished, all the men continued in formation back to camp and, as the King's motor car overtook them, a huge cheer, unrehearsed and spontaneous, filled the air. Back in camp, General Hunter informed them that the King had warmly congratulated Major-General Nugent and told Sir George Richardson what a fine division the Ulster Volunteers had become.

Now the 36th Ulster Division really was deemed ready for war. An advance party of a thousand of the division's engineers was sent over first. The infantry were next, led by the 15th Battalion Royal Irish Rifles. On 3 October many of the men attended a morning church service. In the evening George and the 15th Rifles lined up in formation and marched out of camp down the Portsmouth Road to catch the train for Folkestone. There, on a calm dark night, they boarded an overcrowded boat.

George McBride, aged seventeen, was on his way to war.

To his surprise, the people of France took very little notice of the thousands of troops that were encamped for two weeks in Boulogne. He supposed that they were used, by now, to seeing soldiers arrive but in his young mind he had expected a bit more appreciation for the fact that they were there to help them fight the Germans and might even die in so doing. Instead the French seemed to think that they were in the way and making a nuisance of themselves by trampling over the land.

Each of the three brigades of the Ulster Division that was in Boulogne – the 107th, 108th and 109th – was allocated to a regular army division to learn about life in the trenches. George's brigade, the 107th, was assigned to the 4th Division in exchange for their 12th Brigade. In an area north of the River Ancre, which had been taken over from the French some months before, these regulars of the 4th Division spent the next two months teaching the 107th all they needed to know about trench life.

Even after the months and months of training in Ballykinler, the digging of trenches in France was an entirely different task. It seemed to George that the trenches went on for thousands of miles and learning what the English soldiers called the 'ABCs of the trenches' was exhausting. At the start the ground was chalky and easily dug but as soon as it rained the sides would crumble and have to be reinforced with wood or sandbags. George found it repetitive as well as tiring, as row after row of trenches needed to be built and maintained. The filling of sandbags was hard work too and thousands of these were needed to protect the front and the rear of all fortifications.

The first line of trenches was known as the front line and this would face the enemy, snaking around the contours of the land. A good trench had to allow for good defences as well as give a view over the enemy lines. Behind this had to be dug the support line, trenches that needed to contain dugouts carved into the side walls, each big enough to allow three or four men to shelter in them. Some dugouts were required for the company headquarters or telephone signallers. Finally, communication trenches were needed to link areas behind the lines with both trenches. Equipment, men and supplies all had to travel along these so they needed to be high, so that movement could not be detected, and wide, so that large equipment could be moved. Trenches encased in barbed wire and jutting out from the front line into 'no man's land' had to be dug too, in order to create listening posts for infantrymen.

As well as hours of work digging and building, marching and

weapon cleaning, there were daily manoeuvres to practise bringing supplies up the trenches safely. It was hard work and George and his mates were often hungry. Food rations were poor – hard biscuits and bully beef that was mostly unpalatable – but local orchards were deserted and many evenings were spent raiding them for apples to supplement their poor diet.

Lessons about the use of weapons in war were of great importance and the men had to learn how to oil and clean their .303 Lee Enfield rifles with bayonets attached. The significance of their hand-grenades was stressed, as they could turn out to be more important than a rifle. They had to learn how to use flares and star shells in order to see if any enemies were moving about no man's land at night. Training in the use of gasmasks was also vital as the masks were very primitive and the yell of 'Gas!' struck terror into their hearts. They knew that it could cause a painful death or permanent damage to their respiratory systems and there were wild clashing sounds as they rushed to put on their masks.

In November and December the weather deteriorated and George and the 15th Rifles spent the time alternating with the 10th Brigade on seven-to-ten day stints on the line at Abbeville on the banks of the Somme river. Some days they sank so far into the mud that they had to be dug out. Communication trenches were deep in water and the nightly bringing up of food under cover of darkness often became impossible. Rubber thigh boots were rare and the constant immersion of their feet in water caused many men to develop trench foot, where skin peeled off and exposed raw flesh. The cold caused men's hands to chap, and also led to bleeding and hacked fingers sticking to rifle triggers. Clothing became filthy and damp, and rats, fleas and lice were everywhere. Many men became ill with bronchitis, trembling, fevers and stomach disorders. Sometimes heavy snowfalls prevented food getting to the front line and the scarcity of drinking water was such that some men sucked on snow, even though they knew it would give them stomach cramps.

The only bright spot for George and his mates was Christmas, when packages from home arrived and the food was slightly better. At night they sang carols and were amazed to hear the Germans singing to the same tunes in their trenches not far away. George thought about his parents at home and imagined how they would have spent Christmas Day. One of the other soldiers had received a pair of bedroom slippers as a Christmas present from his sister and George realised that his family probably had very little idea what his life was like. He could only send bland messages home, usually simply stating that he was well and hoping that they were too.

As 1915 ended, life for George McBride was anything but pleasant, but the 107th Brigade had gained an excellent reputation and he and his fellow soldiers had learned just about all they would need to know about taking over their own line of trenches.

1916

Early in 1916 Major-General Nugent recommended that the 36th Division, with its three brigades of Ulstermen, should be reunited and given full responsibility for one section of the front line. Consequently on 7 February, after four days marching, they took over the complete section between the River Ancre and the Mailly-Maillet to Serre road. The 108th Brigade was on the right, the 107th on the left, and the 109th was held in reserve. Divisional headquarters would be situated in Acheux, the large village nearby. In March the division also took over a sector south of the Ancre known as Thiepval Wood.

Conditions in the trenches were poor. The previous troops had dug drains but flooding persisted. After trench-digging at night the men rubbed their feet with thick grease to try to prevent trench foot, or persuaded the ration parties to take their socks back with them for drying. These ration parties brought supplies of tinned stew, army biscuits or rum up each night and gave them into the keeping of the quartermaster, who parcelled out all such goods. They also brought with them letters and packages from home.

During the day George clutched his gun and concentrated on staying alive, avoiding the raucous shell bombardments and the snipers' bullets. Although casualties were still few and far between, he had witnessed men being blown to pieces by shells. After such events the ration of rum was particularly welcome. So too were the open-air Sunday evening services, held in the wood behind, where they could pray for fallen comrades. Chaplains were always on hand, not just to pray but to write letters home for those who could not write, or to visit those who were wounded. George felt that death was never far away.

For relaxation there were card games, reading or listening to other soldiers playing the mouth-organ. After eight days at the front line there was time off at the base depot to visit local villages such as Albert or Amiens, which had restaurants and cinemas. Nearby, they could enjoy entertainment set up in local barns by men from other battalions or even a spot of fishing in the Ancre, a tributary of the River Somme. George enjoyed the endless round of football matches, which became highly competitive. Sports days took place and one battalion set up its own magazine, *The Incinerator*, to report events and share articles, cartoons and mock advertisements.

In March the weather improved and the soldiers celebrated St Patrick's Day with bands and concerts. Soldiers named their trenches after Belfast landmarks – Great Victoria Street, Royal Avenue, Sandy Row – and thought of home. They heard that the Russians had launched an offensive on the Eastern Front at Narocz and hoped that the move had drawn away some of their enemies.

April brought severe bombardments and, in the midst of spring flowers in the Ancre valley, a number of men in the Ulster Division were killed or wounded. At the end of the month news reached them about the bravery of their fellow-countrymen in Hulluch, where the Germans had attacked the 16th Irish Division with gas and killed hundreds of them. They heard too of an uprising in Dublin. George was aghast. He believed that he was fighting the enemies of all the people of Ireland and to learn of treachery in the capital of his country was incomprehensible. Many of the other soldiers admitted to feeling ashamed that their fellow countrymen could stage a rebellion at a time when they were planning a big push to make a breakthrough on the Western Front.

In preparation for this push, two causeways were being built over the River Ancre and all the men were practising to improve their competency with hand grenades. Everyone was preparing for the assault with daily practices of mock attacks on dummy trenches by day. In May and June live raids on the German lines at night were increased, ammunition was moved to new gun positions and assembly trenches were built. By the end of June everything was ready for the major offensive. Well-stocked first aid stations were prepared in dugouts all along the line and each battalion had been assigned thirty-two stretcher-bearers. Field hospitals had been set up behind the lines and casualty evacuation routes had been planned.

The German and British lines were approximately 400 yards apart, with the Ulster Division lined up on a broad line below Thiepval Ridge, which was held by the Germans. Their strong fortifications included a huge system of trenches and bomb-proof underground bunkers known as the Schwaben Redoubt. Fortified machine-guns protected this, the highest ground south of the Ancre. Other strong defences were all around and there were machine guns stationed in old ruins and pillboxes. Major-General Nugent knew how difficult a task taking these defences would be, as the Germans were well prepared and knew an offensive was coming. Furthermore, his men would have to attack uphill with the sun in their eyes. He surmised that his brave men realised the danger as he heard them sing hymns and watched them write final letters to loved ones.

On the night of 30 June George McBride huddled in the trench with his fellow soldiers, Samuel Baxter, James Scott, James McCracken and David Kelly, discussing what was to come. They knew that their task was to cross the ridge and take the German's third line. To do this they would have to cross not only the Germans' front line, but the intermediate line containing the infamous Schwaben Redoubt. They called it the 'Devil's Dwelling-Place'. Both fear and excitement meant that sleep did not come.

In the early morning the soldiers listened to the preliminary bombardment that was intended to damage the German positions. The bombardment would stop at intervals to allow them to progress.

Major-General Nugent had decided that his men would have a head start if they had already gone over the top when the time came. When the whistle blew at half past seven they were standing on the edge of 'no man's land' and fearlessly charged.

At first all went well, as many Germans had not had time to come up from their thirty foot-deep dugouts. The Irish moved rapidly, taking the German first line and Schwaben Redoubt, and by ten o'clock some of them had reached the German third line. The men of the 11th Royal Inniskilling Fusiliers from Donegal and Fermanagh were supposed to follow them, but George could not see them anywhere. The air was full of screams and burning metal. Then the British barrage stopped and the Germans who had survived the bombing manned their machine guns and opened fire. The heavily laden infantry were sitting ducks and hundreds upon hundreds of British soldiers fell.

To George it seemed more like a riot than a battle as disorder set in all around him. His group had reached their objective, the third German line, but when they got there they discovered that they had no officers with them. All of them must have been wounded or killed. They were running out of ammunition and water and could make no further progress. Using shell holes for cover, George and his surviving fellow soldiers made their way back to their own reserve line trenches. The losses were terrible and no ground had been gained. Exhausted Ulstermen were no match for the fresh German reinforcements that kept arriving.

Nearly 2,000 men of the Ulster Division lost their lives that day alone. George's brain was filled with images of the wounded, the dying and the dead. He thought about big Billy McFadzean who, before the battle had even started, sacrificed his own life by throwing himself on top of a box of bombs which could have killed dozens. At roll call there was silence when the names of over eighty men of the 15th Battalion were called out. George wept that night for friends who seemed to have died for no reason.

On 11 July the 36th Division left Picardy and travelled to an area west of St-Omer for training and reorganisation. As they marched through one village a woman shouted 'Up Sandy Row' and they all laughed for the first time in what felt, to George, like a lifetime. Afterwards, as the Germans were still occupied at the Somme, they spent a quiet autumn holding the line in shallow trenches near Bailleul. Large numbers of fresh soldiers arrived to replace those killed or wounded.

The battle of the Somme continued for over four months. Thiepval was not to fall until late September and the Schwaben Redoubt was not taken again until the middle of October. By the time the battle had ended, in the middle of November, the combined losses of both sides were over 1,150,000 men.

1917

Spring approached and activity increased as preparations were made to capture the ridge at Messines. George could see that the organisation of their new commander, General Plumer, for this battle was vastly superior to that at the Somme. He watched great stores of food and ammunition being gathered and was told that aerial photographs of the entire area had been taken. Having been made part of the Lewis-gun section, he was told that they would be able to operate with greater flexibility. The soldiers constructed a model of the ridge and daily manoeuvres took place to familiarise them with the terrain.

The date for the offensive was set for 12 June. The 36th would fight alongside their fellow-countrymen of the 16th Division, which had been formed from the National Volunteers. The Messines-Wytschaete Ridge had been held by the Germans since late 1914 and was an important strategic position on the Western Front. Before the initial assault, as a consequence of the many weeks of tunnelling by the battalions, nineteen mines containing 600 tons of high explosives were detonated under the German front line. Then the carefully co-ordinated artillery advanced, followed by the infantry. German casualties were huge and Allied losses few. By 14 June the whole area had been completely captured.

The battle of Messines, well planned and executed, was the first completely successful battle of the war and the Irish divisions acquitted themselves with bravery and glory. Afterwards, they were informed that they would have some time to rest before preparing for the next battle. Somehow George did not feel like taking part in the celebrations that followed among the men and officers. He felt bad about the men he had killed with his Lewis gun and wondered if they had wives and mothers who would receive telegrams, like thousands of women in Belfast had done throughout the war.

Three months later George found himself up to his knees in stinking muck and water near Ypres in Belgium. The Germans had been shelling this area for years and by July 1917 the buildings were reduced to rubble and the fields to quagmires pitted with holes. The 36th Division was now under the command of the Fifth Army and General Haig wanted to attack eastwards from Belgium into Germany.

For eight days British guns bombarded the German positions and then, in lashing rain, the infantry made their attack on 31 July.

The unrelenting rain meant that men and tanks quickly became stuck in the mud. The 36th was held in reserve but was deployed on 2 August as the other soldiers were exhausted. As they moved up a trench in the dead of night they kept slipping and sliding. The smell was appalling. Only the next morning, to George's horror, did he realise that they had been slipping on the heads of dead men.

During the next fourteen days George and his comrades lay in stinking shallow trenches while the Germans fired at them. There was little food and the water was undrinkable. Some men even shot and ate rats, which they cooked on sticks. Shells rained down on men poorly protected by sandbags and they died in the morass that the trenches had become. There were mustard gas attacks, one of which left George with huge blisters all over his face. Luckily it did not get into his eyes. At least 2,000 soldiers died while waiting for orders to attack.

The order came on 16 August, when the 36th Ulster Division, with the 16th Irish Division on its right, was ordered to advance over two miles. In the clinging mud the soldiers were at the mercy of unrelenting machine-gun fire, gas shells and shrapnel. It was a disaster. By 18 August, when the surviving men were withdrawn, the 36th Division had lost fifty-eight officers and over 3,400 men in the attempt to capture the Passchendaele Ridge. George had thought his time at the Somme was bad but, because of the ground conditions, he considered this to be even more horrendous. He was glad to see the back of it.

The 36th Division moved back into France to rest. They were joined by the 1st Royal Irish Fusiliers, as well as young conscripts from all over the British Isles. At the end of August they relieved the 9th Division at the recently constructed Hindenburg Line of trenches. By November they were preparing to capture further trenches in the battle of Cambrai where tanks were to be in use. At first all seemed successful and losses were few, but falling snow and a German counterattack made the task difficult. The men were delighted to be retired from the line in the middle of December and told that they could rest over Christmas. For George, Cambrai represented another bloody and pointless offensive, another senseless loss of life.

1918

As 1918 dawned the 36th Division again took over the line in the Somme sector. At first it was relatively quiet, but a German assault was expected. Everyone knew that the Germans had withdrawn from the Russian Front and, with the extra soldiers that brought to the Western Front, they would try to make a final push against the Allies. Intelligence came through that a huge German troop build-up was taking place and the men waited for the bombardment that would signal the infantry advance. It came on 21 March and in just two days the German army had broken through the lines at St Quentin. Fighting followed in open countryside and the 36th was forced to retreat, their battalion broken up in the confusion. The Germans captured many of the retreating soldiers. George McBride was one of them.

George and three soldiers from the King's Royal Rifles had been hiding in a trench when they were taken prisoner by a German tank. The tank driver laughed uproariously as they were marched to a big field surrounded by barbed wire. All the soldiers' passbooks had to be handed over. George felt humiliated as he was forced to have his head and all parts of his body shaved, take a bath in disinfectant and then have his clothes fumigated. The Germans spoke little English but managed to make them understand that they would not be badly treated as they were prisoners of war. They were even given a meal.

The next day the long march to Germany began. Day after day the prisoners marched, stopping only at night for food and rest. With bodies already ravaged by a poor diet, they staggered along for days on the verge of exhaustion. Sometimes they would pass fields in which beans grew and men would try to dash in and grab a handful. On one occasion a French girl came out and gave George a piece of bread and he thought nothing had ever tasted so good. As they approached Germany the food got worse and the marches longer. Finally they reached the beautiful town of Giessen in Bavaria.

As the camp at Giessen had been in existence for the duration of the war, it was well organised and planned. It contained spacious huts surrounding a tall tower with a searchlight and machine gun on top. There was even a church hut where regular services took place. Parcels from the Red Cross containing bread and biscuits were distributed among the prisoners. Those Germans who had businesses in and around Giessen were permitted to take prisoners from the camp and have them work for them.

George and two others were taken to a stone quarry in the Black Forest, near the village of Hirschbach. They were billeted in a house in the village and looked after by a guard as well as the owners of the house. Every morning the guard escorted them to the quarry and, after a day's work moving sandstone for the Germans to make a forest fire break, he escorted them back to their lodgings. The guard seemed to trust them and George was bemused when he asked them to carry his rifle as it was heavy and he was old and tired. George was now twenty years old and for the first time in nearly four years he was dry and well fed. The work was hard and his arms ached but, when the foreman went for his dinner, they were all able to lie down and sleep. George enjoyed the company at the quarry though he found that he got on better with the French prisoners than the English ones. Hirschbach was a Catholic village with all the old traditions and processions that seemed strange to George and yet he felt welcome. He was alive and the people around him treated him well. He was even permitted to send letters home so his family knew that he was safe.

A few months later the prisoners were informed that the war was over. Armistice Day was to be on 11 November and all prisoners of war would be set free over the coming months. German guards left their positions and work stopped. The prisoners, now free, set up workmen's councils to keep order until they were able to leave.

In 1919, with hundreds of others, a relieved and wiser George left Germany via Saarbrucken and Metz and travelled on to Calais. As they crossed the channel, someone gave them buns and all around people laughed and sang. The white cliffs of Dover were soon almost within touching distance and, to George's delight, he realised that he would soon see Ireland again. He felt guilty to feel such an emotion when he thought of the hundreds of fine young men from the 15th Battalion who had trained with him and would never be coming home. He tried to recall as many names as he could of boys he had gone to school with, or played games with, or worked beside in Mackie's: Frank Magill, Billy Lindsey, John Agar, Jimmy Boyd, Billy White, Samuel Gray, Isaac Hanna,

Tommy Robinson, Ernest Law, John Montgomery, William Bunting, Robert Stitt, Joseph Cochrane, John Nixon, David Fell, William Kearney, George McCormick, James McGuiggan. As he disembarked with a heavy heart, George realised that he could never remember them all.

15

WINNIE'S WAR

Always a prolific writer, Connolly seemed to intensify his efforts as 1915 ended and 1916 began. As Connolly's secretary, Winnie could sense his mood changing and knew when blackness had descended upon him. As she typed his manifestoes and articles for publication, she thought about his words and no longer questioned a single one. She could feel his intensity and militancy growing, and each article for *The Workers' Republic* was more ominous than the one before. As she reread her work she could pick out the sections that read as dire warnings.

Connolly's article for the first day of January said that it should wish readers a Happy New Year but accompanied that wish with gloom and foreboding:

Over all the world the shadow of war lies heavy on the hearts of every lover of humankind. Over a great part of the world war itself is daily taking its toll, and the gashed and mangled limbs of many thousands are daily scattered abroad, an affront to the sight of God and man. In the British Empire, of which we are unluckily a part, the ruling class has taken the opportunity provided by the war to make a deadly onslaught upon all the rights and liberties acquired by labour in a century of struggling; and found the leaders of labour as a rule only too ready to yield to the attack and surrender the position they ought to have given their lives to hold. Were the war to end tomorrow the working class of these islands would be immediately launched into a bitter fight to resist the attempt of the capitalist class to make permanent all the concessions the too pliant trade union leaders have been swindled into conceding upon the plea of war emergencies. In addition, the whole system of industry has been moulded anew in many of its most important branches. Division of labour has been pushed to an extent hitherto undreamed of. Women have been harnessed to the wheels of production in places and at operations hitherto performed solely by men – and so harnessed with none of the rights with which men safeguarded their positions – and the whole industrial population has been made accustomed to browbeating and driving from those set in authority.

The civil rights of the people have gone, and the ruling class has succeeded in so familiarising the multitude with thoughts of slaughter and bloodshed that the killing of workers on strike will no longer send even a thrill through the nation.

His outlook on the future for Ireland was equally bleak:

Peace will send home millions of men; will dislocate all industry so that those millions will find little employment and will thus be compelled to compete fiercely for work at any price. The terrible taxation caused by the war will send up and keep up the price of everything, whilst the misery of the returned soldier looking for work will hammer down wages.

Nationally Ireland has seen herself betrayed by one set of politicians, her children bartered for sale as hired assassins in the service of her ancient and present enemy. The coming year may see her still linked to that enemy once more at peace with the world, and the 'Irish Nation' finally relegated to the mere status of a gallant tradition, as little useful politically as the Jacobite tradition is to Scotland. With England at peace that country will possess an army of at least one million men, veteran soldiers of the greatest war of all the ages, and when that time arrives the Irish question will trouble England as little as the rivalries of Lancashire and Yorkshire.

With an army of two veteran soldiers for every adult male in Ireland there will no longer be an Irish cause for any uneasiness to the rulers of the British Empire.

Connolly ended the piece promoting the opportunity for a brighter future. Winnie felt that it was, most definitely, a call to arms:

A happy new year! Ah, well! Our readers are, we hope, rebels in heart, and hence may rebel even at our own picture of the future. If that is so let us remind them that opportunities are for those who seize them, and that the coming year may be as bright as we choose to make it. We have sketched out the future as it awaits the slave who fears death more than slavery. For those who choose to advance to meet Fate determined to mould it to their purpose that future may be as bright as our picture is dark.[1]

In the following week's edition, to her extreme pride and pleasure, he used her words. She had written to him the month before with a long criticism of the Irish Volunteers. He had written back to say that it was the best he had ever read because she had gone straight to the heart of the matter and he was going to quote some of it as if it were from a correspondent. On 8 January he did just that and she realised that, apart from the fact that he referred to the writer as male, he valued her opinions.

By the 15 January edition of the journal, Connolly was predicting what would be needed for the establishment of a socialist Irish Republic. To Winnie, it appeared that he thought the day was not far off and he was issuing advance notice to all their readers:

But the human bodies, earthly tenements of human souls, it [the government] will take as ruthlessly and hold as cheaply as possible. For that is the way of governments. Flesh and blood are ever the cheapest things in their eyes.

While we are establishing the Irish Republic we shall need to reverse that process of valuing things. We must imitate those who have so long been our masters, but with a difference.

We must also conscript. We shall not need to conscript our soldiers – enough have already volunteered to carry on the job, and tens of thousands more but await the word. But we shall need to conscript the material; and as the propertied classes have so shamelessly sold themselves to the enemy, the economic conscription of their property will cause few qualms to whomsoever shall administer the Irish Government in the first days of freedom.

All the material of distribution – the railways, the canals, and all their equipment will at once become the national property of the Irish state. All the land stolen from the Irish people in the past, and not since restored in some manner to the actual tillers of the soil, ought at once to be confiscated and made the property of the Irish state. Taken in hand energetically and cultivated under scientific methods such land would go far to make this country independent of the ocean-borne commerce of Great Britain. All factories and workshops owned by people who do not yield allegiance to the

Irish Government immediately upon its proclamation should at once be confiscated, and their productive powers applied to the service of the community loyal to Ireland, and to the army in its service.

The conscription of the natural powers of the land and the conscription of the mechanical forces having been accomplished, the question of the conscription of the men to defend their new-won property and national rights may follow should it be necessary. But as the Irish state will then be in a position to guarantee economic security and individual freedom to its citizens there will be no lack of recruits to take up arms to safeguard that national independence which they will see to be necessary for the perpetuation of both ...

Whosoever in future speaks for Ireland, calls Irishmen to arms, should remember that the first duty of Irishmen is to reconquer their country – to take it back from those whose sole right to its ownership is based upon conquest.[2]

A few days later Winnie was deeply concerned to learn that Connolly seemed to have simply disappeared. She was told that he had not been in their headquarters in Liberty Hall and seemed to have vanished. No letters arrived from him for a week. Usually he wrote several times a week, sometimes daily, and the lack of letters worried her more than anything. She knew that his ICA parades had angered some people, especially those who had joined the IRB. She had been privy to all the discussions about uprisings and disputes between the leadership of the Citizen Army and the IRB. She wondered if they might have taken him.

The next week he simply reappeared and said not a word about where he had been. Winnie noticed that his mood was lighter.

Eventually he revealed that an insurrection was planned and that there was harmony between both groups. They would all work together in the planning and he had been appointed military commander of the republican forces in Dublin, which encompassed the ICA. He said nothing about how this agreement had come to pass.

He never again mentioned his absence but, to Winnie, his thoughts were clearly revealed as she typed up a *Workers' Republic* article he had written in February. It was entitled, 'What is a Free Nation?' In the first half, he savaged Redmond and others who had led Irishmen into war:

The Irish Parliamentary Party, which at every stage of the Home Rule game has been outwitted and bulldozed by Carson and the Unionists, which had surrendered every point and yielded every advantage to the skilful campaign of the aristocratic Orange military clique in times of peace, behaved in equally as cowardly and treacherous a manner in the crisis of war.

There are few men in whom the blast of the bugles of war do not arouse the fighting instinct, do not excite to some chivalrous impulses if only for a moment. But the Irish Parliamentary Party must be reckoned amongst that few. In them the bugles of war only awakened the impulse to sell the bodies of their countrymen as cannon fodder in exchange for the gracious smiles of the rulers of England. In them the call of war sounded only as a call to emulate in prostitution. They heard the call of war – and set out to prove that the nationalists of Ireland were more slavish than the Orangemen of Ireland, would more readily kill and be killed at the bidding of an Empire that despised them both.

The Orangemen had at least the satisfaction that they were called upon to fight abroad in order to save an Empire they had been prepared to fight to retain unaltered at home; but the nationalists were called upon to fight abroad to save an Empire whose rulers in their most generous moments had refused to grant their country the essentials of freedom in nationhood.

Fighting abroad the Orangeman knows that he fights to preserve the power of the aristocratic rulers whom he followed at home; fighting abroad the nationalist soldier is fighting to maintain unimpaired the power of those who conspired to shoot him down at home when he asked for a small instalment of freedom.

The Orangeman says: 'We will fight for the Empire abroad if its rulers will promise not to force us to submit to Home Rule.' And the rulers say heartily: 'It is unthinkable that we should coerce Ulster for any such purpose.'

The Irish Parliamentary Party and its press said: 'We will prove ourselves fit to be in the British Empire by fighting for it, in the hopes that after the war is over we will get Home Rule.' And the rulers of the British Empire say: 'Well, you know what we have promised Carson, but send out the Irish rabble to fight for us, and we will, ahem, consider your application after the war.' Whereat, all the Parliamentary leaders and their press call the world to witness that they have won a wonderful victory!

James Fintan Lalor spoke and conceived of Ireland as a 'discrowned queen, taking back her own with an armed hand'. Our Parliamentarians treat Ireland, their country, as an old prostitute selling her soul for the promise of favours to come, and in the spirit of that conception of their country they are conducting their political campaign.

That they should be able to do so with even the partial success that for a while attended their apostasy was possible only because so few in Ireland really understood the answer to the question that stands at the head of this article.

Connolly went on to explain what exactly a free nation involved. Winnie could feel her mind race and heart stir as she read:

What is a free nation? A free nation is one which possesses absolute control over all its own internal resources and powers, and which has no restriction upon its intercourse with all other nations similarly circumstanced except the restrictions placed upon it by nature. Is that the case of Ireland? If the Home Rule Bill were in operation would that be the case of Ireland? To both questions the answer is: no, most emphatically, NO!

A free nation must have complete control over its own harbours, to open them or close them at will, or shut out any commodity, or allow it to enter in, just as it seemed best to suit the well-being of its own people, and in obedience to their wishes, and entirely free of the interference of any other nation, and in complete disregard of the wishes of any other nation. Short of that power no nation possesses the first essentials of freedom.

Does Ireland possess such control? No. Will the Home Rule Bill give such control over Irish harbours in Ireland? It will not. Ireland must open its harbours when it suits the interests of another nation, England, and must shut its harbours when it suits the interests of another nation, England; and the Home Rule Bill pledges Ireland to accept this loss of national control for ever.

How would you like to live in a house if the keys of all the doors of that house were in the pockets of a rival of yours who had often robbed you in the past? Would you be satisfied if he told you that he and you were going to be friends for ever more, but insisted upon you signing an agreement to leave him control of all your doors, and custody of all your keys? This is the condition of Ireland today, and will be the condition of Ireland under Redmond and Devlin's precious Home Rule Bill.

That is worth dying for in Flanders, the Balkans, Egypt or India, is it not?

A free nation must have full power to nurse industries to health, either by government encouragement or by government prohibition of the sale of goods of foreign rivals. It may be foolish to do either, but a nation is not free unless it has that power, as all free nations in the world have today. Ireland has no such power, will have no such power under Home Rule. The nourishing of industries in Ireland hurts capitalists in England, therefore this power is expressly withheld from Ireland.

A free nation must have full power to alter, amend, or abolish or modify the laws under which the property of its citizens is held in obedience to the demand of its own citizens for any such alteration, amendment, abolition, or modification. Every free nation has that power; Ireland does not have it, and is not allowed it by the Home Rule Bill.[3]

In February 1916 James Connolly came to talk to the Belfast Volunteers, whose captain was Rory Haskin, an ex-British soldier. Republicanism had undergone a revival in Belfast in the early twentieth century. This revival was promoted by young men like Falls Road resident, Denis McCullough, who was a member of the IRB. With Bulmer Hobson, Tom Clarke and Seán MacDermott, McCullough had helped make the IRB a more effective organisation and, by 1916, was the president of its Supreme Council.

Connolly presented a lecture on how the fighting would potentially transpire when the Rising took place. He told them that it would be necessary to fight in the towns where there was a plentiful food supply. This was the first clue they had that this Rising would be based in a city. McCullough was aware that active manoeuvres were taking place in the weeks preceding Easter but he had no knowledge of the final arrangements for the Rising.

On 18 March Connolly made public his views about Germany:

Perhaps after he [a British Socialist] has been here as many years as he has been days he will begin to understand that the instinct of the slave to take sides with whoever is the enemy of his own particular slave-driver is a healthy instinct, and makes for freedom. That every Socialist who knows what he is talking about must be in favour of freedom of the seas, must desire that private property shall be immune from capture at sea during war, must realise that as long as any one nation dominates the water highways of the world neither peace nor free industrial development is possible for the world. If the capitalists of other nations desire the freedom of the seas for selfish reasons of their own that does not affect the matter. Every Socialist anxiously awaits and prays for that full development of the capitalist system which can alone make Socialism possible, but can only come into being by virtue of the efforts of the capitalists inspired by selfish reasons.

The German Empire is a homogeneous Empire of self-governing peoples; the British Empire is a heterogeneous collection in which a very small number of self-governing communities connive at the subjugation, by force, of a vast number of despotically ruled subject populations.

We do not wish to be ruled by either empire, but we certainly believe that the first named contains in germ more of the possibilities of freedom and civilisation than the latter.[4]

Winnie wondered if it was this tacit support of Germany that led to events less than a week later when the number of police raids on homes and businesses increased dramatically. Tensions were running high, especially in Dublin, and police observations of known extremists became twenty-four hour activities. Everyone sensed that something momentous was about to happen and the constant activity around Liberty Hall was being monitored.

On 24 March the military and police began a series of raids in Dublin in search of a new nationalist journal, *The Gael*, which they intended to suppress because its content was clearly critical of those who governed Ireland. The raids started in Liffey Street at Joe Stanley's printing works, known for producing papers such as *The Spark* and *Honesty*, which the Castle authorities referred to as 'rebel papers'. Such raids were not uncommon, but this time the printer's machinery was dismantled and all papers connected to *The Gael* journal were taken to Dublin Castle.

The noted republican journalist, James Upton, quickly smuggled out all papers related to *The Spark* and relocated to Liberty Hall, where the ICA was on guard and printing could be completed on the presses in the basement. At the same time shops all over the city were entered and copies of *The Gael* were confiscated.

Then a number of the Dublin Metropolitan Police entered the Workers' Co-operative Society in Liberty Hall. During the 1913 strike Delia Larkin had established a small co-operative store in the building and a shirt-making factory had also been set up. It gave work to eight or nine girls and specialised in a workman's shirt costing two shillings and sixpence. Usually these were women who could not gain employment elsewhere because of their activities during the strike.

While the police were searching the store, James Connolly, who was its manager, arrived and discovered that they had no warrant to search the premises. Winnie was told later that on hearing this he calmly took out his pistol and said to the policeman who was holding some papers that he would drop him if he didn't drop the papers.[5]

Connolly feared that this was a forerunner of suppression of journals all over the city and decided to rally support. Mobilisation papers were quickly signed and delivered by messengers. During the signing in the machine room, another police raid took place and, although a hot-headed young policeman urged his colleagues to rush Connolly, they withdrew when they realised that reinforcements, including an armed Constance Markievicz, had arrived.

Markievicz handed one of the dispatches to the printer, Christy Brady, and instructed him to take it to Commandant Michael Mallin at Emmet Hall in Inchicore: 'Christy, when you get to Emmet Hall tell him to see Tom Keane and he is to get the guns,' she said.

All over Dublin men dropped what they were doing. Within an hour, 150 armed men, including Michael Mallin, were in place in positions of defence around Liberty Hall. The Irish Volunteers were also placed on alert and the Women's Ambulance Corps and Na Fianna Éireann, the former Irish National Boy Scouts, took their positions inside. The expected raid did not take place but the decision was made henceforth always to have armed guards on duty, twenty-four hours a day.

The authorities in Dublin Castle were still on high alert and knew they needed to suppress the activities in any part of Ireland of those they considered to be involved with seditious plans. The day after she was seen carrying a weapon, Constance Markievicz was served with a notice forbidding her from entering County

Kerry, where she was supposed to deliver a lecture in Tralee the following Sunday. A substitute, Marie Perolz, was sent in her place. On the same day a leading member of the Volunteers, Liam Mellows, was arrested in Athenry in County Galway. Although he was under a banning order, he was visiting Julia Morrissey, who had founded Cumann na mBan in the town. Before being deported to England he managed to send a message to Seán MacDermott to say where he was. MacDermott passed the message to Connolly who sent his daughter, Nora, and Winnie to England on the very next boat. Nora met up with Mellows, who had swapped clothes with his brother Barney to confuse his watchers, and brought him to Glasgow by taxi. There she had obtained a priest's cassock and once he had put it on he was passed into the company of Winnie, who accompanied him back to Dublin by boat. From there he travelled back to Galway where he was needed to lead the imminent uprising. A sign of its imminence was given in James Connolly's next article, which Winnie faithfully typed for the 8 April edition of *The Workers' Republic*:

The Council of the Irish Citizen Army has resolved, after grave and earnest deliberation, to hoist the green flag of Ireland over Liberty Hall, as over a fortress held for Ireland by the arms of Irishmen.

This is a momentous decision in the most serious crisis Ireland has witnessed in our day and generation. It will, we are sure, send a thrill through the hearts of every true Irish man and woman, and send the red blood coursing fiercely along the veins of every lover of the race.

It means that in the midst of and despite the treasons and backslidings of leaders and guides, in the midst of and despite all the weaknesses, corruption and moral cowardice of a section of the people, in the midst of and despite all this there still remains in Ireland a spot where a body of true men and women are ready to hoist, gather round, and to defend the flag made sacred by all the sufferings of all the martyrs of the past.

He concluded with the following, which, Winnie believed, combined his labour values and the cause of a free Ireland:

We are out for Ireland for the Irish. But who are the Irish? Not the rack-renting, slum-owning landlord; not the sweating, profit-grinding capitalist; not the sleek and oily lawyer; not the prostitute pressman – the hired liars of the enemy. Not these are the Irish upon whom the future depends. Not these, but the Irish working class, the only secure foundation upon which a free nation can be reared.

The cause of labour is the cause of Ireland, the cause of Ireland is the cause of labour. They cannot be dissevered. Ireland seeks freedom. Labour seeks that an Ireland free should be the sole mistress of her own destiny, supreme owner of all material things within and upon her soil. Labour seeks to make the free Irish nation the guardian of the interests of the people of Ireland, and to secure that end would vest in that free Irish nation all property rights as against the claims of the individual, with the end in view that the individual may be enriched by the nation, and not by the spoiling of his fellows.

Having in view such a high and holy function for the nation to perform, is it not well and fitting that we of the working class should fight for the freedom of the nation from foreign rule, as the first requisite for the free development of the national powers needed for our class? It is so fitting. Therefore on Sunday, 16 April 1916 the green flag of Ireland will be solemnly hoisted over Liberty Hall as the symbol of our faith in freedom, and as a token to all the world that the working class of Dublin stands for the cause of Ireland, and the cause of Ireland is the cause of a separate and distinct nationality.[6]

From this date onwards preparations for the Rising grew to fever-pitch. Connolly wanted to hoist the green flag of Ireland on top of Liberty Hall. A squad for a guard of honour was picked out and for a week they were put through their paces. Molly O'Reilly, a member of the Irish Women's Workers' Union, was chosen to carry the flag and brothers Bill and George Oman were designated as buglers.

Winnie had not expected to be in Dublin to see the flag being hoisted and was preparing to go to work in the union office on the morning of 14 April when a telegram arrived. It was from Connolly and in it he stated that he was extremely anxious that she should come to Dublin on the afternoon train. She complied immediately. Without telling her mother where she was going she quickly packed a small case and hurried out of the house.

On Sunday 16 April 1916 the green flag of Ireland, inscribed with the words 'Irish Republic', was hoisted and unfurled on top of Liberty Hall. The streets were thronged as crowds gathered to watch the ceremony. The ICA, Na Fianna, the Fintan Lalor Pipers' Band, a sixteen-man colour guard assigned to protect the flag, and the flag-bearer, Molly O'Reilly, all took their places in front of Liberty Hall. Then the colour guard escorted Miss O'Reilly to the roof where she unloosed the lanyard. The green flag flew and everyone cheered. Winnie felt that she would burst with pride; she was thrilled she had travelled down to see this historic event. The whole flag-hoisting ceremony was reported in the 22 April issue of *The Workers' Republic*, as was Commandant Connolly's final command on the day: 'Battalion, present arms.' No one now doubted his intentions. An uprising was imminent and Liberty Hall was where it would all begin.

The austere façade of Liberty Hall in Dublin contrasted sharply with the hive of activity taking place in the numerous rooms and corridors inside. There were men with loaded rifles and fixed bayonets in every corner and doorway. Some were oiling their rifles, others were guarding offices and rooms. Two armed men were at all times outside the door to Connolly's office and others were guarding the print room day and night. Winnie Carney's fingers flew on the typewriter as she tried to keep up with the numerous dispatches being thrust in her direction.

Liberty Hall felt like the right place for such momentous preparations to be made. Standing near Dublin's Custom House, it had once been the Northumberland Hotel where meetings of groups such as the radical Young Irelanders and the Land League had taken place. When almost derelict in 1912 it had become the headquarters of the ITGWU, the offices of *The Irish Worker* and the headquarters of the Irish Women's Workers' Union. The many halls and rooms in Liberty Hall were used as meeting places for workers' groups and nationalist organisations. As it was also the headquarters of the ICA, volunteers were always available to stand guard in case of raids by the authorities.

Copies of Connolly's *The Irish Worker* had rolled off the printing press in the basement and when the newspaper had been banned as seditious by the British government it was quickly replaced by *The Worker* and then, in 1915, *The Workers' Republic*.

In the months leading up to April 1916, Liberty Hall had been the hub where planning had taken place and grenades and bayonets were manufactured. Bombs of all shapes and sizes were made from bagging cans, tin snuff-boxes and tobacco tin cans. The Hall was a maze of rooms and exits and was well suited to secret meetings and privacy. After hours, in a little office leading to the printing press, Connolly entertained visitors for planning meetings. Patrick Pearse, Joe Plunkett and Tom MacDonagh were frequent attendees. Seán MacDermott called weekly and Éamonn Ceannt, one of the founders of the Irish Volunteers and veteran of the Howth gun-running, dropped by occasionally to join in the discussions. Military tactics were usually top of the agenda.

Connolly's own tactics were unique. On the huge blackboard outside Liberty Hall he would place flamboyant notices each Saturday and, in the latter months of 1915 and the early months of 1916, the messages became more and more inflammatory. Such notices as 'Citizen Army, Attack on Howth tomorrow. Arms to be carried' or 'Dublin Castle to be attacked at midnight' were not unusual.[7]

It was commonplace for marches during the day and at midnight to take place and many people believed that the ICA was merely showing off. When Winnie asked him about these tactics he said merely, 'You know the story of Wolf! Wolf!' He believed that the citizens of Dublin, when hearing that a rebellion was about to take place, would simply say, 'We are having it every week for the last six months' and think that this was simply another manoeuvre.[8]

During February and March the activity in Liberty Hall had

increased every weekend. Men would assemble all day and dinner would be served for them. There were two large halls, protected by guards, where arms could be stacked and although massed raids by the British and Irish authorities were always expected, they never took place. As April began, the air of expectation became palpable in the building and every Saturday the ICA would crowd in and, after paying their subscriptions, congregate around the hall in the hope of hearing some major announcement. During the preceding months every member had been assigned a number for identification purposes and all were asked three questions.[9] They were informed that if they could not answer each question in the affirmative they should say so. No one would be thought any less of, but Connolly wanted no one to be forced into a position in the forthcoming fight that they could not face.

The first question asked was whether the individual was prepared to take part in the fight for Ireland's freedom. The second question was whether or not he would be prepared to fight alongside the Irish Volunteers. Finally, each man was asked if he would be prepared to fight without the aid of the Irish Volunteers or any other military force.

On Holy Thursday and Good Friday Winnie sat behind her typewriter and observed all the events. She could feel the air of expectation heightening. When not typing she walked behind Connolly, notebook in hand, ready to take dictation. At one point Connolly brought Pearse into the machine room to speak to Christy Brady, the printer. Pearse asked Brady to come into work on the Sunday between ten and eleven in the morning and to bring his colleagues, Michael Molloy and Liam O'Brien, with him. He intimated that a very important task was going to be asked of them.

A constant stream of people came in and out through the doors as dispatches, mobilisation orders and officers' commissions were carried all over the country. So many had to be typed that Constance Markievicz assisted Winnie in what seemed like an unending task. Men and women had been given commissions in the preceding weeks and were now called into Connolly's office one at a time and informed of their positions in the fight that was soon to take place. They were also told of the number of men who would be at their disposal and were urged to encourage Irishmen in the British Army to come over to their side once the fighting commenced.

Everyone was filled with a feeling of suppressed excitement, especially when they were informed about a shipload of arms that Roger Casement had organised to come from Germany. Joseph MacDonagh, an Irish Volunteer and brother of Thomas Mac-Donagh, the commandant of the Dublin Brigade, gave Winnie a copy of the mobilisation order for the four city battalions in Dublin to type. The battalions were to muster outside the Hall in preparation for starting out for their different commands at noon the next day. Large quantities of provisions were ordered in to make rations for the men. Quantities of meat, bread, butter, tea and sugar arrived every hour. Three-day ration packs were made up for distribution to all those involved.

Sunday, 23 April

Easter Sunday was a day of contrasting emotions in Liberty Hall. Connolly met with Brady, the printer, and his compositors on the steps and took them upstairs to meet Thomas MacDonagh. As MacDonagh read a manuscript to them, words that Winnie had painstakingly typed out the night before, Brady realised that they were hearing words proclaiming an Irish Republic. MacDonagh asked Brady if he could print copies and Brady replied that, as a humble workman, he would consider it a great honour to do such a heroic job. Molloy and O'Brien agreed. 'If we can hold out in this fight in order that Ireland's voice may be heard at the Peace Conference then you boys will not be forgotten,' said MacDonagh as he gave the manuscript to Molloy.[10]

For the rest of the day the men worked tirelessly at setting up the type in the heavily guarded machine room and by half past eight that night the machine was ready for the first printing. The shortage of type meant that the Proclamation had to be set up in two sections. The printing would take hours and one of the guards, Cathal Brugha, a quiet, devout member of the IRB and the Irish Volunteers, even slept on layers of newsprint with his loaded revolver and pistol by his side as the printing progressed. Eventually 2,500 copies were run off and tied up in two parcels and then brought to Helena Molony. Molony had been asked by Connolly to help with the co-operative store in 1913, as well as organise the girls as a unit of the ICA with training in first aid. A labour activist and member of the ICA, she had readily agreed. As an actress in the Abbey Theatre at night, she worked at Liberty Hall during the day and had quickly become secretary of the Irish Women's Workers' Union. When given the printed Proclamations, she put them under her pillow on a couch in the co-operative store.

Meanwhile confusion reigned in many of the other rooms. On arrival early that morning Winnie had been surprised to see her Cumann na mBan friends from Belfast already inside Liberty Hall, preparing breakfast on an open fire. She had thought they were with the men who had been directed to mobilise in Coalisland, County Tyrone. She greeted Eilish and Nell Corr, before pulling Kathleen Murphy into a corner to find out what was going on. Murphy told her that they had indeed travelled to Dungannon by train, as ordered, with a contingent of Belfast Volunteers. From there they had gone to Coalisland in a horse car and billets had been allocated to them. They had visited centres of mobilisation all over the town but on their returns to billets had heard that Eoin MacNeill, the Volunteers' chief of staff, was considering countermanding the order and cancelling the mobilisation.

When Nora Connolly had heard this she insisted that they all catch the midnight train to Dublin so that she could inform her father. They arrived in Liberty Hall at five o'clock that morning and Nora had been taken immediately by an armed guard to her father's bedroom. Shortly afterwards he had come out and all the girls told him how willing the men in the north were and how they had mobilised in Tyrone. Murphy said that Mr Connolly had thought their information of great importance and told them that they should go separately with an escort and find the leaders and tell them about MacNeill. Then they should tell the leaders to come to Liberty Hall immediately for a meeting.

Escorted by armed ICA soldiers, the Belfast women had set off to find the leaders. Murphy could not contain her excitement as she told Winnie about the leader who had been assigned to her: Joseph Plunkett. She had found him, as directed, in the Metropole Hotel. At first the porter had not been willing to admit her but soon changed his mind when he saw her accompanying soldier's gun. She said that Mr Plunkett looked very sick with a bandage on his neck and his overcoat on over his night attire. However, he listened to all she had to impart and she ended by telling him that the leaders were summoned to Liberty Hall.

By eleven o'clock all had arrived. Much of the discussion revolved around whether or not to proceed. Connolly had never been angrier and other heartbroken Volunteers were either crying or cursing. Eoin MacNeill had indeed sent orders around the country to stop the mobilisation and had even had a countermand printed in the *Sunday Independent*. Placards announcing the calling off of the manoeuvres were outside all the newsagents' shops. Winnie heard them surmise that this followed MacNeill learning of the dreadful news that the German merchant ship, the *Aud*, which Roger Casement had organised to bring in 20,000 rifles and 1,000,000 rounds of ammunition, had been intercepted. Casement had also been arrested, after being put ashore by a German submarine.

Cathal Brugha bought a copy of the *Sunday Independent* on his way to Liberty Hall from Mass and read the statement. The same newspaper carried reports of the grim news about the accidental drowning of three Volunteers on their way to set up a transmitter to enable them to signal the *Aud*. Three of the leaders, Pearse, MacDermott and MacDonagh, had visited MacNeill on Good Friday to enlist his support for the rebellion. At first he had been loath to do so but when he heard that arms would be arriving he had been persuaded to change his mind. With the loss of the arms he obviously changed it again.

At one point Connolly went to the machine room to check on the printer's progress. Markievicz entered in uniform. 'I will shoot Eoin MacNeill!' she shouted, in a raging temper as she waved a telegram.

Connolly replied, 'You are not to hurt a hair on MacNeill's head. If anything happens to MacNeill, I will hold you responsible.'[11]

Two schools of thought prevailed inside Liberty Hall. A few felt that they should demobilise and follow MacNeill's orders. Others, including Connolly, thought that they had already lost a day of their plans and, if they did not proceed, the element of surprise would be lost. The majority supported this latter view and Winnie was pleased to hear them decide to proceed. She was instructed to type the orders. Members of Cumann na mBan would carry the messages to remobilise outside Dublin. Nora Connolly and the other Belfast women were told to return to Coalisland the next morning with orders to proceed as planned. Her father told her that it would be too dangerous to give her a copy of the recently printed Proclamation but that she should do her best to memorise its contents. He also gave her a small revolver, a box of cartridges and some money.

Most of the men had expected Easter Sunday to be the day when they went into action. Instead, in the late afternoon, Connolly took the whole ICA on a route march across Butt Bridge, Tara Street, College Green, Dame Street, Christchurch, High Street, Francis Street and back by the quays. He was in a foul mood and barked orders at them as they marched. On returning the men were paraded in front of Liberty Hall and Connolly announced that they had been mobilised for a purpose and, until that purpose was achieved or they went down in the attempt, they were to consider themselves soldiers. He told them that Liberty Hall would be their barracks and Captain Seán Connolly would be the officer on duty. Spirits were raised by the hope of tomorrow.

One incident further spoiled the day for Connolly and his

response reminded some of why he was referred to as 'grim Jim Connolly'.[12] In the midst of all the excitement a young Volunteer, Tom Daly, fired off a shot. That night he became the subject of the Irish Volunteers' first court martial at which Connolly was incandescent with rage. While no punishment was meted out, Daly was subjected to a torrent of verbal abuse. Later, Connolly lectured all the Volunteers about house-to-house fighting, and reminded them that they would be going into a fight massively outnumbered and with everyone against them.

There was plenty of food and the co-operative women were all busy cooking large joints of meat and buttering bread for the men who kept arriving. The usual Sunday night concert took place to cover up for the appearance of so many people in Liberty Hall. The difference this Sunday was that many of the men and women stayed over, some sleeping on overcoats and others talking through the night about the momentous events that were about to unfold. The order for 'lights out' was given at eleven o'clock. Winnie and Constance Markievicz stayed at the home of William O'Brien, Connolly's staunchest ally in the union.

Monday, 24 April

Exhausted, Winnie rose early the next morning and hurried back to Liberty Hall. In the early hours Connolly had sent men out with messages to the leaders of the Volunteers and they met to discuss tactics for the coming day. There was a steady stream of visitors, each one challenged by the sentries on the doors. Very early on Easter Monday morning, Seán MacEntee, an Irish Volunteer from Belfast, visited the Hall to talk to Connolly. He greatly admired Connolly for his track record in uniting Belfast

Catholic and Protestant workers in common cause. MacEntee was greatly disillusioned by parliamentary politics and the fact that, even though the Irish Parliamentary Party had long held four-fifths of Irish seats in Westminster, the implementation of Home Rule had been shelved.

Connolly recognised MacEntee and asked him to wait until Patrick Pearse arrived so that they could discuss his mission. MacEntee fell asleep on a stairway to the left of the main landing, but was wakened at nine o'clock by the clattering of feet and a great stir in the building. Members of the ICA, who had been given passes to go home, were returning. Section mobilisers were leaving on their bicycles every couple of minutes with special mobilisation orders. Dispatch-bearers and orderlies ran up and down the stairs. Soon MacEntee was sent for by James Connolly and Tom MacDonagh, but MacDonagh was called away in the middle of talking and replaced by Éamonn Ceannt and Piaras Béaslaí wearing a long grey waterproof and bowler hat. Although he had been born and educated in England, Béaslaí was a great friend of Pearse's and had helped him infiltrate the Gaelic League and force out its founder, the moderate Douglas Hyde. As Winnie continued to clatter away busily in the corner, there was a great deal of talk, teasing and gaiety, and she thought that the atmosphere was like one of a reunion of old friends, not of those about to stage a rebellion.

'I feel grand, never better,' said MacDonagh as his fingers caressed his Sam Browne belt.[13]

Suddenly the door opened and Pearse entered. It seemed to Winnie that the presence of Pearse filled the room and seemed to dwarf those present. He had a commanding dignified air as he stood wearing his slouch hat and sword to augment the grey-green uniform of the Volunteers. Although his expression was serious, he exchanged greetings with all present. He disappeared into a side room with Connolly and a few moments later MacEntee was brought in to join them. As usual, Winnie took notes. Meetings like this took place all morning and small groups huddled in corners to discuss the momentous events that they hoped would unfold.

Men in civilian clothes were sent off to the Royal Barracks to watch the movement of troops and report back if they saw anything suspicious or out of the ordinary. The plans were formulated. Connolly hoped for 5,000 men with which to launch the Rising. They would march towards the centre of Dublin, block the main routes into the capital and seize a number of strategic official buildings including the General Post Office (GPO), the Four Courts, Jacob's factory and Boland's Bakery. The Provisional Government would then call on all Irish patriots to resist British control of their country.

More and more Volunteers arrived as the morning wore on. George Plunkett, the militant younger brother of Joseph, and over sixty members of the Kimmage Company got off the tram at O'Connell Bridge and marched to Liberty Hall where Connolly and Joseph Plunkett, a member of the IRB's Supreme Council and responsible for the majority of the military strategy, stood to greet them. Connolly looked drab in his bottle-green serge uniform but Plunkett was beautifully dressed with tan leather boots, spurs and a pince-nez. His throat was swathed in bandages following a recent operation and the necessary hospital stay had left him pale and weak. They watched as boxes were loaded onto hired four-wheelers ready for transportation to the GPO. Although it was a bank holiday, the GPO never closed as it was the communications hub for the whole country.

Noon was the given time for mobilisation. By then over a thousand volunteers of the ICA and Cumann na mBan had assembled outside Liberty Hall. Although Connolly was disappointed, he knew that the confusion and change of date had affected the numbers. Supervised by Seamus McGowan, sergeant and quartermaster-general of the ICA, stocks of guns, ammunition, bombs and grenades accompanied the Volunteers, as well as copies of the Proclamation of the Republic of 1916. The women and many of the men had no uniform. Some men wore green coats, others slouch hats and a belt. Helena Molony wore an Irish tweed costume with a Sam Browne. Although her rank was now that of adjutant, Winnie Carney wore a blue coat and carried a Webley gun. Connolly gave out revolvers to members of Cumann na mBan saying, 'Don't use them except in the last resort.' Nine of these women were instructed to go to Dublin Castle under Captain Seán Connolly, a clerk in Eason's in Dublin and an accomplished footballer and hurler. Although a committed republican, the captain's passion was for the theatre and many of the women had enjoyed watching his performances. It was hoped that attacking the castle, seen as the citadel of foreign rule for 700 years, would have a psychological effect on both the British and the Irish public.

Commandant Connolly approached Captain Connolly and shook his hand. 'Good luck Seán! We won't meet again.'[14]

Seán Connolly's party then advanced up Dame Street towards Dublin Castle and City Hall. With only twenty-five men, he knew his task would be nothing short of impossible. It was at Dublin

Castle that the first shot was fired when an unarmed police sergeant who was guarding the gate was killed. However, the rebels failed to occupy the Castle.

Four city battalions were taking part in the rebellion although some of the men still thought this event was just another manoeuvre. Edward Daly, a slight twenty-five-year-old, was commandant of the First Battalion. His command was to be the area west of the GPO and included the Four Courts. He had about 150 men. The Second Battalion, led by Thomas MacDonagh, was to take over and hold Jacob's, a biscuit factory. The Third Battalion, led by Éamon de Valera, was to defend the eastern approaches to the city centre by holding bridges over the canal as well as Boland's Mill. Éamonn Ceannt, with the Fourth Battalion, was to take over the South Dublin Union. Constance Markievicz was to stay with the ICA detachment under Michael Mallin that would dig trenches and build barricades at St Stephen's Green.

Before leaving Liberty Hall, Connolly had spoken to the caretaker, Peter Ennis. He assured him that by teatime no Volunteers or arms would be left in the building. He knew that some of his trade union colleagues did not agree with his part in the Rising and so he had given his word that the building would not be used during it and therefore the union would not be compromised. Connolly also muttered to his close friend, William O'Brien: 'We are going to be slaughtered.'[15]

'Is there any hope?' queried the pacifist O'Brien, who had counselled Connolly against the uprising.

'None whatever,' replied Connolly. 'Go home now and stay there. You can be of no use now but may be of great service later on.'[16]

The two men embraced and O'Brien left for home.

Just then The O'Rahilly arrived in his green touring car. Michael Joseph O'Rahilly was a well-travelled, wealthy man, a staunch Republican and a founding member of the Irish Volunteers. He was their director of arms and had trained them to fight. However, he had taken no part in planning the rebellion and had had several previous disagreements with Pearse about the recklessness of the insurrection. In fact, he had spent the previous twenty-four hours driving around the country and telling leaders in Cork, Kerry, Limerick and Tipperary that they were not to mobilise their forces. Now, when he realised that the insurrection could not be prevented in Dublin, he made a quick decision to join this Headquarters group and go to the GPO. He said that as he had helped wind up the clock, he might as well hear it strike. Spare equipment, homemade bombs, rifles and ammunition were piled into his car and he set off, saying to Countess Markievicz, 'It is madness, but it is glorious madness.'[17]

At that sixteen-year-old Bill Oman's bugle sounded the 'Fall in' and Connolly ordered the men to form into fours. He wondered how many of those present recalled the day that the young ICA member had played 'The Last Post' after Pearse's speech at O'Donovan Rossa's funeral. Now Pearse was at the head of the column and behind him were Connolly and Joseph Plunkett. While church bells chimed midday, Connolly commanded 'quick march'. His whole party, including his fifteen-year-old son, Rory, then proceeded in formation, with the Kimmage Company bringing up the rear. Some of the Volunteers were pushing a cart loaded with ammunition. They marched down Abbey Street and up O'Connell Street to the GPO. Then the order, 'Into line. Left turn', given by

George Plunkett, meant that the two lines now faced the main entrance of the building that was to be their headquarters. Winnie, together with 150 armed men, stood proudly at James Connolly's side.

The GPO in Dublin was a set of fine buildings with elaborate plaster-work and mosaic floors. The buildings were constructed around a quadrangle, part of which was roofed over in glass. Centenary renovations had been completed only six weeks previously. The clerks and customers inside the main building were bewildered when warning shots were fired and armed men rushed through the front columns shouting, 'Everybody out!'

Staff and customers scrambled to leave and a policeman and soldier were taken prisoner. Soon the rebels were in charge of the GPO, annexes and nearby houses in Henry Street. Their first action was to cut the cables that carried messages to Scotland and England. Winnie marvelled at Connolly's organisational skills as he supervised the construction of defences and harried the men to improve their protection. She watched him in action as he moved from window to window to check what was happening and even went outside to supervise the barricade building. For almost four years she had listened to and written down his thoughts and words with which her own became synonymous. For the first time a knot of fear gripped her, a foreboding that she tried to ignore.

As he had instructed, Winnie seated herself at the main stamp counter, made of red teak with brass railings. She marvelled that a few minutes before the person occupying this space had been an unsuspecting and solemn-faced official selling postage stamps. She placed her typewriter and her revolver in front of her and listened as Connolly barked out orders for the Volunteers to smash the windows and bank up the openings with mailbags and ledgers. One of the bags contained registered packages and she couldn't help feeling sorry for those needy people who were waiting for the money orders that the letters might contain.

She encountered her first casualty within minutes, a young Volunteer with an ugly gash on his forearm caused when smashing the windows. Given her first aid training, she was quickly able to bandage him. Some of the nurses had other casualties to help. Liam Clarke had been carrying a homemade grenade that exploded as he entered the post office. He was bleeding profusely from a head wound very close to his eye, and Catherine Byrne, a member of Cumann na mBan, rushed to dress it with strips of material torn from her petticoat.

Winnie began typing instructions to the four city battalions and the various snipers who had slipped away from the main body as they marched. They would be delivered just as soon as the Cumann na mBan contingent arrived and Connolly assigned courier duties to them. Seán T. O'Kelly was standing behind her, seemingly doing nothing. When Connolly realised this, he sent him back to Liberty Hall to collect some flags which, although wrapped in brown paper ready for transportation, had been forgotten.

For a while Winnie looked around her, hardly daring to believe that the rebellion had actually started and she was a part of it. The incongruity of Catherine Byrne, until today a teenage shop assistant, bringing everyone cups of tea in the middle of an armed uprising was not lost on her. Opposite was another counter at which the GPO's military leaders, Pearse, Plunkett and Connolly, were ensconced. Winnie chatted with The O'Rahilly, and with

Joseph Plunkett, trying hard not to show her distaste for the filigree bracelet and antique rings that he was wearing. Then she noticed the young British soldier who was held in a telephone booth with his hands tied with string. She watched as Plunkett offered him a cigarette and lit it for him. Winnie felt sorry for the young lad, Lieutenant Chalmers, who was only doing his job. She went over and shared some of her chocolate with him. Later, kind-hearted O'Rahilly, pipe in hand, ordered that the soldier be untied and brought upstairs to guard the safe and ensure nothing was stolen from it.

Meanwhile some of the armed rebels made their way upstairs to take over the telegraph office. Once they fired through the door the unarmed staff inside quickly surrendered. When this floor was taken, Connolly placed snipers on the roof and ordered that the doors all be closed and barricaded. The O'Rahilly took charge of the upper floors. Less than thirty minutes later, Patrick Pearse stepped outside to read the Proclamation of the Republic in the middle of the street and copies were posted both inside and outside the GPO. His voice rang out solemnly:

POBLACHT NA hÉIREANN
THE PROVISIONAL GOVERNMENT
OF THE
IRISH REPUBLIC
TO THE PEOPLE OF IRELAND

IRISHMEN AND IRISHWOMEN: In the name of God and of the dead generations from which she receives her old tradition of nationhood, Ireland, through us, summons her children to her flag and strikes for her freedom.

Having organised and trained her manhood through her secret revolutionary organisation, the Irish Republican Brotherhood, and through her open military organisations, the Irish Volunteers and the Irish Citizen Army, having patiently perfected her discipline, having resolutely waited for the right moment to reveal itself, she now seizes that moment, and supported by her exiled children in America and by gallant allies in Europe, but relying in the first on her own strength, she strikes in full confidence of victory.

We declare the right of the people of Ireland to the ownership of Ireland and to the unfettered control of Irish destinies, to be sovereign and indefeasible. The long usurpation of that right by a foreign people and government has not extinguished the right, nor can it ever be extinguished except by the destruction of the Irish people. In every generation the Irish people have asserted their right to national freedom and sovereignty; six times during the past three hundred years they have asserted it in arms. Standing on that fundamental right and again asserting it in arms in the face of the world, we hereby proclaim the Irish Republic as a Sovereign Independent State, and we pledge our lives and the lives of our comrades-in-arms to the cause of its freedom, of its welfare, and of its exaltation among the nations.

The Irish Republic is entitled to, and hereby claims, the allegiance of every Irishman and Irishwoman. The Republic guarantees religious and civil liberty, equal rights and equal opportunities to all its citizens, and declares its resolve to pursue the happiness and prosperity of the whole nation and of all its parts, cherishing all of the children of the nation equally, and oblivious of the differences carefully fostered by an alien government, which have divided a minority from the majority in the past.

Until our arms have brought the opportune moment for the establishment of a permanent National Government, representative of the whole people of Ireland and elected by the suffrages of all her men and women, the Provisional Government, hereby constituted, will administer the civil and military affairs of the Republic in trust for the people.

We place the cause of the Irish Republic under the protection of the Most High God, Whose blessing we invoke upon our arms, and we pray that no one who serves that cause will dishonour it by cowardice, inhumanity, or rapine. In this supreme hour the Irish nation must, by its valour and discipline, and by the readiness of its children to sacrifice themselves for the common good, prove itself worthy of the august destiny to which it is called.

Signed on behalf of the Provisional Government:

THOMAS J. CLARKE

SEAN Mac DIARMADA   THOMAS MacDONAGH

P. H. PEARSE   EAMONN CEANNT

JAMES CONNOLLY   JOSEPH PLUNKETT

Shortly afterwards, a high-spirited Connolly stepped out onto the street and called to Winnie to come out as well. 'Isn't it grand?' he asked her. She followed his gaze as he looked at the roof of the GPO from where the union flag had been removed. The Green Flag had been raised at the Princes Street corner, and, at the Henry Street corner, the Tricolour waved in the breeze. Winnie smiled at his obvious pleasure, even greater than her own. In her heart, however, she feared for him and for the outcome of the insurrection. She thought the world of him and knew that he had honoured her with his trust and confidence in a way he had with no other person.

Following this Connolly called her to type up a dispatch that would be sent to everyone. He directed her as to the way it should be set out. She was to head the page with the words, in capitals, ARMY OF THE IRISH REPUBLIC. Below that, in brackets, she should put Dublin Command. It was to be addressed to 'The Officers and Soldiers in Dublin of the Irish Republic'. Proudly, he dictated to her:

> Comrades, we salute you. This day the flag of the Irish Republic has been hoisted in Dublin and the armed forces of the Irish Republic have everywhere met the enemy and defeated them – North, South, East and West. The Irish Army has been in action all day, and at no single point has it been driven in, nor lost a single position it has taken up. In the name of Ireland, we salute you. This is the greatest day in Irish history and it is you who have made it so.[18]

She was to finish it with the words 'Commandant-General, Dublin Division'. Winnie pulled the page from her typewriter and handed it to Connolly, who signed it with a flourish.

Due to a lack of military intelligence on the British side, there was very little fighting on Monday 24 April. MacNeill's published countermand had led the security forces to believe that even if something had been planned, it was now cancelled. Furthermore, the authorities had only 400 troops at their disposal and the commander-in-chief was on holiday in England. All the buildings that had been targeted, many of them mills and bakeries, were captured with almost no resistance and the Volunteers set about making them defensible. The GPO was to be the headquarters and five members of the provisional government were stationed there:

Patrick Pearse, James Connolly, Thomas Clarke, Seán MacDermott and Joseph Plunkett. Winnie realised that, in effect, she was the secretary to the Provisional Government of the Irish Republic.

It was from these headquarters that shots were fired less than an hour later when the British 6th Reserve Cavalry Regiment entered O'Connell Street. Volleys of shots from the rebels reached them, both from the roof and the windows of the GPO. Having suffered the fatal loss of three cavalrymen and two horses, the regiment quickly retreated.

Inside the GPO all was relatively calm and the front doors remained open. Jeremiah O'Leary, who in London had been sworn into the same IRB circle as Michael Collins, arrived with some ammunition he had collected from a safe house in Seville Place. After passing through a barricade he entered and found Connolly and Pearse sitting on high stools downstairs, eating sandwiches and drinking tea. The building was well-stocked with food as beef, bread and milk had been commandeered from nearby hotels. Stretcher beds and bedding had been brought in from the Metropole Hotel. O'Leary informed the leaders that some looting was going on in Earl Street and Abbey Street and that seemed to spoil their appetites. They asked him to take wooden batons and organise a volunteer group to try to prevent such behaviour.

All day Winnie stayed at her post, typing orders at Connolly's request. Runners would take them out and bring back information about what was happening all over the city. Commandant Ceannt, in charge of the forces that occupied the South Dublin Union, sent word that the extensive buildings had been attacked by the British in the afternoon. He and his men had repulsed the attack but did not feel they could keep such a large site secure so would be withdrawing that night to the well-fortified Nurses' Home. As darkness fell, the doors of the GPO were closed and before midnight the crowds that had gathered on the streets had melted away.

Tuesday 25 April

By Tuesday morning the British authorities had gathered information about the rebellion's strength and begun to react with the required force. Army reinforcements arrived by train from the camp at the Curragh and they planned to cordon off the city and attack the buildings held by the rebels, in particular the GPO. The first task, however, was to protect Dublin Castle, the seat of government, and so 4,500 soldiers secured the complex.

They then turned their attention to the Mendicity Institution, held by commanding officer Seán Heuston, a member of the IRB's inner circle, and his Volunteers. It was quickly overrun. In the GPO, Connolly was extremely angry. Some of the men had asked him if they could return to work as they would be losing pay and he wondered if they fully understood that they were in the middle of an insurrection. The rage was apparent in his voice as he dictated to Winnie. The dispatch correspondence between Connolly and the other insurrectionary centres was continuous and always typed by her. She was constantly by his side as he responded to incoming news and changed strategies in light of it.

All day and night, in shifts, the Volunteers guarded the building and waited for an attack. Upstairs, the women prepared food when they weren't carrying dispatches around the city. They found it easier to get past watching soldiers in their plain clothes. Jeremiah O'Leary and Seán McGrath, another member of the Dublin Brigade, who were not well known, travelled around the city gathering information and reporting back to Connolly on the formation of cordons of British troops. As the day wore on, Winnie became concerned about Joseph Plunkett's increasing weakness and her eyes were drawn to the heavy bandages which he clutched around his throat. She confided to Connolly that she found his large rings and bracelet overdramatic. Connolly quickly rebuked her by saying that Plunkett could do and wear what he pleased because he was an expert in military science. As usual, when he spoke sharply to her, Winnie blushed and resolved not to mention the matter again.

Reports came in of two hours of fighting at the Annesley Bridge post where the army was trying to repair the Great Northern Railway line, which had been damaged earlier by rebels. There were numerous casualties and finally the Volunteers were forced to retreat from both the Annesley Bridge and Fairview posts. An exhausted Winnie went to lie down but was depressed by the fact that not one piece of good news had come back from the dozens of dispatches she had typed. In fact the last one had stated that two British Infantry brigades had just landed at Kingstown and that martial law had been declared. John Joseph Scollan, commandant of the Hibernian Rifles who had voted to join the fight, returned to the headquarters. He had been directed earlier to take twenty-five of his men and proceed to the roof of the Exchange Hotel. He reported that the City Hall had been occupied by soldiers but that his men had killed over twenty Inniskilling Fusiliers when they had attempted to storm his position.

Wednesday 26 April

By Wednesday Jeremiah O'Leary found that even he could not manage to get through the cordons that surrounded the inner city. The day began with outbursts of rifle and machine-gun fire aimed mainly at the GPO. Some volunteers from the ICA raised their flag, the Starry Plough, on the top of the Imperial Hotel. Loud cheering erupted and the irony of the fact that the building was owned by William Martin Murphy, the man who had led Dublin employers against workers in the lock-out of 1913, was not lost on them. His actions contributed to their formation as an army and now they were in control of his hotel. Reports were received that Liberty Hall had been shelled, even though it had been evacuated since Monday. Connolly was incensed, remembering the promise he had made to the building's caretaker.

The gunboat *Helga* was stationed on the River Liffey and it joined in the artillery barrage. Many of the Volunteers' smaller posts were overcome and forced to withdraw. In the Four Courts and in the area around North King Street, Commandant Edward Daly's men put up firm resistance and did not retreat. Several buildings were set on fire and fighting continued into the darkness. As the day wore on the gunfire became heavier. The two brigades that landed the night before marched into Dublin as Commandant de Valera's Third Battalion had blocked the railway line.

Information about the fighting all over the city was brought to the GPO where Connolly had just woken from a short nap. He could deduce that the rebels were outnumbered by twenty-to-one in Dublin. His greatest concern was for the morale of his men and he tried to cheer them by suggesting a singsong of the route march songs. They enthusiastically joined in and their voices echoed around the building. Michael Collins, who had been trying to sleep, was indignant at being awakened. He whispered to Winnie that if this was supposed to be a concert then perhaps the men would want a piano in the back room.[19] She gave one of her very rare smiles.

Thursday 27 April

By Thursday morning the main thrust of the British attack on the Volunteers was directed towards the GPO and its surrounding buildings. General Sir John Maxwell, the new British military commander, arrived in Dublin and he had full powers to do as he wished. The GPO was under almost constant fire. While outside surveying the damage, Connolly was wounded in the shoulder by a gunshot. He returned to the building and was put in one of the beds in the area the nurses described as 'front line trenches'.

Winnie ran to his side. 'Why do you expose yourself to danger when so much depends on you?' she asked him irritably.

'Do not blame me now, Winnie,' he whispered. 'I must take risks like the others.'

Connolly rose from the bed when his wound was treated and continued rallying his men, who were returning fire. The building was riddled by gunshots hour after hour and, in the afternoon, a ricocheting bullet caught Connolly in the ankle. He was in agony and forced to lie on a makeshift stretcher. Despite this he immediately dictated a very defiant dispatch to Winnie and ordered that it be sent to all the leaders whose morale needed to be sustained. Dr O'Mahony, who was one of the Volunteers' prisoners, treated his wounds, assisted by a medical student named Desmond Ryan. Dr O'Mahony told Ryan that he thought the wound very serious indeed. Connolly heard him and, fearing for his chances of survival, immediately called over Seán Nunan who was passing. Seán and his brother Ernie were Irish Volunteers from units in England and hailed from Brixton. Connolly asked Nunan if he would take a message to Commandant Pearse on his behalf. Nunan agreed and Connolly said to him, 'Tell him, trust Miss Carney as you would trust me.'[20] Nunan duly delivered the message to Pearse.

That night everyone was exhausted, but sleep did not come easily. The women insisted that Seán MacDermott lay down as he was not physically strong. His leg had been operated on a few years before and had left a weakness that had been exacerbated by all his travelling before the Rising, when he was spreading anti-British and anti-recruitment propaganda. Winnie and Aoife de Burca, a Kildare member of Cumann na mBan and a nurse who had volunteered for first aid duty, carried a mattress to Commandant Pearse in the hope that he, too, would take a rest. Many of the Volunteers slept clutching their shiny traditional Irish rosary beads, made in Dublin from cows' horns. Winnie thought of her mother in Belfast, probably unaware that her daughter was in the midst of this uprising. Winnie wondered if she would ever see her again.

Friday 28 April

Friday morning was beautifully bright and, while Aoife took tea to the rest of the wounded men, Winnie took Connolly's to him. She noted the paleness of his skin and felt the clamminess of his forehead. Everyone in the GPO was told to turn out and present themselves for breakfast upstairs in the staff dining room, now referred to as the men's mess. Men who had been taken prisoner when the building was captured served mugs of tea and bread and margarine to the Volunteers on a scrubbed wooden table.

Most of the men's spirits were good, despite the fact that British forces were closing in around them. Tom Clarke was less optimistic and confided to Aoife – who, in turn, confided to Winnie – that things were looking serious. The first dispatch of the day, however, brought good news to the GPO. Commandant Thomas Ashe, in County Meath, had defeated a large group of RIC officers in a five-hour battle. But as the day wore on, it became obvious that all was lost. Posts all over the city were falling and the constant shelling had left the GPO in flames. It was apparent to all that the GPO could not be held much longer.

At noon the leaders decided that all the women, except those performing nursing duties, should be evacuated. Pearse called the women together and praised them for their great heroism and bravery before ordering them to leave. Twelve women and sixteen wounded men would leave but, although urged by Pearse to do so, Winnie curtly refused to go. Close friends, suffragettes and members of Cumann na mBan, Elizabeth O'Farrell and Julia Grenan said that they, too, would remain with the men. As nurses they had worked tirelessly all week and acted as dispatch carriers when required. The wounded men and the women left, escorted by Father Flanagan and Desmond Fitzgerald, who took the wounded to Jervis Street hospital. Connolly had refused to leave with those wounded, saying that his place was with his men.[21] Thirty men then left in a second group, with Pearse supervising the evacuation.

In dreadful pain, Connolly insisted that he be transferred out of the hospital area in the GPO onto a bed on castors. All afternoon he was rolled around the building so that he could cheer on the men who were still firing from their stations. Winnie walked beside him while he dictated letters as well as his account of the rebellion. As she typed out his words, she ensured that her gun was within reach. In other parts of the building Volunteers were busy trying to extinguish the many fires.

By seven o'clock the flames had spread to the main hall, the heat was intense and it was obvious to all that the GPO must be evacuated. The O'Rahilly volunteered to lead a party of men out of the building in an attempt to reach Williams and Woods, a factory on Great Britain Street (now Parnell Street) that was still intact. As they advanced up Moore Street, he and several others were shot down by machine-gun fire from the British barricade at the street's intersection with Great Britain Street. The O'Rahilly managed to stumble across the road and find shelter in Sackville Lane but, being severely wounded, he could go no further and lay down. He pulled out a piece of paper from his pocket and began writing to his wife. The short letter said:

Written after I was shot – Darling Nancy I was shot leading a rush up Moore Street [and] took refuge in a doorway. While I was there I heard the men pointing out where I was and I made a bolt for the lane I am in now. I got more [than] one bullet I think. Tons and tons of love dearie to you and the boys and to Nell and Anna. It was a good fight anyhow.

Please deliver this to Nannie O'Rahilly, 40 Herbert Park, Dublin. Goodbye darling.[22]

By eight o'clock that night Connolly and Pearse agreed that, if they were not to be buried in burning timber and falling stone, the time had come to leave. They had heard about The O'Rahilly's wounding and the belief that he may no longer be alive. Connolly asked Winnie to sit down and type a final dispatch. He said it was simply to be addressed to 'soldiers'. Tears rolled down her cheeks as he reminded his men of what they had achieved. He said that after five days the flag of a free Irish Republic still flew over the GPO and that it was the first time in 700 years that had happened. He assured them that all the commandants were still holding their positions: Daly in the Linenhall Barracks, MacDonagh from Bishop Street to Stephen's Green, Mallin in the College of Surgeons, de Valera in Boland's Bakery and Ceannt in the South Dublin Union. He informed them that he had been injured twice but had had his bed moved into the firing line so that he could be of use. Finally he exhorted them to have courage because they were winning and never to forget the splendid women who had everywhere stood beside them and cheered them on. He finished with the words, 'Never had man or woman a grander cause, never was a cause more grandly served.'[23]

Winnie broke down completely. She knew that he was saying all this to raise everyone's morale but still it sounded so eloquent and, for his sake, she wished it were true. Her shoulders shuddered and tears streamed down her face as he stroked her hand.

The garrison was by now all on the ground floor as the fires were so close. IRB member Diarmuid Lynch, aide-de-camp to Connolly, was put in charge of removing the bombs from the cellars and the Nunan brothers went to help him. The other groups would carry out food and ammunition. Shortly before nine o'clock the last men and women left the burning GPO by the Henry Street door. Four men carried Connolly out on a stretcher. To protect him from gunfire a young Fianna Éireann boy ran on one side of him and Winnie ran on the other. Nurses O'Farrell and Grenan accompanied them. Pearse is said by some to have been the last man to leave the GPO, dodging bullets that rained down upon him from the army and his own men.

Under severe gunfire from a contingent of soldiers behind a barricade, the dishevelled party arrived in a laneway off Moore Street and took shelter in a cottage. In panic and fear, many of the rebels fired indiscriminately and innocent residents of Moore Street were killed. They barricaded the house and took up their positions in the parlour. Connolly lay on a stretcher in the middle of the room and was obviously in great agony. Arriving just before Pearse, Nurse O'Farrell hurried over to ask how he felt. He told her that he was bad and that the soldier who had shot him had done a good day's work for the British government. Mattresses were procured for Connolly and the other seventeen wounded men to lie on, one of whom was a British soldier. Connolly muttered to Winnie that he would dearly love a cup of tea. She had none but was able to procure some Bovril from one of the Volunteers and she hurried off to make it for him.

The owner of the cottage could see how famished and worn they all were and offered them a ham that she had been boiling on the range. In fear that soldiers would be following the rebels, she and her family then took shelter in the cellar. Winnie divided the ham out among all the men and knelt down to feed Connolly. She looked around at the men and women eating in the small room: Seán MacDermott, Tom Clarke, Patrick Pearse, Willie Pearse, Joseph Plunkett, Julia and Elizabeth. All had been so brave and so full of hope at the start of the week. Now everyone was exhausted and just lay down wherever they could find a space.

Plunkett called Winnie aside and begged a moment to talk to her. Giving her an envelope with 'Somewhere in Moore Street' on the front, along with his filigree bracelet and one of his large antique rings, he asked if she would do him a great service. He requested that she give the items to his fiancée, Grace Gifford. He said that her Protestant family had disowned her because of her conversion to Roman Catholicism and he wanted to ensure that she was taken care of in the event of his death. His cheerfulness while in pain, and his courage, had caused Winnie to change her mind about him during the last five days. She promised him that she would.

His action encouraged her to go round each of the men collecting their addresses and any small treasures that they wished her to give to their wives or mothers. One very young lad asked her if she thought they would win and she avoided giving the honest answer by saying that she had never been in a rebellion before.

All through the night they could hear machine-gun fire hitting the buildings around them and the roar of burning buildings. Sometimes there were loud bangs that they surmised were hand grenades being thrown in their direction. More Volunteers arrived, having dodged British machine-gun fire from Great Britain Street. Throughout the night the three women were kept busy taking it in turns to nurse the wounded.

Saturday 29 April

In Moore Street, after very little sleep, Winnie wakened early and made tea for everyone. Nurses O'Farrell and Grenan helped her while, at the same time, checking on the wounded men. After breakfast, Connolly and the other wounded men were carried through holes that had been knocked in the interior walls of the terraced houses in an attempt by the retreating rebels to reach Great Britain Street in safety. They came to rest in 16 Moore Street and Connolly was placed on a bed in a back room. There, with Pearse, MacDermott, Plunkett and Clarke, a council of war was held and the five men tried to convince themselves that the fight could go on. Willie Pearse was with them too. In all their hearts they knew that it was over. Clarke wept when they finally agreed that surrender was the only option. Winnie went over to comfort him but she, usually so reserved and aloof, also broke down.

Nurse Elizabeth O'Farrell, who had been a dispatch carrier to Galway just five days before, was chosen to carry the letter of surrender. She was a fearless, tall, blonde girl who accepted the task without hesitation. Winnie thought that she was a good choice as she was very strong and capable. Having hung a white flag outside the house, MacDermott provided her with a white handkerchief and instructed her to proceed to the nearest barricade. There she was to inform them that Commandant Pearse wanted to treat with their commander.

As she walked up Moore Street she saw The O'Rahilly's hat and revolver lying on the ground. Having given her message to the officer in charge at the barricade, O'Farrell was escorted up the street to meet another officer, who took her over to the hall of the National Bank. She was searched and the Red Cross was cut from her arm and the front of her apron. Then she was taken to Brigadier General Lowe, who treated her in a gentle fashion. She was told to inform Pearse that he, the Brigadier General, would not treat until there was an unconditional surrender. Pearse was to be the first to hand himself over, with Connolly following on a stretcher. O'Farrell was driven by motor car back to Moore Street and ordered to return in half an hour.

When she returned with the message Winnie knelt down on the floor beside Connolly and, weeping, pleaded that he not give himself up as he would be shot. She believed there must be another way. However, he just shook his head sadly and told her that he could not bear to see all his brave boys burn to death. As her tears fell, Winnie washed Connolly's face and tenderly brushed his hair. Julia Grenan dressed his wounds.

'Thank you, Winnie, for everything,' he said softly.

Pearse drew up the final order for the garrison commanders. It stated:

In order to prevent further slaughter of Dublin citizens, and in the hope of saving the lives of our followers now surrounded and hopelessly outnumbered, the members of the Provisional Government at headquarters have now agreed to an unconditional surrender, and the Commandants of the various districts in the City and Country will order their commands to lay down arms.[24]

Pearse signed and dated the order at 3.45 p.m., 29 April 1916. Below this Connolly wrote and signed, 'I agree to these conditions for the men only under my own command in the Moore Street District and for the men in the Stephen's Green Command.'

While many of the men knelt, rifles in hand, to say the Rosary, Pearse and O'Farrell departed the Moore Street house. They were met at the barricade at half past three by Captain Lowe. Pearse handed over his pistol, sword and ammunition and signed the document of surrender that had been placed on an old wooden bench. O'Farrell agreed to deliver the documents of surrender, which the other commandants would sign, to all the Dublin outposts. Accompanied by two officers and an armed guard, Pearse was taken away in a motor car.

With grief-stricken expressions, the garrison from Moore Street marched into the devastation that was O'Connell Street. When they lined up in front of the Gresham Hotel all were ordered to lay down their arms and equipment at the foot of the Parnell statue. The ambulance corps were instructed to remove their red crosses. Winnie and Julia Grenan were towards the back of the line, near the leaders. One of the British officers laughed at Seán MacDermott and asked if they had cripples in their army.

They were then marched up O'Connell Street to the plot of grass outside the Rotunda Hospital. They were ordered not to leave the small grass area but to lie there, and were told that if they attempted to rise above their knees they would be shot, either by the police and military who surrounded them, or by the machine guns that were trained on them from nearby roofs. Winnie thought the space would hardly have held 200, let alone the 400 of them. Consequently many were almost on top of each other. They were given no food or water during the night as they huddled together in the cold. Their numbers grew by the hour as O'Farrell reached the other occupied buildings and gave the leaders in each location the notes of surrender. Winnie huddled beside Seán MacDermott, who was shivering so much that she lifted her own coat and put it over him. He shared his compressed food lozenges with her but the taste was so dreadful that she could barely swallow them. Nearby, Plunkett also looked to be suffering from the cold. Connolly had given Winnie his coat and, seeing

Plunkett's discomfort, she placed it on the ground for Plunkett to lie on.

Some of the soldiers took great pleasure in surmising loudly about what was going to happen to the prisoners. Others showed their anger by cutting off the Red Cross insignia from a very young Volunteer's coat. Winnie tried to ignore the rude talk of some of the officers but her blood was boiling because so many of the Volunteers were so young. She even saw an officer kick a boy and she whispered to MacDermott what she would do if she had her revolver. He put his arm around her, afraid that the usually placid Miss Carney might attempt something foolish.[25] It was a long uncomfortable night and most were fearful of what the next day would bring. Winnie worried most about what would happen to James Connolly.

Sunday 30 April–8 May

At dawn many of the prisoners knelt to say their prayers. Detectives started to arrive to distinguish between the men and the leaders. Tom Clarke was taken away under armed guard. When he returned he said that he had been searched and everything he had was removed. He told the others that he was amazed at how much they knew about his entire life.

On the stroke of nine the rebels were marched across Dublin to Richmond Barracks with a double line of armed military. Winnie and Julia Grenan waited to assist Seán MacDermott, who was unable to march, but were told to walk on and that he would be escorted alone. With many wrecked buildings, the damage to the city was great; the inhabitants blamed the Volunteers entirely for causing such wanton destruction. Hostile crowds jeered them as they dejectedly walked past. The wives of soldiers who were serving on the Western Front, and the widows of those who had died in the battle in Gallipoli, spat at them and shouted abuse as they approached the barracks. Some threw rotten fruit and vegetables. Winnie wished that she could stop and talk to them, explain that what they had done was necessary for Ireland to be free, and that it was the British Army who had shelled their city. She wanted to tell them that the brave men she had been with in the GPO were fighting to release them from the yoke of British imperialism and that the first stop on the road to freedom had been taken. The flag had flown.

Richmond Barracks was an imposing building that had been occupied by the British Army since 1814. In recent years many Irishmen had been stationed in the barracks before going off to fight in the war. Now it was used as a cavalry depot and housed the four Hussar regiments, as well as members of the Royal Irish Regiment who had so recently been fighting the Irish Volunteer group led by Commandant Éamonn Ceannt. Winnie feared for the future as she watched all her fellow insurrectionists being directed to separate locations. Joseph Plunkett, ill and exhausted, fainted and was taken away by soldiers. She scoured the scene for Connolly but there was no sign of him. Pearse also seemed to have quite simply vanished. MacDermott arrived about forty-five minutes later, completely worn out and pale as death.

Having spent all night out in the open, Winnie was chilled to the bone when she was finally ushered inside the barracks. She was surprised at the lack of harshness from the soldiers who directed Julia Grenan and herself into one of the guardrooms. Still shivering – though from cold or fear she could not be sure

– Winnie asked one of the young officers whether it might be possible to have some tea to warm them up. To her surprise, they were quickly brought tea and shiny buns which, given their state of hunger, they gobbled in a most unladylike fashion. They were delicious. Winnie and Julia were then taken to the married quarters in the barracks where other members of Cumann na nBan from the Four Courts joined them. Countess Markievicz was there too, in uniform, and she rushed over to speak to the familiar faces. As she approached, however, an officer prevented her from reaching Winnie. The officer then ordered that the countess be taken away, but not before Markievicz gleefully declared that it would be penal servitude for her.

Winnie's sojourn in Richmond Barracks was short-lived. As night approached, all the women were lined up and escorted out of the barracks. The group included Helena Molony, Kit and Nell Ryan, Kathleen Lynn, Madeline ffrench-Mullen, Countess Plunkett, Marie Perolz, Nellie Gifford and Annie Higgins. As they marched along, they heard one tall soldier wonder aloud about what the nuns of Loos would think of them.

The group approached Kilmainham Gaol, a grim and desolate building that had become an army detention centre on the outbreak of the war. The building had no light or heating and the flickering candles added to the gloominess. The prisoners were placed in the west wing, which was in a dreadful state of disrepair. The sanitary facilities, for example, were horrendous. The women from the various garrisons were brought together in this wing. Three or four women were placed in each cell, which only contained two hard beds and three dirty blankets. Winnie had to share with Julia Grenan and Nellie Gifford whom she knew well.

She felt this made the situation slightly more bearable. Food was poor: cocoa and dry bread for breakfast, an indescribable type of soup for dinner with some potatoes, cheese and bread, and a bowl of thin gruel for supper. They were also given prison biscuits that – since cutlery was not provided – they kept as eating utensils. To keep their spirits up, the women sang songs and wrote letters. Once a day, to the sound of jeering from their guards, they were allowed out of their cells for exercise. They tried to use this time for a bit of jollity by indulging in Irish dances, but this was soon banned.

The guards taunted them that their leaders would soon be shot. Just three days after arriving at Kilmainham, Winnie was woken very early in the morning by the sound of gunfire. She then heard a low voice, just under her cell window, giving the order to quick march. Her heart sank because she knew that the executions had begun. As it happened, many more such mornings followed when they heard the close noise of rifle fire and the crisp voice of the officer in command. During the next six days they heard the gunfire of eleven more executions. Winnie waited on tenterhooks as each day someone managed to bring them information about who had been killed and each day she waited for the dreaded words: James Connolly.

Late on the evening of 8 May, as they were getting ready to go to bed, they were all ordered out of their cells and ushered into the central hall. The names of many of the women were called out. Those named were instructed to move to one side of the room. After a caution as to their future behaviour, the large group was informed that they were going to be released. Winnie was not in that group, so was escorted back to her cell.

For the next three mornings Winnie heard no shots. She dared to hope that the executions had ended. There was a rumour that Countess Markievicz, who had been second-in-command at St Stephen's Green and a sniper on the roof of the College of Surgeons, had had her death sentence commuted to life imprisonment.

On the fourth morning, gunshots pierced the air twice more. That afternoon she heard the words she most feared. One of the wardresses coldly told her that James Connolly had been carried on a stretcher to the execution yard. Unable to stand before the firing squad, he had been tied to a chair and shot. Winnie fainted at the news.

16

WINNIE:
AFTER THE RISING

When the Easter Rising began there was little popular support in Ireland for the rebellion. On 1 May 1916 the editorial in the Belfast-based *Irish News* stated: 'We have passed through one of the saddest and most deplorable weeks in our nation's history. It is needless to dwell upon the hopelessness, the mad folly, the blind fatuousness of this reckless adventure.' The cost of the Rising in human terms was devastating for Dublin and part of the reason the rebels were jeered as they were escorted to prison. During Easter Week over 450 people died – over half of these had been civilians. On Friday alone, the last day, forty-five ordinary people died as they attempted to go about their business. One hundred and sixteen British Army personnel were killed in the fighting and, in addition, sixteen members of the RIC and Dublin Metropolitan Police lost their lives. Of the 262 civilians who died, twenty-eight were children aged fifteen and under.

The Rising was suppressed after seven days of fighting but the harsh measures that followed led to a change in political attitude among non-militant nationalists. Seventy-nine women and 3,430 men were arrested and of these 1,841 were interned in England and Wales. Those thought to have organised the insurrection were kept in Ireland for trial. Fourteen of the leaders were executed in Dublin between 3 and 12 May 1916. They were Thomas James Clarke,

Thomas MacDonagh, Patrick Pearse, Joseph Mary Plunkett, Edward Daly, William Pearse, Michael O'Hanrahan, John Mac-Bride, Éamonn Ceannt, Michael Mallin, Con Colbert, Seán Heuston, Seán MacDermott (Mac Diarmada) and James Connolly. In Cork, Volunteer Thomas Kent was executed after resisting arrest by British forces.

Winnie Carney wept and mourned for each man who was executed. Their memoriam cards became her most treasured possessions.

The shootings ceased in Kilmainham Gaol on 12 May with Connolly's execution. Winnie knew that this, the day she would forever remember as the one on which poor James had died, was also the day that British Prime Minister Herbert Asquith visited the prison. He was shown around several of the cells and talked to the prisoners. Winnie was not introduced to him but was told that he asked questions, such as what their names were and why they had been arrested. As soon as he left, the mood in the prison changed and Winnie heard shouts of victory as news spread from cell to cell that there would be no more courts martial. In the days that followed there was a noticeable positive difference in the quality and quantity of food, and they were issued with more blankets.

Shortly afterwards, in the middle of the night, the remaining women were moved in a Black Maria police vehicle to Mountjoy Gaol. The conditions were much better in Mountjoy and some of the women said that, compared to Kilmainham, it was like a hotel. Although the beds were still made from planks, they had clean sheets that were regularly washed for them. The wardress, Miss O'Neill, was decent and treated them like human beings. The women were allowed to exercise together twice a day and, after the Bishop of Limerick, Edward Thomas O'Dwyer, had written to the British military commander, General Sir John Maxwell, to intercede on their behalf, their cell doors were left open. They could also have visitors and accept the clothes and food parcels that were sent to them from outside. Often friends sent in sausages, bacon and eggs, which they were able to cook. The six weeks in Mountjoy passed quickly.

At the end of this time some of the women were released. However, on 20 June, Nell Ryan, Helena Molony, Marie Perolz, Brigid Foley and Winnie were deported to England to serve sentences in Lewes Prison in Sussex. All the women were given seven days in which to appeal their sentences; these appeals were heard by an advisory committee and a high court judge. Only Foley and Perolz were released following their appeals. Winnie knew that hundreds of men were also interned in Britain under the Defence of the Realm Act, which had been passed in August 1914 and created a new capital offence of assisting the enemy. This 'internment' meant that no charges had been brought against them and they had been found guilty of nothing.

At the end of July Nell, Helena and Winnie were transferred to the political prisoners' wing in Aylesbury Prison in Buckinghamshire. It was a damp and gloomy old building that was surrounded by a high wall. Their wing was full of women who were assumed to be spies. Winnie was particularly friendly with Nell, whose family came from Wexford and raised all their children to value education and the equality of women. She was a lively and intelligent young woman who had travelled all over Europe, knew many of Winnie's friends and raised spirits with her sparkling wit and conversation.

In letters to friends and family Winnie tried to be jovial and write about the fact that the food was good and they could stay out in the grounds until lighting-up time. However, at times she could not keep up the pretence and wrote that she dreaded the empty life that lay before her.[1]

Countess Markievicz was already being held in the prison but she was in a wing with thieves, prostitutes and murderers. The new arrivals were horrified and offered to forgo their political prisoner privileges, which included sending and receiving letters, visits and food parcels. They wished to accept the same treatment as Markievicz and made a formal appeal to the Home Office to be treated as convicts. Their request was refused.

Winnie was distraught by the fact that she could not exchange a word with Markievicz and was not even allowed to wave at her over the wall. The only time they caught glimpses of her, dressed in convict's clothes, was at Mass. To the three women's joy, the kindly Scottish priest, Father Thomas Scott, offered to pass notes between them. They soon discovered that their friend was quite safe as she was in a cell on her own and shut in from half past five each evening. As she was an armed rebel who had killed a soldier, her food and sanitary conditions were much worse than theirs and she had to endure hard labour in order to receive rations.

Nell Ryan was released on 13 October and in early November an offer was made to Helena Molony and Winnie. They were told that if they wished to be released they could sign an undertaking not to engage in any acts of a seditious character. They both refused to sign.

Letters from home were always welcome and Winnie replied with as many letters as she was permitted to write. She was always anxious to hear news of her mother's health and was delighted that her friends always made an effort to visit her when they were in Belfast. Winnie also worried about her own health, as she seemed to be getting thinner. She could not blame the prison food because, as she wrote to friends, Miss Molony was keeping splendidly and getting fatter.

By December 1916 there was a new Liberal and Conservative coalition government in Westminster. David Lloyd George had become prime minister, Andrew Bonar Law was chancellor of the exchequer and Sir Edward Carson was minister for the navy. They were all well aware of how public opinion regarding the Rising had changed since the ensuing executions and so announced a general amnesty for all political prisoners, except those who had been charged with offences or had death sentences commuted.

Winnie was set free to return to Dublin on Christmas Eve. As she was preparing to leave, she collapsed onto her bed, sobbing – not from relief, but because she did not wish to leave others behind in prison. She did not know if she would ever see Countess Markievicz again.

All the newly released prisoners reached Dublin on Christmas Day and went straight to Liberty Hall. Hampers had been made up to send to them in prison but now they were opened and used for a celebration dinner. Afterwards, there was a great deal of dancing and laughter but, in the absence of Connolly and the others, Winnie felt there was little about which to be joyous. She still dreaded the empty life that she saw stretching before her. She heard about Connolly's last days from Nora, who had gone to visit him with her mother, and she could not remove the image painted to her about how he was so weak and feverish that he was court-martialled while sitting up in bed. Nora said that, on the night before his death, he had shown no regret and told Nora that he was proud of her.

'Father gave me a copy of the last statement he made to the court martial and he was proud of us all. He thanked God for letting him live to see the day when thousands of Irish men and women were willing to give their lives for Irish freedom. Try not to be sad, Winnie, he had no regrets.'

Throughout 1917 Winnie threw herself back into her work for the ITGWU on Corporation Street. Her whole life had been centred around James Connolly and his work for the union. She had espoused his ideals regarding class struggle, women's liberation and industrial unionism, and now she wanted to pursue his dream of a socialist independent Ireland.

She returned to the Workers' Educational Association, of which she had been a member before the events of Easter Week. It had been started in 1910 by her friend, Tom Johnston, who was also the president of the association. They gave her a rousing welcome back.

Winnie still lived at home with her mother beside the shop in Carlisle Circus. Her mother had been overjoyed when Winnie returned home. As an avowed republican, she had supported all of her daughter's actions, although she admitted that the worry during Easter Week had almost sent her to an early grave. Information had been slow filtering through to Belfast and there had been rumours that Winnie had been shot. Fortunately a friend, Father O'Neill, had been in Dublin at the time and had viewed the surrender from the Gresham Hotel. He travelled post-haste to Sarah Carney's home to tell her that he had recognised Winnie in her blue coat and that she was unharmed.

Winnie also continued her association with Cumann na mBan and worked tirelessly to promote her republican ideals. This included escorting women from Dublin to Belfast public houses where they could collect ammunition for transportation.[2] Her hard work was rewarded when Cumann na mBan held a convention a few months later. Markievicz, now released from prison, was confirmed as president and Winnie was appointed as the delegate for the Belfast branch. It was the branch's role to organise protests regarding the ill-treatment of prisoners and to raise funds for the families of those still in prison. As a result, her mother and she had to get used to regular raids by the police throughout 1918 in search of seditious material. The raids would often take place in the early morning when a loud hammering at the door jolted the household awake and members of the RIC searched the house for documents. They usually acted politely towards the women, though Winnie never trusted them and took to sleeping in her clothes so that she was not caught in a state of undress.

She had little time for rejoicing when war came to an end in November, though it was difficult to ignore the joyful celebrations in Belfast. It seemed as though the whole city had taken to the streets to dance and sing.

Now that the vote was to be given to women over thirty, Winnie was active in rallying all the Cumann na mBan members for the upcoming elections, especially as the Home Rule question would have to be addressed. In the past, most of the 105 Members of Parliament elected to Westminster for Ireland had been members of the nationalist Irish Parliamentary Party, which supported the ideal of Home Rule. The rest had been members of the Unionist Party who wished to maintain the union with Great Britain. However, since the Easter Rising of 1916, Sinn Féin, which favoured separation from Britain, had been growing in popularity throughout Ireland. The party was formed in November 1905 by Arthur Griffith and over the next three years absorbed groups such as Cumann na nGaedhael and the republican Dungannon Clubs, organised by Bulmer Hobson. Sinn Féin advocated passive resistance, economic and cultural self-sufficiency and political independence. The party had won three by-elections in 1917 and expected even greater success in this election.

Cumann na mBan urged Sinn Féin to put forward women candidates in the upcoming elections. As a result, two women were nominated to stand for election. One was Countess Markievicz, who would run in the St Patrick's Division in Dublin. The other female candidate would stand in the Victoria Division in Belfast. This was Winnie Carney. Her nomination papers were signed by John Quinn, a foreman docker and member of the ITGWU, and by a barber named Andrew Leonard. Victoria was a staunchly unionist area and Winnie insisted that she stand on a Workers' Republic platform, as she thought Connolly would have done. She tried to enlist the support of some of his friends who were active trade unionists, but found few would help campaign for a woman. She wondered how they could have forgotten the equality promised in the Proclamation just two years previously.

At one meeting in St Mary's Hall, she appealed to women to use their vote wisely and not waste it as men had done in the past. She was supported at the meeting by Miss Cashel, secretary of Cumann na mBan, Countess Plunkett, her friend and poet Alice Milligan, and Agnes McCullough, the wife of the Belfast republican leader, Denis McCullough. Such women were great supporters of Winnie and many had a shared history. Agnes was a sister of Nell Ryan, with whom Winnie had been so friendly in prison, and another sister, Min, was a founder member of Cumann na nBan and had been hoping to marry Seán MacDermott. At this meeting Winnie was vociferous in her condemnation of the police who frequently followed her and came in plain clothes as spies to such meetings. She referred to them as blackguards and was delighted when this made the headlines in the *Irish News* as 'Sinn Féin Feminists Have No Time To Waste On Such Blackguards'.

On 14 December 1918 Countess Markievicz was successfully elected. However, in keeping with Sinn Féin principles, she refused to take her seat in Westminster. Even if she had been willing to take her seat, it would have been impossible as she was imprisoned in Holloway at the time for the making of a seditious speech. She was the first woman in the United Kingdom to be elected.

Winnie polled only four per cent of the vote, though even that was a surprise considering that it was an unwinnable seat and she had received little support from the party. She wrote to complain to Joe McGrath, a member of the IRB and Sinn Féin organiser, that she felt she had lost the £150 deposit she had paid in order to stand for election because she had been provided with no personation agents, committee rooms or canvassers. She was angry that the only people Sinn Féin had sent up to support her were Father O'Flanagan and Seán T. O'Kelly, who had been in and out of the GPO in 1916. In fact, she told McGrath that she was amazed that 395 people had actually turned out to vote for her.

She ended her letter with the following paragraph: 'I wonder in time to come shall we occupy the same bench or shall you have become a conservative while I remain an extreme anarchist because you see I am determined that I too shall one day share the responsibility in directing the government of the country.'[3]

Sinn Féin won seventy-three out of the possible 105 seats in the 1918 elections and the Unionists won twenty-six, twenty-three of which were in the north-east of the country. Ireland was more divided than ever.

17

GEORGE:
AFTER THE GREAT WAR

George McBride was officially discharged on 26 March 1919 as a Class Z reserve. This meant that if war resumed he could be immediately recalled to the army. His parents welcomed him home with great joy while he felt only relief and sadness. He had not reached the age of twenty-one and yet he had already seen thousands die. His Lewis gun had fired forty-seven rounds a minute and he found it hard to think about how many men he must have killed. He had no desire to talk about the war, which his parents found hard to understand. He felt that they did not need to know about the horror and futility of it all.

George thought himself fortunate to be able to resume his apprenticeship in the engineering firm of Mackie's. Other returning soldiers were not so lucky – their jobs taken by men who didn't enlist. Every day he saw former soldiers, in desperation, taking their possessions to pawn shops in order to get money to buy food. Some were even forced to pawn their medals. Others turned to drink in order to escape the desperation of their lives and the memories they had brought back with them. Many solved their problems by emigrating to Canada, Australia or New Zealand.

Some of George's old friends and their families were badly affected by the Spanish influenza epidemic, or 'black flu', that struck Ireland first in 1918 and returned in the spring of 1919. The name arose because as the lungs became infected, blood poisoning set in and many sufferers turned dark purple or even black. This pandemic killed 40 million people worldwide and about 23,000 in Ireland in a period of six months. George saw funerals passing Mackie's every day on their way to Milltown, Friar's Bush or the other city cemeteries. He heard that thousands were being buried all over the country. Newspapers seemed to minimise the effects of the influenza, but talk in workplaces or on street corners told him a different story. What was evident to him, from the newspapers, was the number of advertisements proclaiming remedies or methods of avoiding contracting the disease. Folk were urged to use Jeyes' Fluid or Lifebuoy soap to disinfect their homes and to drink Oxo or Bovril to fortify their bodies against the onslaught of the terrible infection.

The threat of the infection, together with the growing political unrest in Ireland, increased the desire in many to leave the country. Some friends urged George to go with them but he never considered joining the emigrants as he just couldn't face all the travelling involved. He had no political ambitions but resolved to dedicate his life to securing better conditions for the ordinary man in the street. The average working week was five and a half days and he wanted to see this reduced to five days with paid overtime for Saturdays. He felt he could fight for this best from within the trade union of which he was a member.

He watched events unfold across Ireland and heard from his co-workers about the republican success in the election of 1918. The Irish Parliamentary Party was annihilated when Sinn Féin won seventy-three seats. The winning party went on to declare an Irish Republic and set up their own parliament, Dáil Éireann, which met for the first time in Dublin in January 1919. Éamon de Valera, who had escaped execution after the Rising in 1916, was elected president of the new Republic. There was speculation as to where this would all lead and nightly George scoured the newspaper for reports. He had no desire to be involved; he had seen enough fighting and death on the Western Front.

From the newspapers George learned about the fighting that was taking place in the south of the country, where Republican activists, who knew the countryside well, were concentrating on guerrilla actions and assassinations. While they ate their packed sandwiches in work, the men discussed the planned new Home Rule Bill and how it would mean that Ireland would govern itself within the British Empire but would be divided into two parts with two parliaments, one in Belfast and one in Dublin. The northern part would contain six of the nine counties of Ulster: Antrim, Down, Fermanagh, Londonderry, Tyrone and Armagh. The southern part of Ireland would have the other twenty-six counties. George's workmates, like most other northern unionists, seemed happy with that outcome.

The idea of this division caused great anger in the south. The Irish Republican Army (IRA), led by Michael Collins who fought in the GPO in 1916, started a campaign against any form of British government in Ireland. The men in Mackie's with whom George spent his days were delighted when, in the summer of 1919, the British government declared both the Dáil and Sinn Féin illegal. It was a guerrilla war and anyone who was seen as a symbol of British power was targeted. On 2 September 1919 two members of the RIC were shot dead in Tipperary. Violence escalated following this. George had encountered enough bloodshed and was angered to see feelings in Belfast become affected by it.

The IRA began a series of attacks on police stations and policemen whom they saw as the enforcers of British rule. Reinforcements for the RIC were sent to Ireland from March 1920 in an attempt to quell the shootings, ambushes and riots. These men were mostly former soldiers and were nicknamed the 'Black and Tans' because of the colour of their uniforms. They rapidly became hated for their brutal methods. Despite these increased numbers, by June 1920 fifty-five policemen had been killed, sixteen barracks destroyed, hundreds abandoned and many members of the RIC had resigned from their positions. In July the remaining police were further reinforced when members of the Auxiliary Division, a separate unit made up mostly of ex-army officers, started to arrive.

Reprisals and counter-reprisals became regular occurrences and culminated on 21 November when IRA members killed twelve suspected Army Intelligence officers in Dublin and two Auxiliary policemen. Later that day the Auxiliaries and RIC, in search of the killers, went to look for them at a football match in Croke Park. They fired into the crowd and killed fourteen innocent people. Many more were wounded. In reprisal, a week later, two lorry-loads of Auxiliaries were ambushed and sixteen killed at Kilmichael, County Cork, with one survivor being shot later that day. When another British Auxiliary patrol was ambushed in Cork on 11 December, with one of the patrol killed and eleven wounded, the city was sacked and martial law was declared.

By 1921 the violence had spread to Belfast, where many Catholic homes were attacked. Thousands of Catholic employees were expelled from the shipyards and engineering works, and George was horrified when he heard about working men being pelted with metal pieces as they swam for their lives in the lough. Often, as he travelled home from work, he saw the Black and Tans, with their revolvers strapped round their right upper legs, kick in the doors of people's homes and pull the occupants, shaking, onto the streets. On occasion the tram he travelled on was attacked by supporters of the IRA and he and other workmen had to lie on the floor to avoid the rocks and bullets fired at them. He recoiled from the sight of burnt-out shops on the Shankill Road and families loading their possessions onto carts in a bid to flee. Although he understood the need for it, George despised the nine o'clock curfew that was imposed in Belfast and enforced by soldiers travelling around in tall cage vans with a slit through which their guns jutted. It brought back painful memories of the trenches and his enforced march through Germany. In many ways, it felt as if the war had followed him home.

Meanwhile the Government of Ireland Act 1920, which created two governments in Ireland, was passed in Westminster in December 1920 and elections were planned for the following May. There was to be one parliament for the six north-eastern counties and one for the remaining twenty-six counties, with forty-two MPs for the island being elected to sit at Westminster. Both governments would have very limited devolved powers. Unionists in Ulster were quite happy with these powers but Irish nationalists were not. As a result, many who had not previously supported the IRA's campaign of violence were now in favour of it.

In June 1921 George went into town to see King George V and Queen Mary officially open the first session of the new Northern Ireland parliament in Belfast's City Hall. The last time he had seen the King was when he had inspected the 36th Division in

England. He had seen him more clearly then because, this time, the King was surrounded by huge policemen in pointed hats and soldiers with fixed bayonets.

George followed with interest the reports of a Truce between the British and the Irish republicans in July and the ensuing negotiations. He read about the agreement which created the Irish Free State and how Michael Collins and Arthur Griffith had been to London to sign an Anglo-Irish Treaty. He fervently hoped that this would bring an end to the violence.

18

WINNIE:
THE ROAD TO PARTITION

Since her failed election attempt in 1918, Winnie had worked hard for the union, as well as in her role as the secretary of the Irish Republican Prisoners' Dependents' Fund. Her frequent trips to Dublin during 1919 on behalf of the union led to her being of great use as a courier. Winnie worked closely with her comrades in Cumann na mBan and the ICA, and on her visits to Dublin she helped in the setting up of emergency hospitals during the dreadful influenza epidemic. Thousands of Irish people were dying and the organisation wanted to use Cumann na mBan's nursing skills to do what they could.

The influenza affected many of the prisoners and their dependants, and Winnie worked long hours administering funds to them. Some of the prisoners who had been interned under the Defence of the Realm Act had medical training and they were released from prison to assist the authorities in fighting the epidemic. One of these was her friend, Dr Russell McNab, who had stood and been defeated, like herself, for election as a Sinn Féin candidate in 1918.

At the end of 1919 Winnie ended her frequent trips to Dublin, which were attracting too much attention, but she still sheltered many of her republican friends in her home when they visited Belfast. Countess Markievicz who, after her release from prison, had become Minister for Labour in the Dáil, stayed with her often.

Above: The inlaid box owned by George McBride which he gave to Rita Murphy. (*Author's collection*)

Right: Winnie and her sisters. *Left to right*: Mabel, Winnie, Sarah and Maud. (*Courtesy of Jane Austin-Kaneshiro*)

Overleaf: An anti-Home Rule rally in the Ulster Hall. (*Photograph reproduced with the kind permission of the Trustees of the National Museums and Galleries of Northern Ireland*)

Edward Carson signing the Solemn League and Covenant. (*Courtesy of the Billy Nelson collection*)

The Ulster Division march past at Belfast City Hall, in which George took part. (*Courtesy of the Somme Heritage Centre*)

ARMY OF THE IRISH REPUBLIC

(Dublin Command)

Headquarters   Date.25th.April,.1916.

To

Officer in Charge, Henry Street.

     Erect barricades in Henry Street on both sides of
Moore Street. Occupy first floor in houses taken in
Henry Street and top floors also. Se that the men are
instructed to keep their fire under control, not to
fire on sm ll bodies. In all cases wait for word from
a responsible officer before commencing to shoot. A
few men should be placed in the end house on each

side of Moore Street at the Henry Street end. After this
is done find out what available food, water, and water
utensils is at your disposal and report here accordingly.
Be sure and break all the glass in the windows of the
rooms you occupy for fighting purposes.

                             Commandant-General

James Connolly

                             Dublin Division.

One of James Connolly's dispatches issued from the GPO and typed by
Winnie. (*Courtesy of the National Library of Ireland*)

Left: Winifred Carney. (*Courtesy of Kilmainham Gaol Archives, 2012.0243*)

Below: The GPO after the 1916 Easter Rising. Only the shell of the building survived the fire. (*Author's collection*)

R'man GEO. M'BRIDE,
Royal Irish Rifles, 131
Crimea Street, Belfast, prisoner of war.
(Photo: J. Thompson.)

Left: A picture of George which appeared in the *Belfast Telegraph* when he was a prisoner of war.
(*Courtesy of the Belfast Telegraph*)

Below: George's war medals.
(*Courtesy of Conor Dulligan*)

CERTIFIED COPY OF AN ENTRY OF MARRIAGE
COPI DILYS O GOFNOD PRIODAS

GIVEN AT THE GENERAL REGISTER OFFICE
RHODDWYD YN Y GENERAL REGISTER OFFICE

Application Number 6232192-1
Rhif y Cais

1928.	Marriage solemnized at *Register Office* in the District of *Holyhead* in the County of *Anglesey*						
No.	When Married	Name and Surname	Age	Condition	Rank or Profession	Residence at the time of Marriage	Father's Name and Surname	Rank or Profession of Father
80.	Twenty-sixth September 1928	George McBride	30 years	Bachelor	Textile Engineer	Albany Hotel Church Terrace Holyhead	George McBride	Ship yard Fitter
		Winifred Carney	39 years	Spinster	—	Albany Hotel Church Terrace Holyhead	Alfred Carney	Commercial Traveller

Married in the *Register Office* according to the Rites and Ceremonies of the _____ by *Licence* by me.

This Marriage was solemnized between us, { *George McBride* *Winifred Carney* } in the Presence of us, { *E. Roberts* *C. Thomas* } { *R. P. Williams*, Registrar *Owen J. Hughes*, Superintendent Registrar }

CERTIFIED to be a true copy of an entry in the certified copy of a Register of Marriages in the Registration District of } Holyhead
TYSTIOLAETHWYD as fod yn gopi cywir o gofnod mewn copi y tystiolaethwyd iddo o Gofrestr Priodasau yn Nosbarth }

Given at the GENERAL REGISTER OFFICE, under the Seal of the said Office the } 26th day of } January 2015
Fe'i rhoddwyd yn y GENERAL REGISTER OFFICE, o dan sêl y Swyddfa a enwyd y }

CAUTION: THERE ARE OFFENCES RELATING TO FALSIFYING OR ALTERING A CERTIFICATE AND USING OR POSSESSING A FALSE CERTIFICATE ©CROWN COPYRIGHT
GOFAL: MAE YNA DROSEDDAU YN YMWNEUD Â FFUGIO NEU ADDASU TYSTYSGRIF NEU DDEFNYDDIO TYSTYSGRIF FFUG NEU WRTH FOD AG UN YN EICH MEDDIANT. ©HAWLFRAINT Y GORON

WMXZ 350130

WARNING: A CERTIFICATE IS NOT EVIDENCE OF IDENTITY.
RHYBUDD: NID YW TYSTYSGRIF YN PROFI PWY YDYCH CHI.

The marriage certificate of Winnie and George. (*Author's collection*)

The only surviving image of George and Winnie together, along with some local children. (*Courtesy of the District Trades Union Council*)

George in later life, with his favourite nurse, Rita. (*Author's collection*)

So too did Austin Stack, who had commanded the IRB's Kerry Brigade in 1916 and co-ordinated Roger Casement's attempt to bring in arms. He had been elected to the Dáil at the same time as the Countess and, like her, was an abstentionist member of parliament for Westminster.

In February 1920 Winnie joined the Socialist Party of Ireland and in April attended the Independent Labour Party's annual conference in St Andrew's Hall, Glasgow. She found herself intrigued by the 'Treatise on Rise and Progress of Socialism', which dwelt on the growth of trade unionism and progress towards social democracy. She felt that the thoughts expressed were more akin to those of Connolly's than were the present Sinn Féin views. The central theme of the treatise was that economic development should be viewed only as a progress towards a socialist state. When she voiced these thoughts at some of the many meetings she attended, her friends would tease her by calling her 'Carnovitz'. Winnie was unsure if this was because of her views or her friendship with Constance Markievicz.

Winnie's support for republican prisoners, meetings with known activists and continued involvement with Cumann na mBan brought her actions under even greater scrutiny from the local police and their special forces. Raids on her home increased, much to the distress of her mother. The police also knew that some of Winnie's relatives were avowed republicans and so they were followed on occasion.

One day her cousin, Alec Cassidy, came to the house in a state of great agitation – he was carrying a gun and the police were after him. Without making a fuss, Winnie hid the gun under her skirt and stayed calm during the subsequent raid. The police found nothing.

Winnie stayed away from home as often as she could to try to minimise disruption to her elderly mother's life. Part of the reason she tried to find alternative accommodation was because her brother Alfred's marriage had broken down and he had returned to live in the house with them. She did not get on well with Alfred – she thought he lacked ambition – and this led to frequent disagreements in the house. Moreover, he brought his son, Jack, with him, and Winnie did not want the young boy to be privy to the details of her life.

In March 1921 she realised that she was being followed again by some of the Special Forces. She decided to stay with her uncle, in what she considered a safe house in Newington Avenue off the Antrim Road. She used to play there as a child with all the Cassidy cousins. It had always felt homely. As she walked towards the Cassidys' house, she carried her clothes, union documents and some of her most cherished possessions in her valise.

Without warning, during the night, the house was raided by several members of the RIC. They were interested only in Winnie and her possessions. She shoved her valise as far as possible under the bed, but it was quickly found. She tried to cling onto it, but the officers seized it. As well as her change of clothes, the valise contained her copy of Thomas Johnston's *Handbook for Rebels*, some letters, postcards, greeting cards and poetry. It also contained treasured possessions, such as a Christmas card from Mrs Pearse, Patrick and Willie's mother, and memoriam cards for Joseph Plunkett, Patrick Pearse, Willie Pearse, Tom Clarke and John Edward Daly, all of whom had been executed in 1916 (see Appendix 1 for full details of the papers seized).

Three days later, Winnie wrote to the Divisional Commissioner to ask for the return of her possessions. She pointed out that they were not of any political or military significance.

> 2 Carlisle Circus
> Belfast
> 14.03.21

The Divisional Commissioner of Police
Atlantic Buildings
Waring Street
Belfast

Dear Sir

On Friday 11th instant, during raiding operations at the residence of Mrs. Cassidy, 70 Newington Avenue, the following are amongst the articles extracted from my suitcase by the Constable in charge:–

A Christmas Card
Several memoriam cards
Some letters
A pamphlet issued by a philosophical society
A second pamphlet giving extracts from the speeches of loyalist and Unionist members of the British House of Commons.

None of these articles were of any military or political significance or value. The letters were purely personal ones.

I would feel grateful if you would kindly institute inquiries, and order that these things are returned to me at once.

Thanking you in anticipation.

Yours sincerely

Winifred Carney.[1]

The Commissioner did not agree.

> Divisional Commissioner's Office
> Belfast
> 26th March 1921

Dear Madam,

In reply to your letter of 14th instant, I regret that at present none of the documents seized on the occasion of the search at your house can be returned.

> Your obedient Servant,
> For Div. Commissioner.[2]

Winnie was angry but relieved that she had had the sense not to carry with her many of the correspondences she had received during the past four years. These were from a range of people like Michael Collins, Maud Gonne, Joseph MacDonagh, Russell McNab and Sylvia Pankhurst. All were proof of the wide range of seditious activities in which she was involved. She was also glad that she had seen fit to store her most prized possessions in a safe location in a friend's house: original copies of the *Irish War News* and the Proclamation from 1916. They were her greatest mementoes of James Connolly.

19

GEORGE:
LIFE IN NORTHERN IRELAND

George had found it difficult to settle back into his pre-war life, especially at home, where his brothers and sisters had grown up in his absence and understood nothing of his experiences. While he was away his family had moved to a house at 131 Crimea Street just off the Shankill Road. He thought it strange to live in a street named after a war and wondered if, in the future, streets would be named Somme or Passchendaele. The neighbours were strangers to him and many of his friends from his school and YCV days never returned from France. The Belfast of his youth seemed to have disappeared.

His experiences during the war had confirmed some of the beliefs he had grown up with, but challenged others. His father had been a member of the Amalgamated Engineering Union all of his days and George had always believed in trade unions. However, as the fighting in Belfast escalated during 1921, he felt that he needed to do more. One thing that troubled him most was the division between Catholic and Protestant working men. There had been few Catholics in the street where he had grown up, but the village in which he had stayed as a prisoner of war had been totally Catholic and he had not felt out of place. When he saw frequent funerals of children through the streets of Belfast, he realised that poverty knew no religious distinctions. Some of his workmates in Mackie's seemed concerned with what religion a man was, but George felt that was not important. He blamed the churches for a lot of the trouble that was taking place.

George was an avid reader and one of his heroes was Ernest Bevin, a great trade unionist who had just amalgamated several British unions into the Transport and General Workers' Union. George thought that Bevin's strength made him seem like something hewn from the Cave Hill that towered over Belfast. He admired Bevin's values, which emphasised economic and social issues. Although George had not wanted to be involved in politics just two years previously, he decided now, after reading about Bevin's life, to join the Belfast Labour Party.

At the first meeting he attended, George knew that he had made the right decision. Here were people with the same views as his own and those who had lived through similar experiences. He learned that ten Belfast Labour Party candidates had achieved success in the municipal elections the year before and he met one of them, Harry Midgley, who was a councillor on Belfast City Council. To George, Harry was a young man much like himself. He had served during the war and now wanted to make a difference, but was being impeded by old tribal divisions. Harry had stood for election in May to the first ever parliament of Northern Ireland, but had been defeated. He told George that the main reason for his defeat was that James Craig feared that Labour would split the loyalist vote and had sent a mob of shipyard workers to disrupt his final Labour rally in the Ulster Hall.

George also met another Labour councillor, Margaret Mc-Coubrey, who was a staunch trade unionist and suffragette. She too had been elected to the city council and was the general secretary of the Co-operative Women's Guild. George admired her for her strength of character and outspoken views. He heard how she had run a peace and suffrage campaign in Belfast during the war; her reasoning being that she believed that a woman looking at a battlefield would not see dead Germans or English, but rather dead mothers' sons. George felt that for once he could voice his own thoughts. He did not believe that the Battle of the Somme should ever have taken place and he questioned the right of one man to kill another.

The Belfast Labour Party later developed into the Northern Ireland Labour Party. George remained a very active member of the Court Ward in West Belfast. He wanted to be part of a socialist party that treated women equally, believed in non-violence and was neither nationalist nor unionist, Protestant nor Catholic. He was horrified when Catholics and those considered 'bad' Protestants, as well as Labour Party members that he knew, like Harry Midgley, James Baird, Sam Kyle and John Hanna, were expelled from the shipyard and even from Mackie's where he worked. He felt that war pitted young men from working-class backgrounds against one another and he was very dissatisfied at the social conditions under which people were living. George resolved to use his time and energy to try to make the new Northern Ireland a better place.

20

WINNIE:
LIFE IN NORTHERN IRELAND

Winnie found little to celebrate as 1922 dawned. Now in her thirty-fifth year, she had resigned herself to living at home and taking care of her aging mother. She kept herself extremely busy and wondered if she did so to stop herself considering the loneliness she often felt. She had many friends and acquaintances but all were part of the world of work and politics with which she had filled her life. Even in this she had known many heartaches and disappointments. She had visited Dublin a few weeks previously, after a break of almost two years, and had been dismayed by the divisions she found between her friends.

Following the ceasefire in July 1921, Markievicz had kept Winnie informed about the two months of treaty negotiations in London. Winnie was privy to her views and knew that she must be equally distressed by the turn of events. That Michael Collins had been one of the signatories to the document was the hardest blow of all. She could not believe that Collins, one of the men she had stood side-by-side with in the GPO in 1916, had betrayed them all. He had signed the Anglo-Irish Treaty with the British government on 6 December 1921 and now it would be put before the Dáil for ratification. She could only pray that would not happen.

Winnie was aware that, according to this newly signed Treaty,

Ireland would not be the republic for which James and so many had fought and died. It would instead have the status of a self-governing dominion and be associated with the British Commonwealth. The Crown would be recognised as the symbol and accepted head of such an association. Winnie felt betrayed, especially when she learned that the new parliament of Northern Ireland would remain in place. She and her fellow republicans were simply being abandoned.

Winnie was furious when she heard that the Treaty had been approved in the Dáil on 7 January 1922 by a margin of sixty-four votes to fifty-seven. Letters from friends in Dublin brought news to her that Éamon de Valera, the president of the republic, had resigned and that Michael Collins and Arthur Griffith had dissolved the Dáil and formed a provisional government. She was pleased to hear that Countess Markievicz had also resigned.

Despite her anger, in early 1922 Winnie found herself once more in the role of courier, carrying messages relating to discussions that had started between Michael Collins and Sir James Craig, Prime Minister of Northern Ireland. A Conciliation or Peace Committee was to be set up and she was informed that the matters now under discussion would be about adjustments to the border, the return of shipyard workers to their jobs, the southern boycott of Belfast firms and, for problems affecting all Ireland, the devising of a more suitable system than the Council of Ireland. The pact being discussed would attempt to reconcile unionism and nationalism and would contain clauses that would guarantee the release of political prisoners and set up a committee to end sectarianism.

On 30 March the Craig-Collins pact was signed. As a result,

IRA activity was to end in the northern counties and, in exchange, measures would be put in place to make the six counties more acceptable to the Catholics who lived within its borders. A £500,000 imperial grant was to be provided to carry out the measures. In addition, the Corporation and the Harbour Board of Belfast would provide £500,000 to be distributed in proportion between the two sections of unemployed.

Less than twenty-four hours later, however, the pact began to crumble when a policeman was shot dead in Belfast. The police reacted brutally by entering Catholic homes and shooting indiscriminately. Collins demanded an inquiry. However, while engaging in correspondence with Winston Churchill, the then secretary of state for war, he, along with IRA Chief of Staff Liam Lynch, was also planning an offensive along the border area. When intelligence about this reached Churchill, he deployed 1,000 troops to shell Pettigo, a village that lay on the border between Fermanagh and Donegal. It was reported that republicans had attacked the mainly unionist village, driven out Protestants and occupied their houses. The Craig-Collins pact had failed before it ever really started.

For months, debate raged over the Treaty at all the Cumann na mBan meetings that Winnie attended. Some branded Collins a traitor for endorsing such a document. Others argued that he saw it, not as a final settlement, but as the nearest he could get to an independent and unified Ireland. The pro-Treaty and anti-Treaty arguments persisted and tensions grew. While Winnie was still opposed to the Treaty, she listened carefully to all the arguments put forward in its favour and was interested to hear from Eamon O'Duibhir, the IRB's assistant brigade quartermaster in

Tipperary, that the settlement was as good as could be expected and that things missing from it could be secured as Ireland grew in strength under a twenty-six county government. He predicted that the people, including those he commanded, would accept it. Austin Stack, the IRB leader from Kerry, believed the opposite.

As Winnie weighed up all the arguments, she started to consider the possibility that Collins may be correct and the final solution might be achieved in a step-by-step fashion. She knew that he had been sending money and arms to the IRA's northern units and had met both the IRA and the IRB regarding a guerrilla war in the north. He appeared to be looking towards a future in which the thirty-two counties would be reunited. Her anger against Collins gradually dissipated and she found herself remembering how sincere he had seemed in the GPO in 1916. She decided that he would not have settled if there had been the slightest possibility of achieving more. Winnie was swayed completely when Collins wrote to her to say that, while the Treaty did not give them the ultimate freedom that they all desired, it did give them the freedom to achieve it.

Everyone awaited the outcome of the Irish general election in June, which would show how the public viewed the matter. De Valera had formed a new political party, Cumann na Poblachta, and toured the country preaching against the Treaty. On 16 June 1922 fifty-eight pro-Treaty Sinn Féin candidates, led by Collins, were elected. De Valera's new anti-Treaty party got only thirty-five seats. There were also seven independent members, seven Farmers Party, four Unionists and seventeen Labour Party TDs elected, most of whom were in favour of accepting the Treaty.

While the pre-election debates had been taking place, violence broke out again in Ireland. Collins began building a National Army from pro-Treaty IRA units, but the IRA's Army Council called a convention and the majority repudiated Collins' right to dissolve the republic proclaimed in 1919. The violence spread to the new Northern Ireland, where Dawson Bates, the Minister for Home Affairs, declared that they were at war with the IRA and internment was introduced on 22 May.

An IRA offensive was launched and many engagements with British troops took place. The actions were not well co-ordinated and large numbers were imprisoned. When the IRA murdered a policeman, loyalists in Belfast attacked Catholic families in reprisal. On the other side, the IRA murdered Protestants and was also responsible for bombing trams taking shipyard workers to Harland and Wolff.

By late June 1922 civil war had broken out all over Ireland and factions fought in support of their pro- and anti-Treaty views. In Northern Ireland feelings ran high among those who were opposed to the Treaty and the very existence of the new statelet in which they found themselves. The disputed new border, which divided the six counties from the other twenty-six, required thousands of soldiers and police officers to maintain all disputed areas. Meanwhile, assassinations and reprisals became commonplace in the new Free State as the anti-Treaty forces waged a guerrilla campaign. Towns such as Cork, Limerick and Waterford were captured by pro-Treaty forces enhanced with British armoured vehicles and artillery.

The Special Constabulary in Northern Ireland, known as the 'B Specials', began arresting known IRA supporters, including nationalist and republican members of the Peace Committee. A warrant under the Special Powers Act was issued for the arrest of Miss Winifred Carney on 22 July. The reason given for issuing the arrest warrant was that she had been associating with dangerous characters and was believed to be acting as a courier for the IRA.

Winnie had just returned to Belfast from Dublin on the last train on 24 July. She was still in bed at eight o'clock the next morning when she heard the police banging at the door. She instantly knew that her mother's house was about to be raided again. She jumped up and rushed to the fireplace, grabbing papers from the dressing table on the way. She lit the papers and watched them catch fire.

The door swung open as she was about to add more to the flames. A policeman entered and prevented her from doing so. He said that he was the commanding officer of the 49th Platoon and he was there by order of the CID. She asked if she could have a few minutes to tidy herself in the kitchen and the policeman said that he would fetch two women searchers to accompany her. While he was away she tried to pass some of her documents to her mother, who was standing nervously nearby. Winnie was caught in the act on the policeman's return and could do nothing more than protest vociferously as the house was searched and many documents were removed.

She was shown the raid order and was then arrested and taken to Chichester Street. En route, the policeman told her that the union office at 122 Corporation Street was being searched at the same time.

Raid order No. 153.

To. AREA COMMANDANT,
i/e SPECIAL PLATOONS.

24.7.22

Please raid and search the undermentioned premises and effect the arrest of:–

Winnie CARNEY
2a CARLISLE CIRCUS

Ascertain the office address of the Transport Workers' Union, and raid and search the offices in connection with this arrest.

Assistant Commissioner
C.I.D. B.

Danesfort,
Belfast[1]

By the afternoon, Winnie was seated alone at a large wooden table in the police barracks. The commanding officer who had searched her house entered, accompanied by two policemen struggling under the weight of large boxes they carried. They placed the boxes on the floor. Winnie assumed that they held all the materials taken in the raid on her home and her place of work. As her heart raced, she watched the commanding officer slowly empty the contents of one of the boxes onto the table, then lift each item individually, examine them closely and lay them down again.

'Miss Carney, you have been arrested for being in possession of seditious letters and accounts. Can you explain why you are in possession of these receipt forms and relief papers for the Irish Republican Prisoners' Dependents' Fund? These ledgers from your office show the amounts raised on behalf of such prisoners.'

'I can, sir. I am the secretary of the Transport Workers' Union and also the secretary of the Dependents' Fund and therefore there is nothing unusual in those papers being in my possession.'

'And these field dressings and the First Aid outfit, Miss Carney. How do you explain these?'

'I have made no secret of the fact that I have been a member of Cumann na mBan for many years. Those particular items are necessary for first aid activities which we perform.'

'I would suggest that they are related to the subversive activities in which you have long engaged, Miss Carney. Look at these letters I'm placing in front of you. They are from Michael Collins, Joseph MacDonagh, William O'Brien, Russell McNab, the Sinn Féin Demonstration Committee. Such letters are proof that you have been part of actions against the state of Northern Ireland.'

'No, sir, those are all personal letters.' Winnie lifted up one of the cards. 'Look, this is a Christmas card from Michael Collins; nothing more than a simple courteous greeting between friends. That is not an action against any state.'

'I would suggest that most of these documents are proof that you have connections with Bolshevik groups. Look at this: a membership card for the Socialist Party of Ireland, letters from Sylvia Pankhurst, invitations to meetings of the Irish Women's Suffrage Society. Dozens of Sinn Féin pamphlets! Even these letters on IRA headed paper!'

Winnie tried to remain calm. 'Many of those documents have

come into my possession through my work. We deal with people from a variety of backgrounds. There will be letters from prisoners because they ask us for assistance for their dependants.'

'And what about these prison letters, Miss Carney, from Mountjoy and Aylesbury prisons?' The officer waved several letters in her face.

'I wrote those letters to my mother when I was in prison. Those are personal letters and have no connection to my work.'

'But they are proof of your republican past, are they not, Miss Carney?'

'I do not deny my past. I do not deny being a republican. But I am now a member of the committee formed under the Collins-Craig pact and yet, since I became a member, my home has been raided more often than usual.'

After the interrogation, Winnie was taken to a cell and provided with a meagre meal. However, in less than an hour, she was escorted back to the interview room. More boxes had been unpacked and the pile of books and papers on the table had grown considerably. She felt weary and though she had tried to sweep up her hair she knew that she must look rather dishevelled.

'You are accused, Miss Carney, of being involved in actions against the state. You say this is not true, but look at these pamphlets and books that support the charge. The *Significance of Sinn Féin*, the *Life of O'Donovan Rossa*, even a copy of *Sheaves of Revolt* signed by the murderess Markievicz. What about the papers you destroyed and tried to hide? Were they even more seditious and incriminating? Just look at these raid reports. What have you to say about these?'

Winnie was handed several sheets of paper to read:

RAID REPORT

ARDOYNE HOUSE
25-7-22

I beg to report that I raided and searched the undermentioned premises this morning at 6a.m.

No. 2a, CARLISLE CIRCUS. — MISS WINNIE CARNEY

Delay was experienced in gaining admission. Miss Carney was found in bed. She was told to arise and after a slight delay her room was entered. It appears she had been burning some papers. She then asked to be allowed the use of the kitchen for herself. I said I could not let her do this. I fetched two women searchers. Whilst I was away it appears Miss Carney passed a packet of papers to her mother. A/H.C. McGregor noticed the movement and gained possession of the papers. The house was thoroughly searched and some documents were taken away.

122, CORPORATION STREET

55/348. The offices of the Irish Transport Workers Union, of which Miss Carney is Secretary were then searched and some documents were found.

I arrested Miss Carney as instructed, and lodged her at Chichester Street.

D.I.

COMMANDING NO. 49 PLATOON R.U.S.C.[2]

The second paper read:

> City of Belfast
> Ardoyne House
> 49 Platoon
>
> 25/7/22
>
> D.I.
>
> I beg to report. That whilst engaged in a search party in No. 2A Carlisle Circus I went into the kitchen after Miss Carney. I saw her hand her mother a small paper parcel. The mother seemed rather nervous and then Miss Carney took the parcel from her which I took possession of. The parcel contained some newspaper cuttings and letters.
>
> A. McGregor A/H.Const. 6339[3]

A separate document listed all of the items that had been found during the raid:

Exhibits found on Winnie Carney

Exhibit 1.
Label showing where property was found. 2a Carlisle Circus by Sergt. McGregor. Also sack label – Capt. McMahon O'Brien, Ardoyne House.

Exhibit 2.
Assortment of Republican Newspaper Cuttings.

Exhibit 3.

Two notes undated from Madam Markievits [*sic*] to Miss Carney making appointment for 22nd. Address 143 Leinster Road. Postmarked – 27.9.17 and 6.16.17.

Exhibit 4.

Letter from Grace Plunkett to Miss Carney in pencil asking for appointment at 2 o'clock on Monday. No date.

Exhibit 5.

Commemoration card of Easter 1916. Bearing name 'Kathleen Clarke' and on the reverse the following signatures:–

J.M. Plunkett

A name in Irish

Kelly O'Ryan

M. ffrench-Mullen

A name in Irish

Nell Humphries

A name in Irish

Winifred Carney

Kathleen Lynn

20.4.17

9 Belgrave Road

Mountjoy party.

Exhibit 6.

Correspondence received by Miss Carney during June and July 1922. Including letters from Hd. Qrs. No. 1 Bd, 3rd North Div., and the Irish White Cross. On the back of a letter from the latter the following names and addresses are written in pencil:–

Mrs Morton, California Street.   £1
2 children. Husband arrested.

Mrs O'Neill, 15 Hall Street.   £1
Husband and son arrested.

Mrs McCann, Albert Street.   £1
2 children. Husband arrested.

Mulhern, 42 Boundry Street.
2 children. Husband arrested.

Jon Magee
Kamen O'Murcadh
Corvan Divisional Quartermaster

Mrs Scott, Sydney Street
Son arrested.

Largey, -do-   10/-
Son arrested.

Flanagan, Kildare St.   10/-
Son arrested.

Domigan, Catherine St. N.   10/-
Son arrested.

O'Hare, S Peel St.
Husband arrested.[4]

Winnie studied the documents slowly, before replying, 'There is nothing seditious in these papers.'

'Then why did you try to hide them? Why did you pass them to your mother? What papers did you burn?'

'I tried to hide them because they are not the business of anyone else. I am the secretary of the Prisoners' Dependents' Fund and such information is confidential and should remain so. Other documents are personal items that I wanted to keep. How do I know that the papers you take will ever be returned to me?'

Winnie was returned to her cell. The questioning continued for the next two days. Each time she entered the interview room new documents were placed in front of her as further proof of her seditious actions. She was permitted to write one letter from her cell and chose to write to request a business meeting with William McMullen, a close friend and colleague from the ITGWU. A former shipyard worker, McMullen had been one of James Connolly's greatest Belfast supporters, as well as a full-time official in the union. Winnie had worked alongside him for years and she felt she really needed his help. She was also very concerned about the raid on their offices and the fact that they would need to be secured. Two boxes of documents that had been taken in the raid contained the names and addresses of several republican leaders and activists. Warnings needed to be sent to them as quickly as possible.

Winnie was placed in a cell for several hours each day. On the second day, being unused to idleness without so much as a book to read, she asked for paper so that she could write to the major in charge of the station. The commanding officer decided that he would permit this as the correspondence would not be leaving the building. Paper and a pen were brought to her and, sitting on a hard stool in her cell, she poured out her grievances:

Major Leithes

Sir

I assume it was at your instigation my arrest was affected on yesterday morning, 24th inst., at the residence of my mother. I do not know if you also are responsible or aware that since then I have been lodged in the police cells in Chichester Street without any facilities whatsoever for obtaining exercise and fresh air. These cells I would infer from this enclosed situation and this total absence of accommodation are intended solely for prisoners of the criminal class who have been arrested on the streets for detention for one night at the most until charged with their offences at the courts the following morning. They are brought in in a helpless state of drunkenness, create a terrible din for hours and subject their jailers to the foulest language at their command until exhaustion overtakes them and it is amongst this class of men and women of the streets I am to be detained without charge to await your pleasure? For an offence of which you are well aware, against the English Government and of which I was admitting proud, I was indicted in 1916. But if I was, in the very first instance, I was given all the privileges of a prisoner awaiting trial.

At the present moment when men are arrested in Belfast as political suspects they are lodged in the Crumlin Road jail in airy cells which open on to the streets; permitted open air exercise, and I assume other privileges, and yet you detain a woman amongst the lowest of low criminals and under conditions which, even for that class are considered fit only for this detention for one night, indefinitely?

Are you really sane?

I am not a criminal, neither have I been guilty of a political offence that would warrant my arrest. For both these reasons I demand either immediate release or a trial and if I am detained in these police cells for a further night, I shall certainly hold you responsible to an authority much higher than the cabinet of Northern Ireland.

Lack of accommodation cannot be given as a genuine reason for my detention here, or the fact that there are only male prisoners lodged in the Crumlin Road jail. As it is, I am surrounded by male prisoners, and my attendants so far have been men. I do not complain of this because they have shown me every courtesy and consideration. It is not the first time accommodation has been found at the residence of the Governor of the jail for a political prisoner. I need only quote the case of Mrs Sheehy-Skeffington when arrested and taken to London in 1919, but her release came instead.

If I am to be detained for a trial, kindly see if a similar arrangement could not be made on my behalf.

Yours very sincerely, W. Carney[5]

The small cell was damp and airless and Winnie's health had started to deteriorate by the morning of 28 July. The inspector applied to the Inspector General, Charles Wickham, for a detention order, stating that he did not know what charge was to be preferred against her but that the doctor had certified that the detention of her any longer in the cell at the police station would be dangerous to her health. Procedure had to be followed and the inspector, trying to follow the directions with which he had been issued, spent the whole day sending letters back and forward by police messenger:

FORM 38A.

PARTICULARS OF PERSONS ARRESTED UNDER REGULATION 23 OF CIVIL AUTHORITIES (SPECIAL POWERS) ACT.

COUNTY: City of Belfast DISTRICT: 'C' Ardoyne House STATION: No. 49 Platoon

1. Name of Accused: Miss Winifred Carney
2. Address: 2A Carlisle Circus
3. Occupation: Secretary I.T.W.U.   AGE: 30
4. Character, if known, state also if previously convicted or interned.
5. Date & Place of Arrest: 2A Carlisle Circus
6. Reasons for Arrest (as fully as possible, omitting the names of witnesses):

   This woman is reported to have just returned from Dublin, having been released from Gaol where she had been for connection with the recent fighting before the Treaty.

   She has been associating with dangerous characters and is believed to have been acting as courier for the I.R.A.
7. (a) Is a Detention Order requested?   Yes
   (b) Is a prosecution recommended?   Yes
   (c) Is it proposed to recommend internment?   No

Signature ..... Spence   Rank: D.I.   Date: 28-7-22
To

Inspector-General, R.U.C., Atlantic Buildings, Waring Street, Belfast,

Director, C.I.D., Danesfort, Malone Road, Belfast

FORWARDED TO SECRETARY, MINISTRY OF HOME AFFAIRS 28.7.1922[6]

An urgent letter accompanied the application:

> Application for Detention Order for Miss Winnifred [*sic*] Carney
> No. 2A Carlisle Circus.   1345/603
>
> Very Urgent
>
> City of Belfast
>
> Belfast (D) 28.7.22.
>
> Minister of Home Affairs
>
> I beg to apply for a detention order for the detention of the above named lady in Armagh Female Prison. She was arrested by the O.C. 49 Platoon Ardoyne House on 25th inst by order of the C.I.D. I do not know what is the charge to be preferred against her but the Doctor has certified that the detention of her any longer in the cell at the police office is dangerous to her health. I therefore have to request that a Detention Order be at once issued so that she can be removed to Armagh jail this evening.
>
> 2nd D.I.[7]

In fact, the inspector had to apply several times. The Minister for Home Affairs was absent and so the signature of the Inspector General had to be sought:

> Inspector General
>
> R.U.Constabulary
>
> Detention order for Miss Winifred Carney is annexed. As the minister is absent he is not available to sign the Order and it will therefore require to be signed by the Inspector General as Civil Authority.

When signed would you kindly forward it to the Police concerned.

EWS

28 July 1922[8]

All documents collected to date were sent with the application, as well as a recommendation that Winnie be prosecuted:

File No. C.I.D. 23 1345/603

MINUTE SHEET

I.G

55/347) Miss Winnie Carney
55/348) 2A Carlisle Circus,
         Belfast

Raid order, statements of evidence, all exhibits and copies of raid reports and epitome are sent herewith.

This woman should be prosecuted under Regulation 24A for having in her possession documents purporting to emanate from an officer of an unlawful association.

Exhibits 55/347 No.6 and 6A furnish examples of such documents, in the form of letters from officers of Oglaic na Eireann (the Irish Republican Army).

No. 6 was found on Miss Carney's person.

Eustace Stoker

CID. A

28.7.1922[9]

Winnie was removed to Armagh Female Prison that night. She expected to find better conditions in the prison with time allotted daily in the open air. As a political prisoner, she should have been able to receive visitors and food parcels, but her requested meeting with William McMullen had yet to take place.

Her detention was highlighted in the 31 July issue of the *Irish Independent* newspaper:

VICTIMS OF ORANGE ANIMOSITY

Miss Winifred Carney, one of the secretaries of the I.T. and G.W.U. in Belfast, and a member of the Committee formed under the Collins-Craig pact, has been arrested. Since she was appointed on the Committee her house was raided several times, but she had not been found at home until last Wed., according to Dáil Éireann Publicity Department.

At 7.30pm on Wed., a bomb was thrown by loyalists from Newtownards Road into Young's Row (Catholic). One of the children playing in this street, a boy named Walsh, was wounded in the hand by a splinter from the bomb.

As the following documents show, the authorities spent the next few days examining the huge body of evidence in order to decide which charges should be brought against Winnie.

MINISTRY OF HOME AFFAIRS, NORTHERN IRELAND
No. H 1345/603
MINUTE SHEET
Belfast

Winifred Carney | Possession of I.R.A. documents

2a Carlisle Circus

arrested 25.07.22

Under detention order
in Armagh Prison

Attorney-General through Chief Crown Solicitor

Please advise.

There are 2 lots of documents:–

Found at Miss Carney's residence, 2a Carlisle Circus. A letter in Exhibit 6, and Exhibit 6A, are on I.R.A. notepaper.

Found at 122 Corporation Street in the offices of the Irish Transport Workers' Union, of which Miss Carney is said to be Secretary.

Exhibits 2, 3, 4, 7 are on I.R.A. notepaper.

2.8.22   J.W.E. Poynting

Prosecute under regulation 24A
BB

3/8/22

Instructions to military adviser, with order to Governor Armagh Prison to hand over accused to a police escort.

J.W.E. P. 3/8

MINISTRY OF HOME AFFAIRS, NORTHERN IRELAND
No. H 1345/603
MINUTE SHEET
Belfast

Winifred Carney
2a Carlisle Circus
and
122 Corporation Street
Arrested 25.7.22
Under detention order
in Armagh Prison

Possession of I.R.A. documents

Military Adviser

With reference to the Inspector General R.U.C's minute 24/6359 of the 31st inst., the Attorney General directs that Miss Winifred Carney shall be prosecuted under Regulation 24A, Civil Authorities (Special Powers) Act (Northern Ireland), 1922, in respect of the documents purporting to emanate from officers of the I.R.A. An order to the Governor, Armagh Prison, to hand over the accused to a police escort is attached.

Please instruct the police to proceed accordingly, and be good enough to furnish a report of the result in due course.

J.W.E. Poynting

3.8.22

    City Commr
    For compliance please
    D.J. for J.G.[10]

In Armagh Female Prison, Winnie was still waiting for her requested visit from William McMullen. She knew that he would never refuse such a request due to his high regard for James Connolly and his knowledge of their great friendship. She was convinced that the police in Ardoyne House had ignored her letter, so she decided to make the request again, this time to the governor of the prison. She also wrote two letters to the civil authorities in Belfast on 4 August to complain of the treatment she had received since her arrest:

> HM Prison,
> Armagh
> 4 August '22
>
> The Civil Authorities
> Home Office
> Belfast
>
> Sirs
>
> I wish to protest, most strongly against my detention in this prison without charge or trial, and against the treatment I have been subject to since my arrest on the morning of 25th inst. Since my committal to Armagh Prison, I have been supposed to endure the regulations governing ordinary prisoners, that is, confinement in a cell, prison food (which I am unable to eat) and no communication whatsoever with the outside world, in the nature of letters, papers, parcels from friends or visits. In no country that I am aware of or in no period of a political struggle have I known or read of a mere suspect against whom no charge can be referred, being treated as I am being treated in this prison at your instruction. During my internment by the British Government in 1916 for a clearly admitted attempt against this authority in Ireland, I was provided with a properly furnished bedroom, letters, papers and parcels from friends

and many other facilities which I need not here detail, and now when I can not be accused of any actions other than my actions on two Committees for the relief of distress in Belfast, I am being treated as a criminal, and denied even the right of a criminal awaiting trial? Since my arrest I have scarcely touched food and I cannot eat the regulation prison diet.

Will you at least please see that while I am detained I am accorded what one might almost term the international rights of a political suspect?

Yours faithfully,
W. Carney[11]

HM Prison,
Armagh
4 August '22

The Civil Authorities
Home Office
Belfast

Sirs

As an elected delegate to the Irish Trades Union Congress which meets in the Mansion House, Dublin on Monday 7th inst. I desire if I may have parole for the three days during which the Congress will sit, that is, for Monday, Tuesday & Wednesday. Also, would you please issue a permit for a business visit for one of the officials of the Irish Transport Workers' Union with whom I want to comment on this & National Health Insurance matters.

Yours faithfully,
W. Carney[12]

The governor of Armagh Prison, M.A. Wilson, immediately forwarded her requests. The police and J. W. E. Poynting from the Ministry of Home Affairs were quick to respond:

MINISTRY OF HOME AFFAIRS, NORTHERN IRELAND.
No. H 1345/603

MINUTE SHEET

Secretary

Ref. Miss Carney's application I think she should be allowed to get in food if ordered by the Prison Medical Officer.

The visiting Committee can allow her a special cell or room under the rules applicable to interned prisoners provided this is consistent with her safe custody. The police having agreed to a visit.

I think she might be allowed a visit in the presence and hearing of a Prison official, and that parole should be referred. She is to be tried for possession of I.R.A. docts.

H.J. 5/8

MINISTRY OF HOME AFFAIRS, NORTHERN IRELAND.
No. H 1345/603

MINUTE SHEET

Governor, Armagh Prison

With reference to your minute of the 4th inst. forwarding two applications by Winifred Carney, a detention prisoner, I am to say that parole cannot be granted, but you are authorised to allow her to have one interview, under supervision, with Mr

William McMullen, Secretary, Irish Transport and General Workers' Union, of 122 Corporation Street, Belfast, and to allow her to write one letter (to be examined by you) to Mr McMullen for the purpose of arranging the interview, which will take place at Armagh Prison. This authorisation is given in consequence of previous application by Miss Carney, made on the 25th inst.

Miss Carney may be allowed to get in food if this is ordered by the Prison Medical Officer; and the visiting committee can, if they think fit, allow her a special cell or room under the rules applicable to interned prisoners, provided this is consistent with her safe custody.

Please report the action taken.

J W E Poynting

5.8.22[13]

Mr Poynting wrote again to the military advisor on 8 August, asking if the Ministry of Home Affairs would expedite Winnie's prosecution as much as possible. The commissioner replied the next day to inform him that arrangements to have Winnie brought to the Police Court in Belfast had already been made and would happen on 9 August. The case was heard on that date but the magistrates reserved their decision until the next day.

The charges against Winnie had been brought under the Civil Authorities (Special Powers) Act. Her health was wretched and she had to hold on to the dock to prevent herself from falling. She was informed that the commissioner had written about the state of her health and his belief that she appeared to be suffering from a complete nervous breakdown. For this reason, the magistrate told her, he would not be interning her as he felt she would only be a case for hospital. The verdict was guilty and the fine was forty shillings. The fine was paid by William McMullen, who was present in the court. Winnie was discharged and looked exceedingly frail as she walked down the steps. McMullen escorted her to her mother's house and told her to rest and regain her strength before returning to work.

Two reports on the outcome of the case were written. One was typed for the Ministry of Home Affairs:

S.B.24/6359.

SUBJECT: Winifred Carney, 2a Carlisle Circus & 122 Corporation St., (Possession of I.R.A. documents.)

INSPECTOR GENERAL'S OFFICE
Royal Ulster Constabulary

Belfast

15th August 1922

Minister of Home Affairs,
Northern Ireland

Reference Govt., No. H1345/603, dated 3.8.22.

I beg to report that this woman was prosecuted under Reg. 24.A. of Civil Authorities (Special Powers) Act, at Belfast Police Court on the 9th instant. The Magistrates reserved their decision until the 10th instant, when they convicted the prisoner, and fined her 40/-. The fine was paid by a friend in Court and she was discharged.

Her defence was that the communications she received from the I.R.A. were merely in her capacity of Secretary of the Republican Prisoners' Dependent's [*sic*] fund, and not in furtherance of the objects of the I.R.A. After making her defence she informed the Magistrates that she did not recognise the Court.

Owing to this woman's state of health, she is not recommended for internment.

D.I. for I.G.

Copy to C.I.D. (A), for information. (Epitome No.55/105 & 55/348.)[14]

The other, marked secret, was handwritten and sent to the commissioner's office:

SECRET

Subject: Winifred Carney   Crime Special

City of Belfast

Royal Ulster Constabulary

Commissioner's Office

5th [*sic*] August 1922

D.I. 'D'.

For compliance please.

[signature]

Commissioner

I beg to report that the above woman was prosecuted as directed at Belfast Police Court on 9th inst. The magistrate reserved their decision until yesterday, when they convicted the prisoner and fined her 40s/–d (forty shillings). This fine was paid on her behalf by a friend in court, and she was discharged.

The case made by Carney was that the communications she received from the I.R.A. were merely in her capacity as Secretary of the Republican Prisoners Dependents Fund, and not in furtherance of the objects of the I.R.A. Curiously enough after making her defence and cross examining the Crown witnesses, she informed the Magistrates that she did not recognise the Court!

As the question of interning this woman may arise, I know little or nothing about her, but expect her history is well known to the O.A.B. She appears however, to be in wretched health. She was on the point of fainting in the court, and appeared to [be] suffering from a complete nervous breakdown. If interned, she could, I think, be a case for hospital.

All exhibits are returned herewith.

[signature]

Commissioners Office

J.G.   13th August 1922

Submitted. I recommended Miss Carney's internment but did not submit particulars, in view of the condition of her health, I concur with the view that she would only be a case for hospital therefore I am not inclined to recommend her internment.

[signature]
Commissioner.[15]

Everything changed twelve days after Winnie's sentence was handed down. On 22 August Michael Collins, head of the Provisional Government, was killed in an ambush in Cork. Winnie was heartbroken by the death of the handsome young man whose life had been devoted to working for his country. She could not reconcile herself to the fact that men who had once stood side-by-side were now killing each other. W. T. Cosgrave, who had fought under Éamonn Ceannt in the South Dublin Union in 1916, took Collins' position in the government.

Winnie's health gradually improved and she resumed her duties in the office in Corporation Street. She still administered the Prisoners' Dependents' Fund and, as her clients were from the northern counties, she became more and more interested in the workings of the northern parliament and the injustices of the Special Powers Act. By October her strength had fully returned and she waged a campaign of letters at government officials and newspapers about the use of internment under the Act. She used the Irish version of her name to sign the letters. The following letter appeared in the *Irish News* of 17 October 1922:

Interned Without Trial

To the Editor

Dear Sir, – In the report which you gave in Friday's issue of your paper of the discussion which arose at Thursday's meeting of the Northern Parliament over the Home Secretary's report on the cost incurred by the acquisition and maintenance of the SS *Argenta* as an internment ship for political prisoners, an interesting point was made by Mr. Donald at the numbers of innocent young men who were being arrested and detained, sometimes for months at a time, without charge or trial. The reply of the Home Secretary was that cases of this kind are investigated by a Commission appointed by the Home Office, and where innocence is proved, the release of the prisoner is recommended.

For the benefit of those members of the Northern Parliament interested in the question of prisoners, and for the benefit of the public gallery, I would like to draw attention to the case of Miss Mollie Kerr, arrested seventeen weeks ago at her home in Belfast, and at present confined in Armagh Prison, where she is undergoing the treatment of an ordinary prisoner on remand, but with none of the privileges of a prisoner on remand, and given the coarsest of prison food – namely 'D' diet.

The Commission of Inquiry investigated the case of Miss Kerr, and the only evidence that could be produced to incriminate her was that she supplied meals to a prisoner (a neighbour of her own) awaiting sentence in the Crumlin Road Jail, and that in her possession there were found two letters, sealed, from the parents of two other prisoners awaiting sentence at the same time.

These letters she was unable to deliver as the boys had been sentenced before the letters had reached her. She was not cognisant of their contents, which on examination by the Home Office authorities were found to contain only matters of a purely personal and domestic nature. In her efforts on behalf of these three boys Miss Kerr was prompted by the merest feelings of humanity; she had no political reasons for her actions, which were perfectly legitimate and done in the open. Often in her journeyings to and from the prison she was dressed in the uniform of Court Missionary, a position she then held, and for these acts of human kindness, which are being done daily by hundreds of Belfast women for the last six years, of bringing food to prisoners and letters from their friends, the Commission, appointed by the Home Office, refused to recommend her release. Never at any time in her life was she a member of a political organisation, nor held political views of an illegal brand; and from my slight knowledge of her I am convinced that she would not be capable of either lying or evading the truth.

If this is the kind of fair and impartial findings of this Commission, I do not think the prospect of release of any prisoner arrested under the Special Powers Act is so remote as to be absolutely hopeless.

The Sankey Commission which presided over and tried in London Irish prisoners arrested in armed and active rebellion in 1916, against British rule in Ireland, released hundreds of men and women, and recommended only the internment of those who they considered might be leaders of a kind in the Movement.

Yours faithfully,

UNA NI CEARNAIGH

122 Corporation Street, Belfast

16th October, 1922

As the Civil War in the south dragged on, the situation deteriorated rapidly. In November 1922 Cosgrave embarked on a policy of executing captured anti-Treaty fighters. The events that unfolded in Dublin caused Winnie great anguish. One of those executed, on 24 November, was Erskine Childers, a man she had known well. He had been responsible for bringing in the arms to Howth for the Irish Volunteers in 1914.

By the time a ceasefire was called in May 1923, nearly eighty men had been executed. Winnie could not understand how a former Irish Volunteer, who had fought in the Easter Rising and had his death sentence commuted for his participation in that event, had presided over such orders. Many of her friends and acquaintances were emigrating and, for several months, Winnie considered whether she should do the same. However, her continued republican activities ensured that the authorities were still cataloguing her actions and so her application for a passport was refused. The decision had been made for her. Instead she continued in her role in the union in Corporation Street and pledged herself to improving the quality of life for the working men and women of Belfast.

WINNIE AND GEORGE

For years Winnie Carney had been a card-carrying member of the Socialist Party of Ireland. She had also been a member of the Independent Labour Party and attended their annual conference in Glasgow in 1920. In the same year a lady she knew well, Margaret McCoubrey, was elected as a Labour councillor for the Dock Ward in Belfast. Many of Winnie's friends believed that support for the Labour movement was growing in Belfast and this seemed to be confirmed when Harry Midgley won forty-seven per cent of the vote in the 1923 general election.

Winnie's co-worker and friend, William McMullen, had been telling her for weeks that she should join the Court Ward branch of the Labour Party in north Belfast. He said that the members there had a similar outlook to James Connolly and were younger and more revolutionary than other Labour Party branches. They saw Labour as a movement towards Irish unity and lectures on Connolly, as well as Connolly commemorations, were held.

During the dark days between 1920 and 1922 Winnie had despaired that the ideals of Connolly seemed to have been forgotten. There had once been a growing solidarity among Belfast workers and an attempt to forget sectarian divisions in order to achieve objects of common interest. Then sectarian violence reared its ugly head in the shipyards in July 1920, in response to the murder by the IRA of a northern police officer. This led to the worst Belfast rioting for years. Thousands of Catholics and left-wing Protestant workers were driven out of their jobs and homes. There was wholesale looting of shops owned by Catholics, Catholic churches were damaged and Protestant and Catholic homes and businesses were burned. The police and military who tried to intervene were attacked by riotous mobs. Over the two-year period almost 500 people were killed and Belfast was left more polarised than ever.

At the beginning of January 1924 Winnie decided to take her friend's advice and join the Court Ward branch. She discovered right away that William had told her the truth. At the first meeting she met many younger people who had very radical ideas. They included colleagues from the ITGWU, communists and republicans. She was really delighted when her old friends, Nellie and James Grimley, entered the room. Many of the other members had never had any connection with the republican movement and some had little knowledge of the nationalist tradition. This all led to lively debate and Winnie, usually quiet in such situations, found herself becoming flushed and animated. The presence of Nellie and James seemed to give her back some of the confidence she had lost in the last few years. They reminded her of the days when they had protested at factory gates and been part of the 'Don't give a damn league'.

As the discussions continued over a cup of tea, Winnie became aware that a handsome young man seemed to be staring at her, almost in recognition. She kept glancing across the brown wooden chairs to where he was seated but she was sure she had never seen him before. No one introduced him and it would not be seemly to introduce herself. She turned her attention to Nellie and discovered that James and she were very happy and ran a second-hand clothes shop off the Newtownards Road in the east of the city. They had lost none of their socialist fervour and she felt energised by their company.

While working on accounts in her small office the day after, Winnie looked forward to returning to the Court Ward branch the next week. It had been wonderful to see the Grimleys and she liked some of the other flamboyant characters she had met at the meeting. The ideas she heard about infiltrating the labour movement with more revolutionary ideas excited her. She found her thoughts wandering to the identity of the handsome young man but then dismissed them as foolishness. She had turned thirty-seven the month before and felt that she should have no interest in young men. She never embraced the idea of the traditional role for women as housewives and the break-up of her parents' marriage had made her wary of relationships. She was strong-willed and enjoyed her independence. However, each morning as she brushed her thick dark hair, she found herself dreading the appearance of grey strands.

At the next meeting much of the discussion was about a demonstration against the Board of the Poor Law Guardians which the Labour Party was planning for February. Poor Law Guardians administered workhouses and outdoor relief and, with rising unemployment, the situation in Belfast was becoming desperate. Employment in the shipyards had dropped by twenty per cent and in the engineering works was down by fifteen per cent. There seemed to be a distinct lack of co-operation between the Northern Ireland Government and the Guardians and so the Labour Party felt that something had to be done.

During the discussions someone said that Miss Carney should

be good at organising the demonstration as she had already been part of the major one in Dublin in 1916. She replied that she would be of no use as an organiser, but she would be happy to participate. The handsome young man she had noticed the week before said that he too would be happy to take part as many employees of Mackie's, where he worked, had been laid off and were greatly in need of assistance. There were murmurs of support for a demonstration from all corners of the room and the final motion of the evening was in favour of one on 26 February. As usual the meeting was followed with a cup of very strong tea and a great deal of animated discussion. Winnie chatted to Murtagh Morgan, a young republican she knew because he had joined the union the previous year, but she was aware that the young man she noticed before was moving in her direction.

'Excuse me, Miss Carney, I don't believe I have had the pleasure.' With this George proffered his hand.

As Morgan moved away, Winnie could do nothing else but shake his hand. Up close she realised that he was even younger than she had first thought.

'Good evening, sir. You have the advantage over me as I do not believe we have been introduced,' she replied. At this Tommy Geehan, secretary of the Branch, who had been standing close by, intervened.

'Permit me to introduce you, Miss Carney. This is George McBride, one of our comrades and one of our veterans of the 36th Division that fought in the fields of France.'

Winnie couldn't help but smile at the thought of this fresh-faced young man being a veteran of anything.

George mistook the smile as an encouragement to speak. 'And

you, Miss Carney, in what type of demonstration did you take part in 1916?'

'I did not take part in a demonstration, Mr McBride. I took part in an uprising. I bid you goodnight.' With this sharp response Winnie turned on her heel and left the room. George gazed after her with a distinct feeling of déjà vu. The *Titanic* came to mind, for some reason.

For the next week Winnie fumed at the arrogance of the whippersnapper who referred to the great sacrifice of 1916 as a demonstration. She considered whether she would return to Court Ward and then decided that Mr McBride was only one person and she would not be deterred. She would find solace in the company of Nellie and James and ignore Mr McBride.

Over the next few weeks the Court Ward meetings were fully occupied with planning the demonstration. George McBride did not seem deterred by her rebuke to him on their first meeting and sought her out at every possible moment. He was fascinated to learn that she had been in the GPO with Connolly and was one of the last women to leave. Other members joined them and the tactics of Connolly were often debated. While Winnie could never agree with many of George's views, which seemed to dismiss the importance of 1916, she found herself looking forward to their discussions which, at times, became very animated.

'Tell me, Miss Carney,' George asked one evening in February, 'how could Connolly have led his men and women into a venture such as the uprising which was doomed to failure? Did he not know that there was no chance of military success?'

'Somebody had to start,' Winnie replied. 'James never thought the British Army would shell the GPO and the other buildings.

He did not think that they would destroy capitalist property to any great extent.'

'And was that not foolish, Miss Carney, when the capitalist powers of Europe were blasting the whole continent of Europe to ashes? I was there and saw it. I know what dead men look like, thousands of them. All the death and destruction! Connolly must have known it was a suicidal and hopeless venture.'

'You may be right, Mr McBride, but even if there was no hope of military success surely the symbolic display of courage and rebellious spirit was an achievement in itself?'

'I do not dispute their courage, Miss Carney, but I believe the leaders to have been naive. How could anyone have believed that the British would not have destroyed property and use any means possible to crush the rebellion?'

Winnie firmly reiterated, 'Somebody had to start.'

As everyone left the room she heard someone call out, 'Many happy returns, George. You've seen a lot in twenty-six years!' Winnie's heart sank; he was even younger than she had thought.

Winnie and George both attended the demonstration at the end of February and with hundreds of others registered their disapproval of the machinations of the Poor Law Guardians and the new Northern Ireland Government. Afterwards George offered to escort her home. It was a dark night and he did not feel that a woman should be walking the streets of Belfast alone. She protested that she would be perfectly safe but he insisted. As usual their conversation turned to Labour Party policies and the differences between their ideals were highlighted once more. George thought that James Larkin was the greatest of all union leaders, while Winnie's loyalty was always to James Connolly, who had distrusted Larkin.

'I have always admired Larkin,' said George. 'Connolly was the strategist, but not a great one. Larkin was the tactician, and a brilliant one.'

'But Connolly was the one with the courage. Larkin took himself off to America,' argued Winnie.

'Like many others Connolly mistook courage for military knowledge,' replied George. 'Many of those fighting for a republic in 1916 did not even know what the inside of a slum looked like.'

'I cannot dispute that, Mr McBride, but I still feel their actions showed bravery and achieved much,' she responded with conviction.

George thought too highly of her to rebuke her again.

From that evening a pattern developed in their lives. Each week, following the meeting, George would walk Winnie home to Carlisle Circus where she still lived with her mother. They talked of politics and policies, the past and the present, disappointments and hopes. Frequently they disagreed, usually about the past, but their friendship grew stronger. Winnie was an attractive woman and could be very charming. She was extremely independent and had a quick wit and a sharp tongue. George admired these qualities and, although he did not agree with many of her views, he still wanted to hear them.

Over the next two years George and Winnie met each other several times a week. He wanted to understand her ideas and opinions and was interested in meeting her old friends and comrades. On her part she was interested in the path that had taken him to war and how he had come to develop such radical socialist principles.

Their common ground was the work of the Labour Party and they shared in all the branch's activities.

George was fascinated by Winnie and loved to hear her talk about art and literature; subjects that he knew too little about. She asked him to accompany her to the Belfast Municipal Museum and Art Gallery and he was in awe of her knowledge about sculpture, one of her great interests. On such rare outings she would talk about her family and he was keen to listen and learn about her life when she was young.

'I love Belfast. Our life was so much richer when we moved here after our travels around County Down and England. There's so much to see and do here, so much history too.'

'We never learned much about history, I seem to recall just lists of kings and queens of England to be learned off by heart. There was a picture on the wall of every king and queen from William the Conqueror to Edward VII.'

'Oh the Christian Brothers made sure we had lots of history in our school, George. We learned all about Dean Swift, Henry Grattan, the rebellion of 1798, Catholic emancipation, the famine and the land acts. We had some British history too and even learned all about the French Revolution. I loved all the stories when I was young; Brian Boru, Cuchulain and Finn MacCool. We had lots of books at home and I read them all. I was the youngest of six so I read everyone else's books. My mother enjoyed history and reading as well. She said that was because our family had a connection with the rebel press of Dublin.'

George looked perplexed and Winnie hurried to explain.

'After the Act of Union in 1800 many nationalists wanted to overthrow the Act and form an independent Irish nation. Journalists used newspapers such as *The Freeman's Journal* and *Nation* to promote that in the 1840s and that was the start of cultural and political nationalism. We were all brought up to take pride in the fact that forebears of ours were a part of that.'

'Was it a happy childhood, Winnie?'

'Well, my mother never seemed happy after my father left though I can't recall her being happy before. There were happy times and I can't complain. Mother worked hard in our shop and my sisters helped her. We were quite comfortable because my mother's brother, Alexander Cassidy, never married and he treated us like his own family. He had a shop in Mill Street and never seemed short of money. Mother's other brother, Michael, had a confectionary shop, so we got plenty of sweets. The best times were when we all gathered round the piano and sang. Did your family do that, George?'

'Rarely. Only my sister Bella was older than me and my mother always seemed to have her hands full, with four younger than me. I loved it when my father let me help look after the pigeons or took me to clock the birds in on a Saturday after a pigeon race. There wasn't much money with only my father's pay coming in until Bella and I started work. We didn't have many books in the house but there was always the newspaper and I was a good reader. I played a lot of games with the younger ones. My only brother is seven years younger than me and my youngest sister, Mary, is still at school today. Where are all your brothers and sisters now, Winnie?'

'Ernest went to New York when I was in my teens. He travelled on the *Umbria* and then Louis went there too. My sisters Maud and Mabel left home in their twenties and are both nuns. Maud is in Birmingham and Mabel works with people with incurable diseases in America. Alfred is still in Belfast.'

'The rest don't seem to have the same love of the city as you,' George remarked as they prepared to leave the museum.

In 1925 they both campaigned on behalf of William McMullen during the run-up to the second Northern Ireland election held in April. The results were decided using the proportional representation system. McMullen was standing in West Belfast and, although he came bottom of the poll, transfers to him from the Nationalist Party's Joe Devlin ensured he was elected. Two other Labour Party Members of Parliament, Sam Kyle in Belfast North and Jack Beattie in Belfast East, were returned at the same time. Celebrations were held in all the successful branches and George and Winnie were delighted to have helped achieve such results, which would surely help working people.

Belfast was still suffering greatly from the effects of the post-war recession. George and Winnie thought that the tough police state, under the Northern Ireland Home Secretary Dawson Bates, was driving more and more workers towards drastic action, such as street protests, which could end in violence. George became increasingly active in Labour Party work and often chaired branch meetings, as well as meetings with workers' groups. Speakers were frequently brought in and George was appalled when one of their speakers, Sam Patterson, a labour activist and critic of Sir James Craig, was arrested for seditious language following one meeting. As George was in the chair when the arrest occurred he felt it necessary to attend Patterson's court hearing. The usually mild George was incandescent with rage when the judge, in trying to define sedition, said that to mention the price of bread at a time of bread shortage could be construed as seditious.[1]

George embarked on a series of lectures to Labour members

in other constituencies. At one such lecture, in the Andrew's Memorial Hall in the very unionist village of Comber, he was questioned about the Labour Party's attitude to the border question and the debate about redrawing the boundary of Northern Ireland. He replied that the Labour Party was neutral but that, really, the border question was irrelevant as they were all controlled by banks and international finance. His comments were booed loudly.

Throughout 1925 Winnie supported George in his work for the branch and faithfully attended all his lectures. She knew that they could only ever be friends, but she valued his company and their animated debates made her feel more alive than she had felt since May 1916. If she had been ten years younger she might have considered more than just friendship but she was wise enough to know that too much divided them. She would settle for friendship.

Winnie's frequent debates with George stirred up a lot of memories of 1916 and over the months that followed she told him a little about her time during the Rising. They compared notes about having been what she described as prisoners of war in foreign countries. She also told him about being arrested in 1922 and how often her home had been raided and dozens of documents seized. The thought of the lost personal mementoes brought a tear to her eye.

'What type of papers did they keep?' he asked as he used his big white handkerchief to gently wipe away her tears.

'I'm not sure you'd understand, George. The most precious were memoriam cards for dead friends, people I thought highly of and stood beside in the past.'

'Tell me about them,' he encouraged softly and after a few minutes she replied.

'One memoriam card was for Thomas James Clarke who was nearly sixty and in the GPO with us in 1916. In deference to his age he was the first man to sign the Proclamation of Independence. His father had been a soldier in the British Army and Thomas, as a young man, joined Clan na Gael in America. He was the treasurer of the IRB and spent fifteen years in penal servitude for his part in a bombing campaign but I found him a kindly, brave man. Indeed in my heart I thought him the bravest. He was executed on 3 May 1916.

'Then there was a card for Patrick Pearse who was in the GPO too. He had a great interest in Irish cultural matters and was a member of the Executive Committee of the Gaelic League. He was intellectual and poetical, with a university degree in Arts and Law. Pearse had been one of the founding members of the Irish Volunteers and the author of the Proclamation. He was executed on the same day as Thomas.

'I'd another card for Patrick's younger brother, Willie. He shared his brother's passion for an independent Ireland and helped him in running St Enda's school. They were very close and fought side by side with us too. Willie was executed on the day after his brother. That was terribly hard on their mother, who wrote to me often. I felt very sorry for her loss.'

'Many mothers lost two sons in the war, Winnie, and I used to think about how awful it must be for two telegrams to arrive. I heard of one mother from Comber who lost three of her sons on the first day of the Somme. I'm sure there were German mothers who suffered in the same way. What a waste!'

'All untimely deaths are sad. One of my cards was for a man who stood with us in the GPO even though he was recovering from an operation. He was very courageous and, although I didn't warm to him at first, he turned out to be very loyal. He was the son of a Papal count and was called Joseph Mary Plunkett. He went to university in Dublin and then joined the Irish Volunteers. It was he who travelled to Germany to meet Roger Casement in 1915. During the planning of the Rising, he was appointed director of military operations. I really treasured his card because it reminded me of the message he gave me for his sweetheart Grace Gifford. They were married in prison and he was executed the next day, on 4 May.'

'Were they all cards for men who were in the GPO?'

'No, I had some others. Tom Clarke's wife, Kathleen, was always very good to me and her younger brother was executed too. Poor Ned Daly was only twenty-five and he was the youngest commandant in 1916. Imagine, she lost a husband and a brother. And then her uncle, John Daly, died a few months later in June. I treasured the cards for both men.'

'Was there no memoriam card for James Connolly?' interrupted George.

As usual Winnie was reticent when it came to discussing Connolly. George admired her loyalty to her former employer and comrade but had noticed that she never wanted to discuss any details about the time they had worked together. Nellie Grimley told him that Winnie never had talked about Connolly's visits and maybe that was because she was the only one in his confidence in those days.

'I never had one,' was the simple reply.

'And why were they not returned to you when you were released?'

'I suppose they thought they were too republican, but to me they were reminders and things to be cherished. There were letters too, and photographs and cuttings. I asked for them to be returned some years ago but the request was refused.'

'Then you should ask for them back now. This is supposed to be a new Northern Ireland. Pursue the matter. Write to Dawson Bates. They may be in storage somewhere and they are yours by rights.'

Winnie was delighted to have his support and nodded fiercely. 'I will, George. You are quite correct. I will write tomorrow when I am in the office.' She used official paper for the letter:

IRISH TRANSPORT & GENERAL WORKERS' UNION
Head Office – 35 PARNELL SQUARE, DUBLIN

Belfast *Branch*

Dated 22nd March, 1926   *Address* 122, Corporation Street.

The Minister for Home Affairs,
Ocean Buildings,
Belfast.

Sir,
Sometime in March 1921 I wrote to the Divisional Commissioner of Police asking for a return of the documents seized at my mother's residence, 2a Carlisle Circus, and at 70, Newington Avenue, the residence of my late uncle. He replied that for the time being the documents could not be returned to me.

I would be glad to know if I may expect their return now, and would like if they were delivered to the above address.

I would point out that the documents in question were of really no political or military significance. They consisted of a group photograph, cuttings from newspapers, letters, Christmas and memoriam cards, an original copy of the *Irish War News* and a leaflet issued by the Irish Provisional Government in 1916. Both of these documents are of considerable historical value, the former one being valued at £200 in the London *Times* some years ago.

Thanking you.

Yours sincerely,
Winifred Carney[2]

She received a reply three weeks later:

H.1345/603   13th April, 1926.

Madam,

With further reference to your letter of the 22nd ultimo, I am directed by the Minister of Home Affairs to return to you the documents as per attached list which were seized during the search of No. 2a Carlisle Circus on the 11th March, 1921.

A careful list of the documents was made at the time of seizure and there is no record of a copy of the *Irish War News* or of the leaflet issued by the Irish Provisional Government in 1916 being included in the documents seized.

I am, Madam,
Your obedient Servant,
EWS
for Secretary[3]

Not all of the items were returned and, having discussed the matter with George, Winnie replied. She was again unsuccessful.

122 Corporation Street,
Belfast.
21/5/'26

Dear Sir

I am much obliged for your registered letter of 13th April containing some of the documents about which I wrote.

There is no doubt whatever as to the seizure of the documents issued by the Irish Provisional Government which were framed and were taken in the first of three raids which took place in 1922. There was also taken a copy (framed) of the Deportation order served on me in 1916 by his Majesty's Government.

The large group photograph mentioned in my letter, and which is of no interest to anyone outside myself has not been returned, and minor other unimportant letters; and maybe if a search were made these things might be found together?

I would be greatly obliged if these things could be traced as I place considerable value on some of them.

Thanking you
Yours sincerely
Winifred Carney

Minister for Home Affairs
Ocean Buildings
Belfast[4]

She received the following reply:

H.1345/603.   8th June, 1926.

Madam,

With further reference to your letter of the 27th ultimo, I am directed by the Minister of Home Affairs to inform you that a very careful search has again been made amongst the documents which were taken during all the searches at Carlisle Circus.

As you have been informed, a careful list of all documents was made at the time of seizure, and there is no record in these lists nor is there any trace among the documents themselves of the particular documents referred to in your letter.

I am, Madam,

Your obedient Servant,

EWS

for Secretary.[5]

Winnie was horrified. She had typed the 1916 Proclamation that was read on the steps of the GPO and now her only copy had disappeared. Not only were some of her most treasured possessions gone but the last letter implied that she was a liar. As had become her habit, she brought the letter to her next meeting with George. He consoled her but said that he was not surprised and surely she realised that government officials could not be trusted. He reminded her that, like him, she had sat in meetings and lectures when Dawson Bates' drumming clubs had been sent around to beat their drums to drown out the speakers, and so even free speech was at risk. For once she felt comforted and not alone. It was a good feeling.

22

WINNIE AND GEORGE:
AN UNLIKELY UNION

Conditions for the working person throughout the United Kingdom continued to worsen in 1926. Unemployment soared, wage reductions were planned and over a million miners were locked out in Great Britain. The Trades Union Congress called for a general strike in May to try to force the government to act. Nearly 1,750,000 workers responded.

Socialists in Belfast rallied to the cause and tried to show solidarity by holding a meeting and inviting one of the miners' leaders to address those present. George chaired the meeting and, as usual, Winnie marvelled at the quiet and yet firm way with which he conducted all meetings. Near the end of the meeting he was faced with the problem of taking up a collection, which was considered illegal at the time. Winnie watched as he calmly stood up and, picking up an empty box, threw money into it. He then passed the box around the room while he warned all present that they were, on no account, to put any money in the box. A substantial collection was raised.

As was usually the case at all these meetings, there was a plainclothes police officer in the room. George was therefore brought to court for illegal collection. In the court he inquired if anyone had heard him ask another person to make a donation. Of course no one had and so he was acquitted.

In any event the general strike lasted only nine days as the government enlisted middle-class volunteers to maintain essential services and the Trades Union Congress admitted defeat.

George and Winnie continued to fight for better wages for many of the people of Belfast who lived in slum conditions. They became used to policemen following them to meetings as well as when George walked Winnie home afterwards.

'You would think we were a couple of agitators,' he remarked angrily to Winnie one night as they reached Carlisle Circus.

'You know, George, I think that might be what we are,' she replied with a laugh. As ever, hearing her laugh could lighten his spirits.

'I suppose so, Winnie, but lately it seems the only thing that unions do is fight with employers and Tories. Maybe we'd be better just to fling obscenities at them and not argue at all.'

'I'm not sure I'd like you as much, George, if all you could use were swear words,' she replied as she linked arms with him.

'And do you like me, Winnie?'

'You are my very dear friend,' she replied.

In spite of their audience, their relationship had grown and George would kiss her as they said goodnight on the doorstep. Winnie could not bring him into her home as she was only too aware of how her mother would react if she was introduced to this Protestant former UVF soldier.

Neither could George take Winnie to his home. He knew that his father would not forgive the fact that she had played a large part in the rebellion of 1916 and was still an unrepentant republican. He thought that his mother would be even more appalled by the thought of him courting a woman over ten years older than himself.

Suddenly he really didn't care what they thought.

'Do you like me enough to be my wife, Winnie? You are very dear to me and I love you very much. I would like to spend the rest of my life with you.' He leaned in closer and asked again: 'Would you be my wife?'

Winnie stood on the doorstep in silence. Minutes passed as she formulated her reply. 'I'm sorry, George, I can't. Too much divides us and I am too old. I am used to my independence and I have made my own life and my own achievements. I love being your friend and want that to continue more than anything. But that is all we can ever have.'

George was greatly disappointed but not altogether surprised. When he had told James Grimley that he wanted to marry Winnie, James had said that, according to Nellie, other men had proposed to Winnie – the list included Joe McGrath and William O'Brien – but she had turned them down. She preferred spinsterhood. George accepted her decision but resolved in his quiet, stubborn manner not to give up.

In the summer of 1927 Winnie was transferred to the ITGWU in Dublin. This had happened to her twice in the past when there was a lack of work in the Belfast office and it was an arrangement that was not to her liking. This time she enjoyed being in Dublin even less, as she desperately missed George. He had become the most important person in her life, she realised, and costly though it was, she tried to travel to Belfast as many weekends as possible to see him. Between visits they wrote to each other every day and her letters always pleaded with him to look after himself until they could meet again.

In Winnie's absence George filled his time with his favourite pursuit – reading. His friendship with Winnie had made him painfully aware of the gaps in his knowledge and he became an avid reader of history, economics and sociology. Winnie often told him that she worried about his health because he spent so many hours reading old books. Then in August his local branch, Court Ward, decided to send him on a training course to the National Council of Labour Colleges in London. His love of learning meant that the lectures were inspirational to him but he was aware that something was missing.

Winnie.

In September George stood nervously outside the Great Northern Railway station on the west side of Great Victoria Street in Belfast. Known locally as the GNR, it was a fine sturdy building with two platforms and three tracks. George walked between the pair of impressive columns that protected the entrance and watched as the Dublin train puffed into the station. The doors clanged open and, with dozens of others, Winnie appeared. As always, he was struck by her dignified beauty and the dainty way in which she walked. Her dark hair was swept up and her eyes and mouth smiled as she saw him. He hugged her, conscious of the fact that she felt as if she would break if he squeezed too hard.

'Winnie, Winnie, I have missed you so much. The weeks have seemed interminable.'

'I must admit I have missed you too. But I have asked for a transfer back to Belfast so we can go back to our old ways,' she replied.

'I don't want to go back to our old ways, Winnie.'

She pulled out of his arms and looked up in alarm. 'You don't want to continue our friendship?'

'No, Winnie, I don't. These last months have taught me that I want more than friendship. I want to be your husband. I want you to be my wife. I don't want us to be apart again. Please say yes, Winnie. I love you.'

'No one will speak to us, George. We will be ostracised. Our families will never see us.'

'I don't care about any of that. I know only one thing – I want to spend my life with you. Please, Winnie, say yes.'

Winnie was silent as they left the station and walked slowly down the street. During their enforced separation he had constantly been in her thoughts and her resolve never to marry had weakened bit by bit. She missed him so much when they were apart and she knew that she loved him.

'I would have to be the boss,' she replied with a smile. 'All I know is ordering men about.'

George's hopes were raised and he stopped beneath a street lamp opposite the Grand Opera House. 'If you say yes, then you can be the boss.'

'You will only be allowed to read old books at certain times,' she giggled.

'I would accept that rule too,' he replied with a laugh.

'Then, Mr McBride, I accept your proposal.'

To the amusement of the long queue waiting to gain admission into the Grand Opera House, the usually reserved George swept Winnie up in his arms until her legs dangled above the ground. He swung her around before setting her down with a gentle kiss on the lips. He felt that he had never known such happiness.

Winnie looked back at the GNR and thought of the dozens of times she had come to that very spot to meet James Connolly getting off the train, or to catch the train to meet him in Dublin. She felt that this was a new beginning and she would live now for all the things George had promised her and all the places they would go together.

Everyone in the Court Ward branch was delighted by the announcement that George and Winnie were to be married. They had watched the friendship grow into love and thought they were admirably suited, even if Winnie could be a bit bossy at times. James and Nellie Grimley were especially pleased. They had spent a lot of the past three years in George and Winnie's company and a firm friendship had grown between the two couples.

As expected, not one member of their families was pleased by the betrothal. For months, while they planned their wedding, George and Winnie listened to all the arguments against their marriage. They were of different religions. They came from different backgrounds. She was republican. He was unionist. She had been a member of Cumann na mBan. He had been in the YCV. She had carried a Webley gun in the GPO in 1916. He had fought the Germans in France as a Lewis gunner. She had fought against England. He had fought for England. She was too old for him. He was too young for her. They could not get married in church because she was Catholic and he was Protestant and neither was willing to change. Winnie's mother even brought the priest to the house to try to dissuade Winnie, but she was strong-willed and politely showed him the door. She was a practising Catholic, but her distrust of the hierarchy meant that she would not be subservient to any dubious, man-made rules of the church.

Finally, George and Winnie decided that they would get married far away from everyone they knew. For several months they made plans and by September 1928 everything was arranged. George left his engineering job in Mackie's as he knew only too well the reaction he would receive from his workmates when he married a republican. He had taken premises in Queen Street and opened a small leather goods business. He also took on a position as a National Council of Labour Colleges' lecturer in Economic History and this, with his small army pension, meant that he could afford to keep a wife. They found a house to rent in Whitewell Parade, off the Shore Road in the north of Belfast. Winnie tendered her resignation to the ITGWU in Corporation Street, prepared to start a new life as George's wife.

Sarah Carney sobbed when she was informed of her daughter's plan. She refused to give the marriage her blessing and said that it would not be a real marriage. She would not even say goodbye and turned her back as Winnie left the house. George's parents would not give their blessing either and informed George that, as he was now making his bed, he would have to lie in it. George had told them of his love for Winnie so many times that he knew it would be futile to argue any more. He said goodbye and left.

On 18 September 1928 George and Winnie returned to the Great Northern Railway station where they had agreed to marry a year earlier. This time it was to catch the train from Belfast to Dublin. A short train journey to Dún Laoghaire followed, where they boarded the mailboat, *Hibernia 3*, which was bound for Holyhead in Wales.

It was a delightful three-hour journey across the sea. The *Hibernia 3* was a most pleasantly designed steamship, with lattice-windowed tea-lounges that made Winnie feel that she was in a country inn. George held her hand as they sipped afternoon tea and all the anxieties of the past year slipped away.

'This reminds me of afternoon tea when I was a girl. My mother loved afternoon tea and with Mabel and Maud we would go to the Grand Central Hotel as a treat.'

'Weren't you very grand at the Grand?' George quipped as he lifted her hand and kissed it. Winnie giggled like a young girl. 'We had a stomach cake and a glass of milk for a treat when I was a boy.'

'That must be why you grew into such a fine figure of a man, Mr McBride,' she laughed.

'It must, indeed, Miss Carney. Your fancy afternoon teas didn't spoil your appearance either. You will be a very beautiful bride.'

Winnie blushed.

Once they alighted in Holyhead they made their way to the Albany Hotel in Church Terrace, Holyhead, where George had booked two rooms. It was a very modest hotel but the rooms were clean and comfortably furnished. This would be their home while their licence was organised.

George and Winnie spent the next seven days exploring the bustling ferry port and Holy Island on which it was built. Each morning, after breakfast in the hotel, they strolled arm-in-arm through the busy streets, taking time to gaze into the well-stocked shop windows. Their first stop was at the town hall, a splendid sandstone edifice built fifty years earlier. The clerk was extremely helpful and arrangements were made for a ceremony the following week.

There was much to see on the island, which was connected to

Anglesey by a causeway. The greater part of one day was spent in the centre of the town where Roman arches led them to St Cybi's Church and they learned all about the saint from a churchwarden. Winnie was fascinated to discover that the church was built on a monastic settlement dating back to the sixth century and had been sacked by Henry IV's army when they invaded from Ireland. After the sacking, they had taken St Cybi's shrine and relics to Christ Church Cathedral in Dublin.

On Saturday they visited the stone breakwater and marvelled at the Victorian structure which, at over a mile-and-a-half long, was the longest in the British Isles. It was pleasant to stroll along with hundreds of other visitors to view the spectacular South Stack lighthouse. Winnie could scarcely recall feeling so carefree. The next morning George and she walked along to the huge Admiralty Pier where they had disembarked and he described to her how, as a young soldier, he and thousands of others had tried to catch some sleep here on arrival from Ireland.

'How naive I was then, Winnie, I knew nothing of war and we all thought we were going on a great adventure. How wrong we were!'

For a while their mood darkened and they wandered back into the town. A lunch in the Queen's Head in Market Street lifted their spirits and their conversation returned to wedding plans.

On Wednesday 26 September, in the Register Office in the district of Holyhead, George McBride married Winnie Carney. No family attended the wedding and two Register Office employees, E. Roberts and C. Thomas, were the only witnesses. Nonetheless George thought his chest would burst with pride as Winnie smiled radiantly and said, 'I do.'

23

WINNIE AND GEORGE: MARRIED LIFE

Mr and Mrs George McBride travelled back to Belfast to their new home in Whitewell Parade. George returned to work in his little shop and resumed his lecturing duties. Winnie's life changed completely as, for the first time in almost twenty years, she took over the duties of running a home instead of going out to work. She discovered that she rather enjoyed it and eagerly awaited George's return each day. Only one thing troubled her and that was the fact that no one was properly caring for her elderly mother. She recalled how she had felt in prison in 1916 when her main concern had been for her mother. She had thought then that revolutionaries ought not to have relatives. Now her mother was even older and more infirm.

Shortly after her return to Belfast, Winnie decided to visit her mother, even though she feared that the door might be slammed in her face. To her surprise, her mother did not turn her away and pragmatically declared that there was no point in crying over spilt milk. Winnie could see that her brother Alfred was not taking proper care of their mother and she resolved to ask George if she could invite her mother to live with them. George could not bear to see his wife worried and unhappy, so he agreed. Within a matter of days, Sarah Carney, who had been so vehemently opposed to her daughter's marriage, was installed in their spare bedroom. Shortly after the move, news reached them that Sarah's husband and Winnie's father, Alfred, had died in London. Neither of them shed a tear.

For the next five years, life settled into a pattern that suited both George and Winnie. In the morning George rose first and lit the fire while she attended to her mother. He left early for work carrying his lunch of a sandwich or some cold meat that she had prepared. During the day Winnie attended to the needs of her mother, kept house, shopped, prepared dinners for George's return after six o'clock and occasionally visited her friend, Margaret McGuinness, whom Winnie was delighted to discover lived nearby. Margaret's parents had once been great friends of James Connolly and founding members of the ICA in Belfast. Margaret's uncle, Alfie McClean, was the first General Secretary of the ITGWU in Belfast and was also James Connolly's election agent in 1907 and 1911. Over the years Margaret had often dropped into the union offices and, although much younger than Winnie, they had many interests in common and enjoyed each other's company.

On Sundays she and George would go for long walks in the countryside around Belfast and discuss George's lectures and current issues affecting the Labour Party. They discussed the government in Northern Ireland and the Irish Free State. Frequently their debates would return to whether Connolly or Larkin was right and often they were forced to agree to disagree. They talked about the Easter Rising, which Winnie still felt had altered the course of history in Ireland. George was still puzzled by the philosophy of the death sacrifice and the glorification of rebels. She could never convince him that the deaths had been worth it. They talked about members of their families who still did not speak to them. Winnie's brothers and George's parents were the most unforgiving.

Both George and Winnie were still members of Court Ward and, if a neighbour was willing to sit with Sarah Carney, they both attended meetings and helped with canvassing. If no neighbour was available, or if Winnie's mother was particularly unwell, George had to go alone. In 1929 they once again supported William Mc-Mullen, by then President of the Irish Trades Union Congress, in his bid to be re-elected to the Northern Ireland Government for Belfast Falls. However, by this time proportional representation had been abolished, costing Labour three of their four seats, including McMullen's.

As the 1930s began, unemployment was still high and the world was in the throes of a recession. The shipyards were sitting idle and outdoor relief was insufficient. Strikes were commonplace and by 1932 many people in Belfast were starving. George and Winnie were part of an Outdoor Relief Workers' Committee and spent their evenings going door-to-door to collect money and food for striking workers. The committee represented the nearly 2,000 people on outdoor relief who were striking to gain better conditions and pay. The strike united both Catholic and Protestant, unionist and nationalist, as all of them were hungry workers. George and Winnie took part in a major protest demonstration in October. Extra police had been drafted in for the demonstration and attacked the strikers indiscriminately with batons and, at times, guns. Two men were killed, a hundred were injured and seventy arrests were made.

The demand for decent standards of living was universal and, after a concerted effort and the threat of a Belfast Trades Council strike, the Belfast Board of Guardians was forced to increase benefits to outdoor relief workers from eight shillings to twenty-four shillings a week for married men. Single men and women would get eighteen shillings a week. The Outdoor Relief Workers' Committee accepted these terms and there was a great deal of celebrating around Belfast.

Sarah Carney, aged eighty-two, died in 1933. Winnie was distraught, although she knew that she had taken good care of her mother until the very end. Once more, Winnie could accompany George on all occasions. They worked hard together to help their Labour friend, Harry Midgley, get elected for Dock Ward.

Many of their friends from Court Ward had moved to Dublin to escape the discrimination they suffered in a unionist state and, apart from visits to the Grimleys and the Kellys – after John Kelly married Margaret McGuinness – Winnie and George spent their time in each other's company. They were not fond of large social gatherings, though they had enjoyed John and Margaret's wedding, where Winnie was delighted to perform the role of matron of honour.

When the Republican Congress was founded in 1934, they discussed becoming members and agreed that there might be something in it to appeal to them both. The Congress had grown out of a meeting in Athlone when former IRA officers, socialists and trade unionists decided that a review of the political and social field, as well as actions required to meet the needs of the country, should be undertaken. The meeting pledged to form a Republican Congress to carry out the necessary work and a conference of trade unionists in Belfast supported the pledge. The Belfast statement supported the call for a Republican Congress and stated:

We are convinced that the horrors of capitalism, the menace of fascism and the question of Irish unity are interrelated problems, the solution of which can only be found in the solidarity of workers, small farmers and peasants, north and south.[1]

This was signed by many union leaders, including William Mc-Mullen, Chairman, Trades Council, and Murtagh Morgan, now the Belfast President of the ITGWU.

Congress branches opened all over the country and regular meetings were held. *The Republican Congress*, a weekly paper, was launched, though in Northern Ireland it was called *The Northern Worker*. In 1934 George and Winnie finally decided to join the Belfast branch. Winnie's old friend, William McMullen, and Victor Halley, a friend of George's from Court Ward, were regional organisers in Belfast. The Marxist-Leninist aspects of the association appealed to George, while the Republican anti-Treaty element inspired Winnie. She was pleased to hear that James Connolly's daughter Nora was actively involved.

The Congress, allied to the Northern Ireland Socialist Party, attracted many supporters from Protestant, working-class areas, and groups were established in the Shankill and Newtownards Road districts. In June many of these Congress members decided to travel to Bodenstown to attend the annual Wolfe Tone commemoration. They were transported in a fleet of buses and, before the commemoration, made a stop at Arbour Hill Cemetery in Dublin to lay a wreath at Connolly's grave. Winnie trembled by the graveside and George had to support her as she boarded the bus to travel onwards.

The majority of the 17,000 who attended the commemoration were members of the IRA, whereas about 2,000 were members of the Congress. Like some other groups, the Belfast group carried a banner that read, 'Break the connection with Capitalism'. Both George and Winnie were happy to follow behind such a banner, not realising that the IRA had warned all political groups not to carry any. The IRA ordered that the banner be seized. When the Congress members refused to hand it over, clashes broke out. The Belfast banner was torn in half and George and Winnie, with many others, left Bodenstown shaken, saddened and disillusioned.

The Republican Congress conference was scheduled to take place in Rathmines Town Hall in September. George and Winnie attended as delegates, along with a strong contingent from Belfast that included McMullen and Halley. The first person Winnie met on arrival was Nora, who flung her arms around her and said she was so pleased to see her attend this, the first truly socialist conference to be held in Ireland since her father's death. Winnie was moved to see James' son, Roddy, there as well. He had been with them in the GPO when he was little more than a boy, but he was now a grown man.

Almost 200 delegates from all parts of Ireland were present, mostly from trade unions, socialist and communist parties, unemployed movements and the Labour Party. While all wanted to mobilise independent workers' forces, the Congress was split as to whether this should be done by forming a separate new socialist party or amalgamating the existing individual groups. The united front resolution was carried by ninety-nine votes to eighty-four and many who thought that a party to fight for a workers' republic should have been newly formed left the meeting. George and Winnie stayed but travelled home feeling disillusioned once more.

From this moment on the Republican Congress went into decline.

24

WINNIE:
INTO DECLINE

As time passed, Winnie realised that her mother's death in March 1933 had left a void in her life. She had cared for her faithfully for five years and was more saddened by her loss than she expected. The next year George's mother died at just sixty-three and Winnie had to comfort George, who was distraught because his mother and he had never reconciled.

Then news reached her that her brother Louie, who had emigrated to America so long ago, had died in an accident on a building site. His wife, Mary, whom he had married in New York in 1922, wrote to ask if she could come to Belfast with her three children. Now that Winnie had a vacant room she invited them to stay. They lived with George and her for six months and the noise of the children playing in the garden lifted Winnie's spirits.

Winnie's brother Ernest returned from America and got married in Dublin, where he settled down. He was extremely angry when he discovered that his sister had married a Protestant and said that he would never forgive her. He rarely visited Belfast and, when he did, relations between them were strained and left Winnie emotionally exhausted.

Winnie had become used to police vans parked outside her home and knew she was regularly under surveillance. Many of her republican friends found life difficult within what they described as 'a unionist regime' in Northern Ireland. They were constantly being harassed because of their political or religious views. The worst blow to her came in 1935, when James and Nellie Grimley moved to Dublin after being intimidated by local residents and forced to leave their second-hand clothes shop on the Newtownards Road. They had been frequent visitors to Winnie and George's home, and their company would be missed. George asked if she would like to move to Dublin as he was willing to consider anything that would make her happier. She was appalled at the suggestion, however, as she thought the Free State was a capitalist system and not at all what she had fought for.

A few years later Winnie received news that her nephew, Jack, had died in an accident when he was travelling as a stowaway on a boat to England. His father, her brother Alfred, died soon afterwards in May 1938. It seemed to her as though sadnesses kept piling up. Her health began to deteriorate, frequent bouts of coughing weakened her and she became less able to take an active role in politics. In the early 1940s she was rarely able to leave the house. She encouraged George to attend all the meetings and report everything to her on his return. Her enthusiasm for debate with him was undiminished and, as she rested in bed or pottered around her home during the day, she looked forward to his return. As always they ate together and discussed his business and the customers who frequented the shop.

When the Second World War began, George was inconsolable at the thought of the waste of young lives. Winnie and he spent many hours discussing the events in Europe and scouring newspapers for reports from war correspondents. The use of aeroplanes made this war very different from the last and, like most people in Belfast, initially they were relieved to be out of the range of the Luftwaffe. However, that changed when the Germans took France. After that they had listened to over twenty air raid siren alerts but each proved to be a false alarm. Nonetheless when George came home each night he carefully pulled down the blackout blinds and checked that the space under the stairs, known as the 'glory hole', contained a bottle of water. There were only 200 air raid shelters in Belfast and, as George did not feel that Winnie had the strength to walk the distance to the nearest shelter, they would have to take cover there. He was quite sure the Germans would want to attack Belfast where aircraft carriers, mine sweepers and planes were being built by tens of thousands of workers.

On the night of 7 April 1941 George and Winnie huddled under the stairs after hearing the warning sirens and listened to the drone of bombers flying over nearby Belfast Lough. The whistling of hundreds of incendiaries, high explosives and landmines could be heard dropping from the sky. Winnie and George held each other, waiting for that terrible whistling sound to stop.

When the all-clear came George went outside and could see the red sky over the city. The next day he learned that homes, timber yards, the shipyards and flour mills had all been hit by incendiary bombs and thirteen people had died. Customers who came into his shop could talk of only one thing: the lack of defences around Belfast. Many of them said that they would be spending their nights under the stars in the hills.

A week later, at Easter, the Luftwaffe returned and Belfast was bombarded with tons of high explosives. George and Winnie once again clung together and waited for the all-clear. The sound of the bombs made George tremble as he felt the same sickening dread he had in the trenches when he had waited for grenades and mortars to land nearby, and had watched his comrades being blown to smithereens. After the bombing ended the couple discovered that the nearby waterworks had been a target and thousands of homes were destroyed. Shelters near them had suffered in the raid and fires blazed all over the city. So great was the damage that the Dublin government sent fire crews and engines to help. Over a thousand people died that Easter and even more were injured. As George remarked to Winnie, 'German bombs do not discriminate between Catholics and Protestants.'

The Germans returned on the night of 4 May 1941 and this time the docks were the main target. George and Winnie listened to the seemingly endless drone as over 250 aircraft passed overhead. Parts of Harland and Wolff's shipyard and Short and Harland's aircraft factory were destroyed, and the city centre suffered major damage.

With great regularity their talk turned to war and politics. During these discussions Winnie became so animated that George almost believed her health was improving. For years he had been telling her that she should seek a pension for all she did in 1916 and afterwards. She always refused, saying that Ireland had not become the country for which she had fought. Now he pointed out that her poor health was probably caused by her imprisonments and she finally agreed to write to the Irish government. Winnie informed them that she had been James Connolly's aide-de-camp in the GPO during Easter Week 1916 and that she had also been a founding member of Cumann na mBan in Belfast, service number 56077. Her request was investigated.

By the time Winnie received news that she was entitled to a

pension, however, she had been admitted to Whiteabbey Hospital. For several months she was treated for latent tuberculosis. Every night, after he closed his shop, George travelled to the hospital to sit with her, holding her hand and talking together as they had always done. Each Sunday through the summer of 1943 he packed a picnic and spent the day with her. If she was well enough he would wheel her outside where they would gaze at the surrounding hills of Belfast and talk about their lives and the fifteen years they had spent together as husband and wife.

'Do you ever regret marrying me, Winnie?' George asked as they sat in the August sunshine.

'Never for even one second,' she replied. 'I have loved you and you have loved me. We have fought the good fight together.'

On Sunday 21 November 1943 George arrived at the hospital but Winnie was too weak to leave the bed or even lift her head. She was fifty-five years old. He held her hand, kissed and stroked it, and told her how much he loved her. She squeezed his hand and, as tears flowed down George's cheeks, she slowly slipped away.

25

GOODBYE WINNIE

George arranged his beloved Winnie's funeral exactly as she had requested. The funeral was to be held in St Mary's, Greencastle's Catholic parish church, and she was to be interred in Milltown cemetery. He placed notice of her death in the 22 November edition of the *Belfast Telegraph*:

> McBRIDE (nee Carney) – November 21st 1943, WINIFRED, beloved Wife of GEORGE McBRIDE, 3 Whitewell Parade, Belfast – R.I.P.
>
> Remains will be removed from Greencastle Catholic Church tomorrow (Tuesday) at 2.30 p.m. for interment in Milltown Cemetery.
>
> Deeply regretted.

The small funeral took place two days after her death and was reported the next day in the *Irish News*.

> 24th November 1943
>
> Belfast woman involved in 1916 dies
>
> The funeral took place in Milltown Cemetery of Mrs Winifred McBride, Whitewell Parade Belfast. Mrs McBride, who before her marriage to a Mr George McBride was a prominent figure in the Dublin General Post Office in the 1916 Rising, was a

close friend of the late James Connolly and had taken a great interest in the trade union movement.

Mrs McBride was interned in British jails subsequent to the rising in 1917. In the 1918 general election she stood as a Sinn Féin candidate for the Victoria constituency of Belfast.

She was a strong supporter of the trade union movement and was closely associated with the Irish Transport and General Workers' Union.

The prayers in Greencastle Church and at the graveside were recited by Rev Fr McGinn, CC, Whitehouse. Rev Arthur Haughey, CC was also present.

The chief mourners were Mr George McBride (husband), Mr and Mrs Ernest Carney (brother and sister-in-law), and Mr John McBride (brother-in-law).

Laity who attended included Mr Joseph MacEntee who represented Mr Seán MacEntee, Irish minister for local government; Mr Hugh Corvin and Mr Cal McCrystal (representing the Gaelic League), Mrs E. Delaney, Cumann na mBan; Mr Daniel McAllister (secretary of the Belfast Branch of the ITGWU), Mr John McLaverty, Mr P. O'Connor, secretary of the Socialist Party with Mr Robert McLeish and Mr Victor Halley, representing the party.

Although the funeral was small, George was pleased to see that someone had been sent on behalf of the Free State government. He thought that if Winnie had been there she may have berated Joseph MacEntee for his brother's government's failure to follow Connolly's ideals. She would have appreciated fellow members of the Socialist Party showing their respect, regardless of creed. She would have been less enamoured to witness the actions of her brother Ernest, who came into their home and removed many of her personal belongings. George was too overcome with grief to argue with him, although George's brother Jack said that he should have stopped him. George's parents were both dead and he was grateful that Jack had come to represent his family.

Ernest also arranged that her grave in Milltown should remain unmarked so that the name of McBride was not associated with her. George was greatly relieved when Ernest returned to Dublin and hoped never to set eyes on him again.

The next week he read an obituary for Winnie in the Dublin Labour paper, *The Torch*. It had been written by her old friend Cathal O'Shannon, and George was warmed by the fact that someone who actually knew his wife's wonderful qualities had committed them to paper for all to see. The Winnie described by O'Shannon was the Winnie George loved so dearly:

> She was the quiet studious type, more built for the role of good comrade, loyal follower and silent good worker, than for leadership, either on the platform or in council or meetings. She could always be depended upon to answer a call for service and to give of whatever she had without stint and without ostentation. Beneath her placid, almost timid exterior, there burned fires which could scorch when anybody provoked her and withal she had a good sense of humour that revealed something unsuspected in her ... Above all she was deep and loyal in her friendships and in her allegiances, political as well as personal ... And her friendship was intimate, understanding and selfless – she was a great and trusted custodian of confidences.[1]

George clipped out the obituary and placed it on the front page of a scrapbook he had bought. He decided that from now on he would keep everything in memory of Winnie. He was a forty-five-year-old widower.

26

LIFE AFTER WINNIE

For the thirty-five years that followed, George continued to live in their home in Whitewell Parade. By day he worked in his shop opposite the barracks on Queen Street and by night he read voraciously. His favourite subjects were sociology, mythology and industrial matters. He had a passion for philosophy and Irish history and, in an attempt to understand Winnie's views on the past, he became an authority on the Irish famine and the Easter Rising.

He attended socialist and communist meetings, but it was at such events that he felt the loss of Winnie most keenly. He scoured Smithfield's second-hand bookshops and felt that Belfast had the best and cheapest selection of books of any city. He firmly believed that the advent of the paperback was a God-send for the working classes and that through them any person could receive a university education. His library grew over the years. Any interesting bits of information in newspapers and journals about Winnie were cut out and stuck in his ever-growing collection of scrapbooks; he also bought any book that mentioned her. By the time George retired, at the age of seventy-two, there were over 3,000 books just in his living room. The books that mentioned his beloved Winnie held pride of place.

He was content with his own company, but when friends did call by, nothing pleased him more than to talk about Winnie and the formation of the socialist movement in Northern Ireland and the fact that people were better off nowadays because the socialists had pointed out their needs and the government had been forced to supply them. He felt that Winnie and he had been a part of that.

Throughout the 1960s he watched and read as Belfast hurtled towards civil disorder. He applauded the attempts of Prime Minister Terence O'Neill to improve relations with the Irish Republic and thought how pleased Winnie would have been to see the taoiseach, Seán Lemass, invited to Belfast. George firmly believed that bridge-building policies must be implemented and that both sides must give and take a little. He supported the idea of civil rights marches but was appalled when they led to violence that spiralled out of control. To him the sacrifice of even one man's life was a waste.

George often heard bombs exploding in Belfast from his home and he dreaded the news of how many lives had been lost. On Saturday 4 December 1971, just before nine o'clock in the evening, there was a large explosion which blew up a pub just around the corner from his shop. On his way to work on Monday morning, he walked past the site where McGurk's bar had stood two days previously on North Queen Street. Throughout the day customers told him of the horror in which fifteen Catholic civilians had died. That night he read a statement placed in the *Belfast Telegraph* by the Empire Loyalists, who claimed to have placed the thirty pounds of explosives outside the bar. The dead included two children.

Seven months later George was in his shop on the afternoon of Friday 21 July when over twenty bombs exploded around Belfast. One was in Smithfield bus station, so close that the glass in his front window shattered. Many were car bombs and seemed to target the transport network. Nine people were killed and 130 were injured. The IRA claimed responsibility. George could hardly comprehend that the city Winnie and he had loved so much had descended into such horror and senseless death.

In 1972 alone, 497 people were killed in Northern Ireland, over half of them civilians. George now lived in a world where armed soldiers were on patrol, checkpoints stood at the ends of streets, people were searched entering shops and death and destruction continued year after year.

In 1978, at the age of almost eighty, George decided that he could no longer live alone. His mind was as sharp as ever but he struggled with cleaning, cooking, washing and ironing. His niece, Mabel, could only visit occasionally as she lived in Dublin, so he had no one he could rely on. He discussed the matter with some of his old friends and consulted his doctor, who advised him to look at homes for the elderly. One old friend, whom he had occasionally helped out in the local Boys' Brigade, told him of a place on the other side of Belfast which was specifically for retired UVF soldiers. George went to visit the facility in December 1978 and immediately felt at home.

Craigavon House had been the family home of James Craig. During the First World War he had offered it as a hospital for wounded soldiers. A hospital wing was added and, in 1917, it became known as the UVF Hospital. As the years passed, it developed into a retirement home. Many old soldiers lived there and when George questioned them they said that their care was excellent. He decided he would move in for Christmas. The irony of the husband of James Connolly's adjutant living in the UVF Hospital was not lost on him, but he decided not to mention the fact to other residents. He placed Winnie's photograph on the locker where he could look at it each night when he lay down.

Although he missed the home he had shared with Winnie, George never regretted his decision to move. He brought with him many of the books that were dear to him and arranged them on the windowsill near his bed. He also placed his books on the sills near the other men's beds, if they were empty. More were piled into lockers and drawers, which left him with no room for his clothes. When one of the nurses, Rita, saw his dilemma she dragged a bookcase from the corridor and placed it at the foot of his bed. She carefully carried the books and arranged them according to size. This was the beginning of years of friendship.

Every day when Rita came on duty she would make her rounds and always had a cheery word for each of the old gentlemen in her care. She tried to spend an extra minute or two with George, who seemed to have few visitors. There was sadness in his eyes and she cajoled him to take his head out of a book and chat to the other men.

'You sound just like my wife,' he said. 'She always said that I read too much.'

'Well she was right, George, you do. What was her name?'

'Winnie. My beloved Winnie! I miss her every day.'

'How long ago did she pass away, George?'

'Let's see, this is 1979, so nearly thirty-six years. And still it seems like yesterday. Life is just not the same without her.'

'Well you must tell me all about her,' replied Rita, hiding her surprise as she moved along to the next bed. She had expected him to say that his wife died only recently.

Rita found George reluctant to go into any detail about his wife's life and yet in most conversations he mentioned her name. Over the months Rita learned only that they had been very happy and that he missed her sorely. He would chat to the other residents about the war and his experiences there but would say little about his wife.

As months merged into years, Rita grew closer to George. She sometimes visited him on her days off. He liked to be clean-shaven, so she always brought him a supply of extra razor blades. He was also fastidious about his clothes and, as the hospital laundry was not to his liking, on many occasions, she took his items home and washed and ironed them. Her husband, Roly, always teased her about having another man's trousers on his washing line.

As a thank you George would try to press a book into her hand. He was forever ordering books from catalogues and his eyes lit up when a package arrived. He tried again and again to give Rita a book.

'Thanks, George, but I never read.'

George was incredulous. 'Then how do you know about history and what happens in the world?'

'I'd really rather not know about history; it's always the cause of trouble in this country. I see enough to do me on the television. Before I came here I worked on the ambulances, George, and being called to the scene after a bomb showed me what history does. My life has been blighted by history.'

George could see the tears in Rita's eyes and decided not to press the matter. He changed the subject and asked her to help him select his best tie as he was going on an outing. He had been invited to speak at an anniversary seminar, organised by the Irish Congress of Trades Union, as part of the fiftieth anniversary of the

Outdoor Relief strike of 1932. He was proud to be remembered as part of that momentous event and, even though he was eighty-four, he wanted to look his best.

His speech was well received and suddenly George found himself of interest to those gathering recollections about the Great War. One afternoon a man called Billy Ervine came to visit him. He asked if he could record George's memories of the First World War for research that Friends of the Somme, a group formed to remember the 36th Ulster Division, was undertaking for their journal, *Battlelines*. George was delighted to share his memories and also to state his views on the futility of it all. The young man had read an article about George, entitled 'He Lives for His Library,' in *The Irish Press* from 1969 and knew that his wife had been Winnie Carney. George decided that, as he already knew about Winnie, there would be no harm in telling him about meeting her and how that changed his life.

'Shortly after joining the party, I met my future wife, Miss Winnie Carney. It was an unlikely partnership; I was a Protestant from the Shankill Road, and an ex-member of the UVF. Winnie was a Roman Catholic and had in fact taken part in the Easter Rising of 1916. She had been secretary to James Connolly who was later executed for his part in the Rising and Winnie was imprisoned with Countess Markievicz. The countess was sentenced to death but this was commuted to life imprisonment. I believe she was released one year later. My wife had set her mind to a certain idea, the Connolly idea of a Republic. She didn't agree with the Free State government and was entirely opposed to partition. We debated it often but, right up to her death, she maintained the Connolly line. She would have made a great politician.'

Billy asked George if he had ever harboured any political ambitions.

'No, not really. I was more interested in trying to secure better working conditions for the ordinary man in the street. I thought I could do this best from within the trade union movement.'

That night, when Rita brought him hot chocolate, George told her all about his visitor and what he had told him about Winnie. He told her that the National Graves Association were going to erect a headstone on Winnie's grave and he would be taken to see it. He described to Rita the day Winnie had been to where James Connolly was buried and how much she had cried. Rita had never heard of James Connolly but she returned later because George had seemed somewhat distressed about Winnie's grave. He was fine and the other men were snoring. He struggled to sit upright in the bed.

'Did your mother and father speak to you after you married Winnie?' she whispered.

'Barely,' he replied. 'They wouldn't come to the wedding and they never came to visit me. My mother died about five years after I got married. Maybe if she had lived a bit longer we would have been reconciled but I'll never know. My father died a few months before Winnie. My brother came to Winnie's funeral in Milltown and that was something, I suppose. Why do you ask?'

Rita was silent for a few minutes and George could sense her distress. 'My father never spoke to me again,' she sighed.

George patted her hand.

'I've never talked about this to anyone and you must promise not to let the other staff or men know.'

'Like my wife, I'm good at keeping secrets. She never told anyone of the last orders James Connolly dictated to her in the

General Post Office. Not even me. You know she was once offered a lot of money to write a book about everything she had been involved in but she wouldn't do it.'

Rita felt reassured and continued her story for George.

'You know that I go to the Church of Ireland, George, but I was baptised in St Patrick's Roman Catholic Church in Donegall Street in Belfast. Do you know it?'

'Of course I know it. Winnie went to the school attached to St Patrick's and she worked there as a junior teacher. I think her parents got married there.'

'Well that's where I was baptised. My father was called Constantine O'Neill and he was the manager of a marine chandlery business. He married in 1899 and then again in 1920 when his first wife died. My mother was his second wife and she died before I was one year old. That left five of us with no mother. My half-sister, from my father's first marriage, took us in and raised us. She had just married. I suppose my father didn't want wee children about the place when he had a business to run. Sometimes Father took us out and even took us on holiday. He was a very handsome man but he frightened me.

'When I was fifteen he said I was to come and live at his house and look after him. I suppose he was nearly seventy then and needed a housekeeper. He was a hard man to please. It was a lonely life as I wasn't allowed to go out at night. I had been at St Catherine's school where I had lots of friends and I missed them. Father decided that I should go to Orange's Academy and learn shorthand and typing. One afternoon, when I was seventeen, some girls and I went roller-skating. I fell and cut my finger very badly. A very handsome young soldier, dressed in his uniform, came over and helped me up and said that my finger would definitely need stitched. He told me that he was just back from Burma and he offered to walk with me to the hospital. He had the kindest eyes I had ever seen. He was six years older than me but we talked for ages while I waited in the hospital and then he walked me to the end of my street.

'I saw him again the next day and soon we were meeting secretly. He wanted to meet my father but I told him that he couldn't. I knew my father, you see: he would never accept a Protestant soldier as a suitor for me. Eventually, when I tried to tell my father, he ordered me never to see or mention him again. My half-sister, Ena, came and met my young man, Roly, but told him that Father would never accept him. She said my eldest brother had been imprisoned for something in 1921 when he was in the IRA and Father had never forgiven the army for it. Ena was kind-hearted, though, and she could see how much we cared for one another. She said that we could meet in her house but Father must never know.'

Rita started to sob as George asked, 'And did he ever find out?'

Just then she was called away to an emergency in another ward. When she did not return George settled down to sleep. He decided that he would wait until she wanted to talk to him again.

Two nights passed before Rita came on night duty. George was delighted to see her. She brought him freshly washed and ironed trousers and squeezed them into his wardrobe, still crammed with books. He was worried that she might have regretted telling him about herself and when she brought him a cup of tea at suppertime he tried to reassure her.

'I would never tell anyone anything you told me Rita, you can be sure of that.'

'I know George, that's why I feel I can talk to you.' Before leaving she took an old photograph from her uniform pocket and left it with him. He studied the face on it closely, the stern features of the moustached man.

Later that night, when he was reading while others slept, Rita returned and pulled up the armchair that always sat by his bed. He pulled the photograph from between the pages of his book.

'Was this your young man?'

'Oh no! That was my father. The man I never saw again. I worried that you might think that so I brought these photographs too. One showed a smiling, dark-haired girl wearing a school blouse with a tie; the other was of a young man in a soldier's shirt. This is us when we first met.'

George studied the two photographs closely before speaking. 'Did he ever find out that you were seeing your young man?'

'He did, and he did his best to stop it, but I married my soldier,' Rita replied with defiance.

'You were married!'

'Oh yes we were. My soldier arranged it all. We planned for months and months. Roly booked the church and I packed my clothes and one night when Father was out I left a note and ran away. Roly was waiting for me at the end of the street and his mother took me in. A few days later we were married. That was nearly forty years ago.' She choked back the tears.

'Have you not been happy, Rita? Why are you crying?'

'Telling me about your wedding and your wife brought it all back. The sadness of it all. None of my brothers or sisters came to the wedding because it was in St Anne's Cathedral, a Protestant church, and Father sent word that he never wanted to set eyes on me again. I tried to go and see him but he wouldn't open the door. When my daughter, Ena, was born – I named her after my sister who raised me – I tried again but it was no use. Ena still talked to me but couldn't be godparent because I had my daughter christened in the Church of Ireland. I wrote to Father when my son, Rowland, was born, but the letter was sent back. The next year, in 1951, I got a telegram to say that he had died on 12 July. From the day I left I never saw his face or heard his voice. He was a hard man but he was my father and I would have loved him to see my children. I don't even know where his grave is in Milltown.'

'But have you been happy with your husband and children, Rita?'

'Yes I have but the ache is still there. That's why I became a nurse, I think. To fill the gap.' She looked at him again, something imploring in her eyes. 'You can't tell any of the staff. I have gone to the Church of Ireland for the last thirty-eight years and they think that's what I am. I used to work in the hospital at Dundonald but a relative of my husband's told them I was a Catholic and I was forced to leave. I just wanted to be a nurse.'

'And you are a great nurse, Rita. You have made me content in my last years and isn't it great that you can talk to me about your father and I can talk to you about my lovely Winnie? She seemed to be happy with me, and I hope I was worthy of her. But you and I, Rita, we have both fought the good fight!'

Rita smiled. 'Yes we have, George. Now you better get to sleep or I'll be getting the sack and then where will we be?'

27

GEORGE:
THE LAST POST

George's last Christmas was pleasant. He enjoyed the carol singers who came to the nursing home and the camaraderie of Christmas dinner with the remaining soldiers who had no families to take them home. Rita came in especially to visit him and bring presents of sweets, razor blades and Brylcream.

Every shift that Rita worked she made time to talk to him. George knew so much about her family that, to Rita, he felt a part of it. There had been many sad times in her life and religion and politics had been at the root of them all. All these events she shared with George. He knew that Winnie would have liked her and would have appreciated the care and kindness that Rita had shown him over the last nine years. He made up his mind to give her a special gift, a wooden writing box that Winnie had treasured. Rita didn't want to accept it but, as he told her, he was nearly ninety and where else would it go? When he said, to close the matter, 'Winnie would have wanted you to have it, Rita,' she knew she could not refuse.

George and Rita frequently talked together about their earlier lives. That Winnie and Rita's father were both buried in Milltown was like a bond between them.

'My greatest sadness,' said George one day, 'is that I won't be buried with Winnie. I'm delighted that there is a headstone to remember her now, but I won't be buried there.'

'Why not? Can Catholics and Protestants not be buried together?'

George could hear the onset of panic in her voice.

'Yes, they can, Rita. Don't worry about that. But Winnie's brother has the grave papers so I have no access to the grave. The rest of the family isn't like him. When Winnie's sister retired as a nun she came back to live in Ireland and I went to visit her. She made me very welcome and I think she must have known how happy Winnie and I were. Not everyone is bitter in this world. So don't you be worrying, you'll be buried with the man you love. And no one can cut Winnie out of my heart; we will always be together there.'

On 10 February everyone in the nursing home gathered round to celebrate George's ninetieth birthday. Rita brought her husband and son to the celebration; two men came from the Somme Association, and his niece, Mabel, travelled all the way from Dublin. George smiled and joked and blew out the candles with obvious pleasure.

He thanked Rita later that night as she got him ready for bed.

'No thanks needed, George, we all had a lovely time. Did you enjoy the day?'

'I did, Rita, I did but one thing was missing. Winnie. Life's been awful without Winnie.'

At the end of March he took ill and Rita sat by his bed every spare minute. On Thursday 21 April 1988 George McBride passed away.

Rita was heartbroken at George's small funeral in the windswept cemetery at Clandeboye near Bangor. The saddest part was when his coffin was lowered and she realised that he would lie in the ground alone. She wondered if he had chosen Bangor because Winnie had actually been born in the town. She supposed she would never know.

28

LIFE AFTER GEORGE

Rita missed George and found that she did not look forward to going into work with the same pleasure. She told herself that all the other old gentlemen needed her too but she could not talk to them in the way she had talked to George. They did not know her secrets.

She was very moved when a letter arrived from a solicitor to inform her that George had left her some money in his will. He had written: *To Mrs Rita Murphy of 38 Cloghan Park, Knock, Belfast, the sum of Five Hundred Pounds (£500) absolutely*. She had not expected that; she had simply been proud to be the friend of a man who had fought for his country and had not let age, religion or politics come above love.

Rita was an ardent churchgoer and every day she prayed that George and Winnie were together in Heaven. A photograph of her standing with George outside the Somme nursing home took pride of place on her mantelpiece and she talked about him to all her family.

'George was never on the side of violence; he believed in talking and learning and love. He hated the glorification of anything to do with war. He never agreed with Winnie's politics and yet he loved her and he missed her every day for forty-five years. He told me that love was the greatest force of all.'

Rita said all this as she told her son, Rowland, about his grandfather, Constantine O'Neill, who never wanted to see him and never spoke to her again.

'I have been angry at my father my whole life. I let the memory of him destroy a lot of happy times. George taught me to try to understand and he told me all about the history of those days and why it was so hard for my father after the war. I might never forgive my father but George said I have to try.'

At her request, Rita's son took her to visit Milltown cemetery in an attempt to locate her father's grave. No one had ever shown her where he was buried and although they walked for hours on the windswept site they were unable to discover where he lay. To her delight, however, they did find Winnie's grave on which the National Graves Association had erected a headstone. Rita felt tears in her eyes as she read the inscription and, when she reached the line 'BELOVED WIFE OF GEORGE MCBRIDE', was overjoyed by the realisation that both George and Winnie would be remembered together forever.

EPILOGUE

The issue of how to best commemorate the events that occurred during the years 1912–1923 has been a major one a hundred years on in Ireland. This is mostly due to the possibility of creating even more divisions than those that are already a legacy of the island's fractured history and the 'Troubles'.

Guidelines have been drawn up for the Community Relations Council for Northern Ireland to assist councils and other organisations in planning events during this 'Decade of Centenaries'. These guidelines, entitled 'Ethical and Shared Remembering: Commemoration in a New Context' encourage people to 'reappraise the decade 1912–1922 in Ireland, the sands of time also enlarging our perspective and opening up more honest, critical evaluation'.

For the last two years, in Northern Ireland's attempts to find greater links to the Easter Rising, the story of Winnie Carney, Connolly's secretary, has become more widely known. In writing the text for the council's exhibition, 'Reflections on 1916', I included a panel on Winnie and her image was even included in Belfast City Council's commemoration logo.

As knowledge of her role has grown, so too has an interest in Winnie's life following 1916. This is especially true regarding the fact that she married a former UVF soldier. This has been invaluable in the attempt in Northern Ireland to present history in a way that will appeal to what is often perceived as two separate communities. A 2016 television, radio and online series produced by the BBC, *Voices 16,* used both Winnie and George's words as part of the narrative.

Ann Hope, past president and secretary of the Belfast and District Trades Union Council, highlighted the fact that George lies in an unmarked grave. This was rectified when, on 7 May 2016, a headstone was erected by that council on George's grave in Clandeboye Cemetery in Bangor, County Down. Relatives of both George and Winnie stood together at the grave and attended a lunch afterwards in the Somme Heritage Centre.

The pair's Cumann na mBan and First World War medals were uncovered in a private collection and are on loan to Belfast City Council for the period of the 2016 'Reflections on 1916' exhibition. They sit, side by side, in a glass cabinet in the City Hall in Belfast, the city in which they met, loved and died. The description below the medals states:

> These medals are placed together as a message of reconciliation. They belonged to Shankill Road man, George McBride, a member of the Ulster Volunteer Force and a soldier in the 15th Battalion of the 36th Ulster Division which fought at the Somme; and Winifred Carney, a founding member of Belfast's Cumann na mBan, secretary to James Connolly and his adjutant in the GPO during every minute of the Easter Rising. From opposite religious and political spheres these two people later met, found love and married.

There is a growing realisation that the past in Ireland is really a web of tangled histories and interconnected communities and that we need to accommodate all angles and perspectives while sharing a common island. The story of Winnie and George is a lesson for everyone who lives on this island, because if their love could be greater than the sum of all their divisions then surely their story is a beacon of hope for us all.

APPENDIX 1

All appendices are transcribed from documents held in the Public Record Office of Northern Ireland in Winifred Carney – Home Affairs File HA/5/2018.

This appendix reproduces a list from Winnie Carney's Home Affairs file of the papers and books seized in the raid on her aunt's home, where she was staying overnight, on 11 March 1921. The epitome is typed but has no reference number. Items taken included her treasured memoriam cards of some of those executed in 1916.

EPITOME (No number)

Date of Raid:	11th March, 1921
Premises Searched:	70 Newington Avenue, Belfast
Occupier:	Mrs Cassidy
Lodger:	Miss Winnie Carney
Raid carried out by:	R.I.C.

Exhibit 1.

Memoriam card of Joseph Mary Plunkett, an executed rebel.

Exhibit 2.

Memoriam card of Patrick Henry Pearse and William James Pearse – executed rebels.

Exhibit 3.

Memoriam card of –

John Daly ⎫
Thos J. Clarke ⎬ executed rebels [*sic*]
John Edward Daly ⎭

Exhibit 4.

Greeting card from Mrs Pearse to Miss Carney.

Exhibit 5.

Postcard addressed to Miss Carney in Lewes Gaol England.

Exhibit 6.

Letter to Miss Carney from 63 Moyne Rd., Dublin.

Exhibit 7.

Letter from 'Alice M' (undated) asking 'Dear Miss Carney' to 'try and get enclosed in to Terence McSweeney [*sic*] a few days before deportation'.

NOTE. The 'enclosed' was obviously some literature connected with Spiritualism, as will be seen from context of covering letter.

Exhibit 8.

Letter dated 27.12.20 to 'Dear Winnie' from 'Willie' (Wm. O'Brien at that time Treasurer of I.T. & G.W.U. and residing at 77 Botanic Road, Dublin) mainly about I.T. & G.W.U. affairs.

Exhibit 9.

Newspaper cutting containing Poetry by Louis Untermeyer and entitled 'To England'.

Exhibit 10.

Letter to Miss Carney, d/1st May, 1918, from Corrigan Solicitor, Dublin.

Exhibit 11.

'Handbook for Rebels' compiled by Thos. Johnston, Dublin, containing extracts from Unionist speeches &c.

Appendix 2

Epitome number 55/105, which details the dozens of items seized during the second documented raid place at Winnie Carney's home on 1 June 1922. Property belonging to her mother and brother was included.

EPITOME   55/105.

Raid on 2a, Carlisle Circus, Belfast.

1.6.22.

Property seized belonging to:–

MRS CARNEY

WINNIE CARNEY

ERNEST CARNEY. No arrest.

1.   (a) Christmas card from Thomas Foran, I.T.&G.W.U.
     (b) Membership card of Irish Land Union dated 1881.

2.   Box containing miscellaneous First Aid outfit, also 3 field dressings.

3.   Bundle of photographs containing pictures of Maud Carney, Edward B. Fitzgerald, and others.

4.   Notebook containing report of weekly meetings of the Election Finance Committee at 25, Mill Street, Belfast, to raise funds to contest West Belfast.

5.   MISCELLANEOUS CORRESPONDENCE. (old and of no apparent value).

(a) Letter in shorthand signed A. STACK.

(b) Receipts for subscriptions printing in Irish.

(c) Letter to PATRICK DORAN. 106, Ballymagee St., Bangor, Co. Down, from National Sailors and Firemen's Union of Gt. Britain & Ireland, dated 21.5.19, also membership card of Seamen's National Insurance Society signed by PATRICK DORAN.

(d) Letter with typed signatures of AUSTIN STACK and DARRELL FIGGIS, from Sinn Féin Offices, 6, Harcourt St., Dublin, dated 17.4.18. addressed to representatives of Comhaile Ceanntair.

(e) Letter signed M. ffrench-Mullen.

55/105

5. MISCELLANEOUS CORRESPONDENCE. (continued).

(f) Two letters signed P. PLUNKETT, 2, Upper Fitzwilliam Street, Dublin, dated 22.8.17 and 28.8.17.

(g) Letter from Sinn Féin H.Q. re election, beginning and ending in Irish.

(h) Report of Republican Meeting (name in Irish) dated 8.7.20.

(i) Letter from Lord Mayor of Dublin acknowledging letter from Winnie Carney, dated 5.2.19.

(j) Letter from G.H.Q., Irish Volunteers, Dublin to Comdt. Belfast instructing JAMES MONAGHAN not to recognise the court – the other prisoners being allowed to act as they please.

(k) Visiting cards – names as follows:–

Winnie Carney.

T. McShane,

41, Durham St., Belfast.

Neil Devine (Vocalist & Dancer)

Law Lake's Co. 'Pretty Peggy'.

Walter Kelly,

9, Castle Arcade, Belfast.

P. Addison-Smyth, (Teeth Specialist)

Main Street, Coothill. (Address of a Paris convent on back)

Ernest Carney,

79, Greenwich Avenue, New York.

Joseph Plunkett,

(on the book is written 'Miss Kearney' and three words in Irish).

Representative card of Mssrs. Doyle and McEvoy,

283, Newtownards Road,

Signed Austin Doyle.

Piece of paper with following name and address:-

Mr Alex. Herron,

113, Hamilton Street, Motherwill.

(l)   Odd letters and Papers. From H. Russell Macnabb [*sic*], Kelly, one signed in Irish from Senior House, All Hallows College, Drumcondra, Dublin, all dated 1918. Receipted bill for 200 circulars from Joseph Cahill. Balance sheet National Executive. Card beginning and ending in Irish from 78, Lr. Mount St., Dublin, dated 8.10.16. National Health Insurance card signed John Carney, 2 Carlisle

Circus, Belfast. 3 typed copies of Mountjoy Treaty and copy of instructions to persons visiting Lewes Prison. Odd addresses and newspaper cutting re JAMES MAGENNIS (see Epitome 55/109); 3 poems; 2 letters signed in Irish re employment of R.C.'s in Belfast dated 13.8.20 & 3.9.20.

6. LETTERS RE I.R.P.D.F.

(a) Correspondence between Seán O'Dolain, 92, University St., Belfast and H.Q. I.R.P.D.F., Dublin, dated 1920.

(b) Letter to Seán O'Dolain dated 12.6.20, in Irish, signed Lili ni Bhraenain. Letter beginning A Chara dated 5.6.22. from Lili ni Bhraenain, 44, Oakley Road, Dublin. Stamped I.R.P.D.F.

(c) Letter from Seán O'Dolain beginning A Chara, undated, re change of secretaryship and transfer of correspondence to 25, Mill St., Belfast.

(d) Two letters mentioning Miss O'Reilly, 90 Aughrim St., beginning A Chara and signed in Irish dated 23.5.20 and 11.6.20.

(e) Letter acknowledging money signed E.A. Dobbyn, The Blackbirds Nest, Toomebridge, Co. Antrim, dated 14.6.20.

(f) Letter mentioning Miss Carney and Miss Brenian [sic] beginning A Chara and signed in Irish, dated 21.9.20.

(g) Bill and receipt from 'Irish News' 1920, to Seán O'Dolain for advertisement re I.R.P.D.F.

(h) Receipt forms for I.R.P.D.F., used and unused. Also odd receipts for some on pieces of paper together with rough accounts.

(i) Relief forms for I.R.P.D.F.

7. LETTERS TO WINNIE CARNEY – MISCELLANEOUS

(a) From Michael Collins dated Nov. 11th 1917, 29th April 1918 and 2nd May 1918 re recovery of money taken by military in 1917. Also card dated 21st Nov. 1918, and a Christmas card 1920.

Two letters from Corrigan & Corrigan, solicitors, Dublin, re above money.

(b) Three letters from William O'Brien, dated 1920. Imprisoned in Belfast. Also wire as follows:–

'Good meeting satisfactory decision charge to be investigated by Dail. Foran retires for a month BRIAN'. Dated 22.6.19.

(c) Two letters from Russell MacNabb [sic] – Birmingham Prison – dated 1918.

(d) Letter from CUMANN-NA-MBAN H.Q. Dublin, dated 13.8.20. signed NANCY P.

(e) Letter from THOMAS FORAN, Liberty Hall, Dublin, dated 1.1.21.

(f) Letter from MARIE ANITA J., 130 Ranfurly Drive, Belmont Road, Belfast, dated 9.11.16.

(g) From member (signature in Irish) of Monaghan Sinn Féin Demonstration Committee dated 25.9.17.

(h) Two letters signed 'MICK' Mountjoy Prison dated 21.3.20., and 09.4.20.

(i) Letter signed H. SPENCER, Aylesbury Prison – 14.11.17.

(j) Letter from Governor of Belfast Prison re visiting dated 20.7.18.

(k) Letter from JOSEPH MACDONAGH, Belfast Prison – 12.5.18.

(l) Letter signed MAUD GONNE dated 14th May 191?

(m) Two telegrams – signed – MILROY – dated 1918

– STACK FIGGIS – dated 1918

8 LETTERS TO WINNIE CARNEY – (CONTD.) Showing her connection with Bolshevism & etc.

(a) Four letters from EDWARD B. FITZGERALD. Three from Editor's Office of 'The Red Hand Magazine', 316, Crumlin Road, Belfast dated 7th and 20th Feb. 1920 and 28th July 1922. One from Glasgow office of 'The Red Hand Magazine', 48, Ingram Street, dated 5th Oct. 1921. Prospectuses of publication of 'The Red Hand Magazine'. Rough notes of chapter headings by Edward B. Fitzgerald.

(b) Postcard signed 'C. O'SHANNON' from Paris.

(c) Letter from 'C. O'SHANNON' from Berne – reporting on the International Labour and Socialist Conference of 1919 – dated 14.3.1919.

(d) Note beginning 'Dearest Carnovitz', without date or address and initialled in Irish.

(e) Membership card of 'The Socialist Party of Ireland' signed WINIFRED CARNEY, dated 08.2.20.

(f) Letter from SYLVIA PANKHURST, dated 20.12.18.

(g) Invitation card to meeting of 'The Irish Women's Suffrage Society' meeting addressed by Mrs Cousins. Letter signed J.H. COUSINS, headed 'The Irish Citizen', 12, D'Olier St., Dublin, dated 29.11.12.

(h) Pamphlet – address to Electors of Victoria – signed WINNIE CARNEY.

9.   LETTERS FROM WINNIE CARNEY.

    (a)   To:- Mrs CARNEY (Mother to Winnie Carney).

        (i)   1 from 43, Belvidere Place, Dublin, undated.

        (ii)   3 from Mountjoy Prison dated 11.5.16, 23.5.16, and 26.5.16.

    (b)   To ERNEST CARNEY (Brother to Winnie Carney).

Letters from Mountjoy and Lewes Prisons 1916.

10.   ERNEST CARNEY. Age 42, height 5'8". Plasterer by profession. Had odd jobs in various parts of U.S.A.

    (a)   Personal letters – addresses U.S.A. 1907–9.

    (b)   Business letters – addresses U.S.A. 1907–9.

    (c)   Personal letters – addresses Belfast 1916–17.

    (d)   Membership cards of various societies etc.

    (e)   Bundle Sinn Féin ribbons.

    (f)   Diary 1920 – few addresses.

    (g)   Map of Chicago, U.S.A.

11.   Postcard addressed to Mrs Carney, 2, Carlisle Circus signed CONNIE BENNETT.

12.   (a)   Sinn Féin pamphlet – address by Rev. J. CLANCY, P.P., delivered at Ennis 13.12.17, on Freedom of Ireland and abolition of Irish representative at Westminster.

    (b)   Pamphlet on Life of O'DONOVAN ROSSA by Terence J. MACSWINEY – dated 25.7.15.

    (c)   Notice of the 10th Convention of Ard Feis for 25th April 1917 – subjects dealt with:–

        1.   Principles of Policy and Constitution of Sinn Féin.

        2.   Organisation and Propaganda.

3. Relations between Sinn Féin and Labour and other organisations.

4. The Food question.

5. Arrests and treatment of prisoners.

(d) Pamphlet on Sinn Féin and the Labour Movement. Deals with the latter as a national movement in Ireland in connection with the eventual establishment of an Irish Republic.

(e) Pamphlet – Ireland's case against Conscription published in 1918.

(f) Copy of 'The Catholic Bulletin' for Oct. 1918.

13. (a) Book – 'The Significance of Sinn Féin' by J.R. WHITE, 1918. Shows Sinn Féin as a starting point for International Socialism.

(b) Book – 'Towards the Republic, 1918 – by A de B. Diatribe against England as a ruling country.

(c) 'Memories of Mountjoy' by Seán Milroy.

(d) 'Sheaves of Revolt' by Maive [sic] Cavanagh – dedicated to Countess Markievitz [sic] 1914.

(e) Pamphlet 'What about Ulster' by E.B. Fitzgerald, suggests methods for coercing Ulster.

14. (a) Book – Independent Labour Party Annual Conference. A souvenir book for the Delegates attending the 28th Annual Conference of the I.L.P at St. Andrews Hall, Glasgow – 4th, 5th and 6th April 1920. Treatise on Rise and Progress of Socialism with illustrations of leaders and biographical notes.

(b) Ticket for Annual Conference of I.L.P. St. Andrews Hall, Glasgow, 4th, 5th and 6th April 1920.

(c) Pamphlet – Report of the N.A.C. of the I.L.P. St. Andrews Hall, Glasgow on the 4th, 5th and 6th April 1920.

(d) Two copies of Pamphlet – Order of Business Arrangements, Resolutions and Nominations. One copy annotated.

(e) Two copies of 'The Red Hand Magazine' for Sept. 1920 and Oct. 1920. That of Sept. appears to be the first issue.

(f) Pamphlet – 'Labour Revolt and Larkinism' by W.P. Ryan – 1913 – Assist. Ed. 'Daily Herald'.

(g) 'The Complete Grammar of Anarchy' by J.J.H. 1918. Uses the resistance of Ulster to Home Rule in 1914 as an argument in favour of the Irish Rebellion of 1916.

(h) Pamphlet '98 Readings' printed by T.U. Labour.

(i) Belfast Co-operative Society – Rules, papers and share notes.

15. (a) Pamphlet – 'The Bolshevik Revolution, its rise and meaning' – by Maxim Litvinoff 1919. Quite useful for propaganda purposes.

(b) Pamphlet – 'The Proletariat' by Karl Kautsky translated from the German by Florence Baldwin. Old publication voicing the usual cry of abolish the capitalist.

16. (a) Bundle of Sinn Féin pamphlets.

(b) Publisher's agreement (unsigned) for book by Winnie Carney.

Appendix 3

A handwritten note drawn up by one of the policemen who carried out the third documented raid, when her home and office were searched on 25 July 1922.

City of Belfast
Ardoyne House
49 Platoon

25/7/22

D.I.

I beg to report. That [*sic*] whilst engaged in a search party in No. 2A Carlisle Circus I went into the kitchen after Miss Carney. I saw her hand her mother a small paper parcel. The mother seemed rather nervous and then Miss Carney took the parcel from her which I took possession of. The parcel contained some newspaper cuttings and letters.

A. McGregor A.H.Const. 6339

APPENDIX 4

Epitome 55/317, which was typed up following the raid of 27 July 1922. Exhibit 6 has two lines beside the entry added in pen and the words Bde. 3rd are underlined. The section Exhibit 12 has brackets inserted in pen with the annotation 'These names are scratched out on original.' The names below are marked 'These names added in pencil.'

EPITOME 55/317

(Please see also 55/138 and 55/166)

PREMISES   2A CARLISLE CIRCUS
OCCUPANT   MISS WINNIE CARNEY
DATE   25.7.22

PERSONS DETAINED   MISS WINNIE CARNEY

PROPERTY SEIZED   SEDITIOUS LITERATURE

Exhibits 1 to 6 found on Winnie Carney

Exhibit 1.

Label showing where property was found. 2a Carlisle Circus by Sergt. McGregor. Also sack label – Capt. McMahon O'Brien, Ardoyne House.

Exhibit 2.

Assortment of Republican Newspaper Cuttings.

Exhibit 3.

Two notes undated from Madam Markievits [*sic*] to Miss Carney making appointment for 22nd. Address 143 Leinster Road. Postmarked – 27.9.17 and 6.16.17.

Exhibit 4.

Letter from Grace Plunkett to Miss Carney in pencil asking for appointment at 2 o'clock on Monday. No date.

Exhibit 5.

Commemoration card of Easter 1916. Bearing name 'Kathleen Clarke' and on the reverse the following signatures:–

J.M. Plunkett

A name in Irish

Kelly O'Ryan

M. ffrench-Mullen

A name in Irish

Nell Humphries

A name in Irish

Winifred Carney

Kathleen Lynn

20.4.17

9 Belgrave Road

Mountjoy party.

Exhibit 6.

Correspondence received by Miss Carney during June and July 1922. Including letters from Hd. Qrs. No.1. Bde. 3rd. North Div., and the Irish White Cross. On the back of a letter from the latter the following names and addresses are written in pencil:-

Mrs Morton, California Street.   £1

2 children. Husband arrested.

Mrs O'Neill, 15 Hall Street.   £1
Husband and son arrested.

Mrs McCann, Albert Street.   £1
2 children. Husband arrested.

Mulhern, 42 Boundry Street.
2 children. Husband arrested.

Jon Magee
Kamen O'Murcadh
Corvan Divisional Quartermaster

Mrs Scott, Sydney Street
Son arrested.

Largey, -do-   10/-
Son arrested.

Flanagan, Kildare St.   10/-
Son arrested.

Domigan, Catherine St. N.   10/-
Son arrested.

O'Hare, S Peel St.
Husband arrested.

6A   The following is an extract from a letter headed Hd. Qrs. No.1 Brigade, 3rd Northern Division, dated 13th June 1922. 'The Prisoners' Dependents' Fund.' 'James Connolly, 9b Joy Street. Three weeks in jail without trial … Holds the rank of Lieut. Engineers.' 'B. Boomer, Clondara St, Falls Road. This man was shot through the chest but recovered. Afterwards he had the misfortune to be arrested with ammunition and is at present undergoing a sentence of, I think, 18 months.'

6B   A letter from Michael Coburn, Fort Road, Dundalk, delegate to the Amalgamated Union of Building Trade Workers of Great Britain and Ireland. Dated June 17th, 1922. From his letter this man is evidently an extremist. Mentions that John Kenny of 19 Railway Street, Banbridge, whose claims for relief he urges, is a relative of Dan Monaghan, which 'I suppose is evidence enough in the eyes of the assassin gang.'

6C   A letter from E.F. Smyth, Circular Road, Downpatrick, sending information re the following Portaferry men who have been arrested. Edward McKeating, John Bell, Hugh McManus. Relatives of the latter need help from the White Cross. Money sent to 'Mr P.S. McGrath, Solicitor, Portaferry, or his brother, Mr James McGrath, Erenagh, Portaferry' will be handed over to Mrs McManus.

Exhibit 7.

Letter from 'Your fond Alfred' to Mrs Sarah Carney, postmarked July 21st 1922. (Personal letter of no importance).

Exhibit 8.

Selection of Seditious handbills – ie.

'How Ireland is gagged'

'Irish Bishop speaks'

National Series, No. 4. 'Free State Promises'

Exhibit 9.

Part of a typed poem. Having reference to Mr Lloyd George and other Ministers.

Exhibit 10.
Copy of 'The Voice of Labour' dated Dublin 1.7.22.

Exhibit 11.
Theatre Royal, Belfast. Poster – 'The Bank of England' having on the reverse some calculations and 16 initials and names.

Exhibit 12.
Paper headed 'Ardoyne District' bearing the following:–

Wheatfield Gardens & Crumlin Road, Kerrs St.	: :	Miss Davy and Miss Murphy
Leopold Street	:	Miss O'Brien and Miss M'Auley
Oakfield Street	:	
Fairfield Street and	:	
Elmfield Street.	:	Miss Tussell and Miss McBride
Chatham Street and	:	Miss Curry and Miss Hughes
Herbert Street	:	
Butler Street	:	Miss Clarke, Miss Gillespie, Miss McCallam
Brookfield Street Crumlin Sy. & Hooker Street.	: :	Miss McDonald and Miss Quinn
Havana Street & Jamaica St.	: :	Miss McEvoy and Miss Mullan
Chief St. Bray St.	:	Miss Matthews
Palmor St. Rosebank Street	:	Miss M'Evoy, and Miss Mullan
Ligoneal [*sic*]	:	Miss Martin & Miss Clarke
Wheatfield Gdns. & Leopold St.	:	Miss O'Brien
Kerra St.	:	
Oakfield St.	:	Mary McConnell
Elmfield St.	:	

Butler Street   :   Miss O'Brien, M. Caughey
(Caugheny ?)

Jamaica St.
Havana St. & Flax St.
Left hand side   :   Miss McAuley (?) (Manley?)

Elmfield St. &   :   Annie Johnson
Crumlin Road, Chief St. :   Maggie McAuley

Herbert Street   :   Maggie Martin
Chatham Street   :   Miss Matthews

Brookfield St.   :   Evelyn McGovern (?)
Crumlin St.   :   Kathleen ?

APPENDIX 5

Epitome 55/348, which lists all the literature deemed seditious that was seized in the raid on the union offices on 25 July 1922. Blue lines were added to highlight exhibits 2, 3, 4 and 7. A handwritten note corrects exhibit 2 to read 'There is no Volunteer Defence Fund and until such is established men on your fund must remain on.'

55/348.

(see also Epitome 55/136.)

EPITOME

of

Raid on 122 Corporation Street

Occupant	The Office of the Irish Transport Works Union.
Date	25th July 1922
Persons Detained	Miss Winnie Carney. (*arrested at her residence No. 2a Carlisle Circus*)
Property Seized	Seditious Literature

EXHIBITS

1.   Label showing place and date when literature was found, signed by C.C. 49 Platoon.

2.   Letter from J. McKelvey (O.C. Division), headed 3rd Northern Division, dated 13th September 1921, to Miss

Carney 122 Corporation Street, in which it is stated that:- 'here is no volunteer Defence Fund and until such is established. In future communications to be addressed to O/C 3rd Northern Division and not to O/C Belfast. I do not know O/C Carlow, but am having enquiries made'.

3. Memo from J. McKelvey to Secretary P.O.F., dated 1.10.21, from Headquarters, 3rd Northern Division, contains instruction to forward despatches intended for O/C Carlow to McKelvey for delivery.

4. Letter from J. McKelvey. Headquarters 3rd Northern Division dated 20th September 1921 to Miss Carney, Sec. I.E. Prisoners Dependents Fund, 122 Corporation Street, Belfast, giving following names as requiring assistance:–

    Mrs Clarke, 54 Harrybook Street, Belfast, sister of Manus O'Boyle, 'B' Company 2nd Battn. Belfast Brigade, interned.

5. Note from Brigade I.E., 1st Belfast Brigade, undated, giving name of Mrs Bennett, 7 Iris Street, for assistance, and stating her son Patrick was arrested in Dungannon after shooting at D.I. Welsh.

6. Letter from F.J. McCurry, 59 Cullingtree Road, Belfast dated 17-1-22 to W. Carney, Sec. P.D.F., enclosing cheque for £3-2-0 as result of vote from Cuman na ban [*sic*].

7. Names and addresses of those drawing monies from the Irish Republican Prisoners' Dependant [*sic*] Fund.

James Furnelly	Ross Street.
Mick Walters	30 Lady Street.
Arthur McLarnon	Omar Street.
George Hamill	Ward Street.

Joe Maguinne	Springfield Road.
J. Cunningham	Comber Street.
Mrs Morgan	7 Kells Street.
Pat Fleming	8 Kildare Street. (vide) 55/296.
Pat Walsh	38 Alton Street (city).
And Largey	8 Sidney Street (city).
Henry O'Neil	21 Samuel Street (city).
Jas Carrol	Carrick Place.
Pat Loughlin　）	Wine Tavern Street.
Jas Cunningham)	
Frank Crummly	17 Noo? Street.
Thes Trainor	(late) Hartly Street.
Pat Devlin	13 Lowry Street.
P. McMahon	Independent Street.
J. Sharp	55 Sheriff Street.
Danl. Cough	36 Dock Lane.
Jack O'Brien	Sydney Street.
Seán McCarty	28 Norfolk Street.
Seán Gaynor	236 Springfield Road.
Danl. Duffing	64 Clonard Gardens.
Fredk. Fox	98 Durham Street.
Edw. Trodden	Falls Road.
I. Leslie	Barker Street.
Edw. Gilmore	Falls Road.
Thos. Corr	York Street.
Bernard Vallily	Kemps Lane.
Manus O'Boyle	34 Harrybrook Street.
Mrs Harper	275 Falls Road.
Vol. H. Young	?5 Laundry Street.
Vol. H. McGraw	34 Laundry Street.
Vol. D. Kane	4 Vulcan Street.

Vol. P. Kane	4 Vulcan Street.
M. Guinne	135A Springfield Road.
Mrs M. Kenny	19 Railway Street, Banbridge.
John Laverty	10 Hartwell Street.
Joseph McLoughlin	7 Martin Street.
Jas Hughes	Hudlow Street.
Patk McPhillips	Sand Street.
Jas Comerford	Cullingtree Road.
Edw. Grant	Palmer Street (?) or Falls Road (?).

The following are names and addresses of women who have received assistance in cash from the I.R.P.D. Fund:

Mrs Burns	Lindon Street.
Mrs Bradley	2C Herbert Street.
Mrs Brady	3C Getty Street.
Mrs Branney	Stuart Street.
Mrs Cullen	4 Milligan Street.
Mrs Dobbyn	Duneane, T'bridge.
Mrs Dillon	49 Gibson Street.
Mrs Dobbyn	Stuart Street.
Mrs Duggan	Cupar Street.
Mrs Foley	20 Locan Street.
Mrs Goodman	15 Quadrant Street.
Mrs Harvey	265 Hillman Street.
Mrs King	142 New Lodge Road.
Mrs Leathem	Lurgan.
Mrs Maguire	3E Fernwood Street.
Mrs Magee	North Queen Street.
Mrs Maguire	Derby Street.
Mrs Curley	Mt. Collyer Street.

Mrs McCormick	Jerusalem Street.
Mrs M'Cann	Duncairn Gardens.
Mrs McDermott	2B Lady Street.
Mrs McClinchy	8 Theodore Street.
Mrs McAllister	Ardilea Street.
Mrs McKee	19 Bombay Street.
Mrs McCann	Tanaghmore West, Lurgan.
Mrs McDade	Getty Street.
Mrs Nash	Gibson Street.
Mrs O'Brien	13 East Street.
Mrs O'Neill	102 Balkan Street.
Miss Rogan	Springfield Road.
Mrs Reid	Grace Street.
Mrs Rea	Spamount Street.
Mrs Reid	Catherine Street.
Miss Trodden	Falls Road.
Mrs Thornberry	Lurgan.
Mrs Davidson	Divis Street.
Mrs Fury	10 Violet Street.

EXHIBITS. (continued)

8. Report of Irish Republican Prisoners' Dependents' Fund Jumble Sale, held on the 27th, 28th and 29th October 1921, which realised the amount of £280-3-5. The following list of persons comprises subscribers to the Sale:–

Mrs Murtagh, Lisburn	£1-0-0
F. Kerr, Solicitor	£1-0-0
A. Serridge	10-0
Miss Minnie Hall	£3-5-0
Miss McPhillips	6-6
Miss McBrierly	£1-3-0

M.O.	7-0
Miss F. Byrne	14-6
Mrs Hayes	£1-19-6
Ballot(?)	£1-0-0
Mrs McAllister	10-6
Miss Smythe	10-0
Per Mollie Smythe	2-6
Miss McCrory	1-11-6
Mrs McInerney	1-5-6
C.F. Ridgway	5-0
R. Henderson	£1-0-0
Miss McMahon	2-0

The following items of expenditure appear:–

Rent St. Mary's Hall	£22-15-0
Advt 'Independent'…. (Receipted)	19-6
Advt 'Irish News' …… (Receipted)	10-0
Roll Tickets (2)	2-6
Refreshments	£1-9-6
Perquisites	6-0
Trams (Saturday)	2-0
Cartage to Mr Griffiths	7-6
Square oilcloth …. (Receipt. J. Robb, Castle Place)	4-0

9. Receipt to 'Mrs Ward' from W.J. M'Manus & Sons, 70 Servis Street, Belfast dated 16-12-1921, for £1-10-0, on a/c of posting 300 Large posters for the Republican Prisoners' Fund.

10. Eight memos. On official paper of Irish Republican Prisoners' Dependents' Fund Dublin:–

    (a) Dated 4-7-21. Forwards List of cases.

    (b) Dated 5-2-21. Forwards sum of £83 to Miss Carney,

for cases in areas outside Dublin. Note at foot of sheet 'Above sum returned to Headquarters D.C.'

(c)   Dated 4-7-21. Suggests Belfast Committee should amalgamate with Committee of Irish White Cross.

(d)   Dated 28-9-21. Re grant of £10 to Mrs Carolan.

(e)   Dated 01-9-21.   -do-   -do-

(f)   Dated 22-7-21. States that Irish White Cross has been requested to pass a weekly cheque to branch of I.R.P.D. Fund.

(g)   Dated 15-11-21. Stating cases 'were sent in to us' through 'Sinn Féin'.

(h)   Dated 13-7-21, re case of William McDevitt, Merchant sailor of Belfast.

11.   Three letters from 'The Park', Ardkeen, signature believed to be Miss McKeating, dated 1-9-21, 6-8-21 and 12-8-21 respectively. References made to a friend 'P.C.' and to collections being made in aid of the I.R.P.D. Fund.

12.   Memo dated 16-6-21, from the Secretary, Irish National Foresters Benefit Society, 39 Divis Street, Belfast, states that they have decided not to rent the hall for any purpose.

13.   Letter from S. McElroy, 43 Thames Street, dated 2-2-22, asking for assistance on the ground of having been incarcerated in Northampton Gaol from 26-9-20 to 13-1-22, and having lost his Army pension thereby. Note on letter states '£5 granted 2nd Feby 1922.'

14.   Letter from Miss Annie Ball, (Secretary of Cushendun Cumman [sic] Knocknacarry), dated 3-1-21, asking whether the sum of £5 has been received. (addressee not stated).

15.   Minute Books (two), Irish Republican Prisoners' Dependents' Fund, Belfast Branch, from which the following extracts are made for information:–

Minutes entered 8-12-21, state 'A suggestion was handed in from the Volunteers recommending that a 'church door' collection should be taken up at all the churches in the City on Sunday 18-12-21'.

Minutes entered 22-12-21 state 'The total amount subscribed at the Church door collection was £220'. The following released prisoners each received a grant of £10 from this sum:–

Andy Furlong.	O'Dempsey.
Jeff Allen.	Tom Corr.
Joe Allen.	Vincent Watters.
M. Carolan.	Edw. Gilmore.
Leo Close.	Hugh Magill.
Eamonn Hayes.	Seán Dolan.
Jimmy Cohan.	Joe O'Boyle.
Eamon Cooney.	Willie Loughran.
Tom Glennon.	Manus O'Boyle.
George M'Neill.	Jas. F. Stewart.
W.J. Casey.	
Paid on 2-2-22.	
Lee O'Neill...£10.	
Smith..........£10.	

The minute books cover the periods as under:–

(a)   14th April 1920 to 28th April 1921.

(b)   9-11-21 to 18-5-22.

The procedure, according to information gleaned from the

minute books, would appear to be that issues on Cash are regularly made to the relatives of all needy Republicans undergoing sentences of imprisonment, such issues averaging about £1 weekly, and being paid for the period of imprisonment only. The cash issues are supported by receipts obtained by the distributors in the various areas, and all monies distributed are subject to the approval of the Irish White Cross Committee, who audit the accounts. Claimants for relief are considered weekly at the Belfast Branch Meeting of the I.R.P.D. Fund Committee. These weekly meetings of the Belfast Branch have been presided over by a Miss A. Ward (who is in direct touch with I.R.A. in Belfast.) from Feb. 1922 to May 1922 inclusive.

APPENDIX 6

Ministry of Home Affairs internal memos relating to the search for Winnie Carney's missing documents. A handwritten addition to the first one shows that a reminder was sent to 'I.G.' on 8 April 1926.

MINISTRY OF HOME AFFAIRS FOR NORTHERN IRELAND

H.1345/603

INSPECTOR GENERAL. R.U.C.

With reference to attached copy of a letter from Miss Winifred Carney, will you please report in whose possession the documents now are, and whether there is any objection to their return.

Your 24/6359 refers.

EWS
for Secretary,
23rd March, 1926.

MINISTRY OF HOME AFFAIRS, NORTHERN IRELAND.

H.1345/603.

Inspector General, R.U.C.

The attached copy of a letter received from Miss Winifred Carney is forwarded for your observations.

Please state if the articles mentioned were seized in the raid referred to in 1922 or in any subsequent raid.

Your 24/635 of 1/4/26 refers.

EWS

for SECRETARY.

29th May, 1926.

APPENDIX 7

Winnie's request for the return of documents seized in 1921. Her letter was referred to the Secretary in the Ministry of Home Affairs, together with a copy of the original epitome shown in Appendix 1.

SUBJECT: MISS WINIFRED CARNEY.

24/6359

INSPECTOR GENERAL'S OFFICE,

Royal Ulster Constabulary,

BELFAST.

10th April 1926.

The Secretary,

Ministry of Home Affairs.

Your Ref: H.1345/603 d/23.03.26

I beg to report that Miss Carney would appear to refer to a raid carried out by members of the R.I.C. on the 11th March, 1921, at the residence of Mrs. Cassidy of 70 Newington Avenue, Belfast, when the documents as shewn in the attached epitome were seized, the originals of which are now forwarded to you for disposal. The documents are very old and are of no great value. Though objectionable at the time of seizure, this does not apply to the same extent at the present moment. If it is considered in the Ministry that any of the exhibits should be returned, there is no objection to this being done.

It is, however, pointed out that several of the documents enumerated in Miss Carney's letter addressed to you, and dated

22.03.26 do not appear to have ever comprised any portion of the seizure and this would appear to be borne out by Miss Carney's letter dated 14.03.21 and addressed to the Divisional Commissioner, copy of which is now given for your information:–

2 Carlisle Circus

Belfast

14.03.21

The Divisional Commissioner of Police

Atlantic Buildings

Waring Street

Belfast

Dear Sir

On Friday 11th instant, during raiding operations at the residence of Mrs. Cassidy, 70 Newington Avenue, the following are amongst the articles extracted from my suitcase by the Constable in charge:–

A Christmas Card

Several memoriam cards

Some letters

A pamphlet issued by a philosophical society

A second pamphlet giving extracts from the speeches of Loyalist and Unionist members of the British House of Commons.

None of these articles were of any military or political significance or value. The letters were purely personal ones.

I would feel grateful if you would kindly institute inquiries, and order that these things are returned to me at once.

Thanking you in anticipation.

Yours sincerely,

Winifred Carney.

APPENDIX 8

A handwritten memo sent to Principal H in an attempt to resolve the matter of the missing documents.

MINUTE SHEET

Reference: 1345/603

Principal H

Please see letter from Miss Winifred Carney (tab 1) & I.G.'s report attached.

The documents attached are all old stuff & if Miss Carney wants them I don't think that any of them will do much harm.

The 2 documents on which she lays most stress by: 'Irish War News' & the leaflet issued by the Provisional Govt are not forthcoming & as I.G. points out she made no reference to it before & there is no reference to it in the epitome of documents seized in subsequent raids (tabs 2 & 3).

This woman was prosecuted for the possession of I.R.A. documents in Aug 1922 and fined 40/-. She was not recommended for internment owing to her state of health.

She is an extreme Republican & one of the principal organisers of the 'Cuman-na-Ban' [*sic*] in Belfast.

I suggest that we should send her back these documents & inform her that there is no record of the seizure of the 2 she specially refers to.

E.W. Newill

12/4/26

Appendix 9

In this document the writer casts doubt on whether Winnie was ever in possession of the missing items mentioned in Appendix 8. The document was stamped SECRET in large letters.

Subject: Miss Winifred Carney, 122 Corporation Street, Belfast.

24/6359.

INSPECTOR GENERAL'S OFFICE,
Royal Ulster Constabulary,
BELFAST.

7th June 1926

The Secretary
Ministry of Home Affairs

Your reference H.1345/603 dated 29th May, 1926

I beg to inform you that a very thorough scrutiny has been made of all exhibits seized in raids at 2a Carlisle Circus, Belfast, during 1922, which has, however, failed to discover any of the documents mentioned in Miss Carney's letter.

It is worthy of note that the whole of the 1922 raids were carried out by the late C.I.D. Military Adviser's Department and at that time a regular system of epitomization of seized articles was carried out, though in none of the Epitomes, i.e. 55/1105, 55/347 and 55/348, is any mention made of any of the articles now claimed shewn as being seized in any of the searches.

In Miss Carney's letter of 22nd March, 1926, she alleges that the specified articles comprised a portion of seizure regarding which she wrote to the Divisional Commissioner, R.I.C., asking for their return, sometime in March 1921, though in her letter of 27.5.26, she states they were taken in the first raid of 1922. There would appear to be reason to doubt if the specified articles ever were in the possession of Miss Carney.

[signature]
D.I. for I.G.

ENDNOTES

5 George: February–September 1912

1   Ulster Covenant Jubilee Committee, *Ulster Covenant Jubilee Souvenir 1912–1962* (Belfast, 1962), p. 21.

2   *Ibid.*, p. 18.

3   *Ibid.*

4   'The Alternative Ulster Covenant', *Irish Republican News*, 28 September 2012.

5   'Celebrating the Ulster Covenant 1912–2007'. Available at http://quis. qub.ac.uk/ulster/Ulster_Covenant.pdf

6 Winnie: February 1913

1   'Belfast Municipal Elections January 1913 – Dock Ward: Election of a Councillor'. Available on the Connolly Society of USA and Canada website: https://www.marxists.org/archive/connolly/1913/01/ dockward.htm

2   Chapter 5, 'Belfast and its Problems', in Connolly, James, *The Reconquest of Ireland*. Available at http://www.ucc.ie/celt/online/E900002-002/ text006.html

3   Helga Woggon, *Silent Radical: Winifred Carney, 1887–1943: a Reconstruction of her Biography*, Studies in Irish Labour 6 (SIPTU, Dublin, 2000), p. 5.

8 George: April 1913

1   Transcript of an address to the YCV given by Francis Forth, principal of the Belfast Municipal Technical Institute on 10 December 1912, PRONI D 1568/5A.

2   Further information on supplies can be found in Philip Orr, *The Road to the Somme: Men of the Ulster Division Tell Their Story* (Blackstaff Press, Belfast, 1987), p. 12.

9 Winnie: March–December 1913

1   To the Linen Slaves of Belfast – Manifesto of the Irish Textile Workers' Union. Available on the Connolly Society of USA and Canada website: https://www.marxists.org/archive/connolly/1913/xx/linslavs.htm

2   See letter from James Connolly to William O'Brien, dated 6 June 1913 reprinted in Donal Nevin (ed.), *Between Comrades. James Connolly: Letters and Correspondence 1889–1916* (Gill & Macmillan, 2007), p. 493.

3   *Ibid.*

10 Gun-running 1914

1   The British government considered taking strong action to crush unionist resistance to the Home Rule Bill. Sir Arthur Paget, commander of the troops in Ireland, was instructed to move 800 men into Ulster. When he passed the orders to his brigadiers in the Curragh army base in County Kildare, over 80 per cent said they would resign rather than act against Ulster.

2   'The Liberals and Ulster', from *Forward*, 30 May 1914. Available on the Connolly Society of USA and Canada website: https://www.marxists.org/archive/connolly/1914/05/lbsulst.htm

3   '1914 – Irish Volunteers during the Howth Gun Running', https://stair naheireann.net/2016/07/26/1914-irish-volunteers-during-the-howth -gun-running/

11 Winnie: August 1914

1   Letter to James Larkin, 15 July 1914, quoted in Nevin, *Between Comrades*, pp. 516–17.

12 George: September 1914–May 1915

1 Quoted in Philip Orr, *Ballykinler Camp – The First Seven Decades. 1900–1969* (Down County Museum, 2012) p. 40.

13 Winnie: 1914–1915

1 For the complete text of P. H. Pearse's oration at the graveside of O'Donovan Rossa see www.easter1916.net/oration.htm

2 'Trust Your Leaders' from *The Workers Republic*, 4 December 1915. Available on the Connolly Society of USA and Canada website, https://www.marxists.org/archive/connolly/1915/

3 'Two Fateful Christmas Weeks', from *The Workers' Republic*, 25 December 1915. Available on the Connolly Society of USA and Canada website, https://www.marxists.org/archive/connolly/1915/12/fatxmas.htm

15 Winnie's War

1 'A Happy New Year', from *The Workers' Republic*, 1 January 1916. Available on the Connolly Society of USA and Canada website, https://www.marxists.org/archive/connolly/1916/01/newyear.htm

2 'Economic Conscription II', from *The Workers' Republic*, 15 January 1916. Available on the Connolly Society of USA and Canada website: https://www.marxists.org/archive/connolly/1916/01/econscr2.htm

3 'What is a Free Nation?' from *The Workers' Republic*, 12 February 1916. Available on the Connolly Society of USA and Canada website: https://www.marxists.org/archive/connolly/1916/02/whtfrnat.htm

4 'The German or the British Empire', from *The Workers' Republic*, 18 March 1916. Available on the Connolly Society of USA and Canada website: https://www.marxists.org/archive/connolly/1916/03/germbrit.htm

5   Christopher Brady, Bureau of Military History (BMH) Witness Statement (WS) 705, p. 2.

6   'The Irish Flag' from *The Workers' Republic*, 8 April 1916. Available on the Connolly Society of USA and Canada website: https://www.marxists.org/archive/connolly/1916/04/irshflag.htm

7   Helena Molony, BMH WS 391, p. 27.

8   *Ibid.*

9   Frank Robbins, BMH WS 585, pp. 27–8.

10 Christopher Brady, BMH WS 705, p. 4.

11 *Ibid.*, p. 7.

12 James O'Shea, BMH WS 733, p. 35.

13 Seán MacEntee, BMH WS 1052, p. 30.

14 William Oman, BMH WS 421, p. 7. See also Helena Molony, BMH WS 391, p. 27.

15 Bulmer Hobson, BMH WS 81, p. 12.

16 William O'Brien, BMH WS 1766, p. 1.

17 http://irishvolunteers.org/tag/the-orahilly/

18 Quoted in Seán MacEntee, *Episode at Easter* (Gill & Son, Dublin, 1966), p. 148. Copy of dispatch found on Major John McBride.

19 Samuel Levenson, *James Connolly: A Biography* (Quartet Books London, 1977), p. 310.

20 Seán Nunan, BMH WS 1744, p. 3.

21 Levenson, *James Connolly*, p. 316.

22 This note is incorporated on a plaque, designed by Shane Cullen, which was erected at O'Rahilly Parade, Dublin on 29 April 2005.

23 James Connolly – last statement to soldiers, 28 April 1916, quoted in Nevin, *Between Comrades*, pp. 544–6.

24 http://news.bbc.co.uk/2/hi/uk_news/northern_ireland/4594388.stm.

25 Winnie's recollection of this can be found in R. M. Fox, *Green Banners: The Story of the Irish Struggle* (Martin, Secker & Warburgh Ltd, London, 1938), p. 291.

16 Winnie: After the Rising

1 Letters of Winifred Carney to Miss O'Brien describing prison conditions in England, 14 August and 16 October 1916, National Library of Ireland, William O'Brien Papers, MS 20,766.

2 Addendum to statement by Mrs Catherine Rooney (Byrne), BMH WS 648.

3 Winifred Carney to Joe McGrath, 10 and 24 January 1919, quoted in Woggon, *Silent Radical*, p. 12.

18 Winnie: The Road to Partition

1 PRONI, Home Affairs File HA/5/2108, Letter from Winifred Carney to Divisional Commander, dated 14/3/21.

2 *Ibid.*, Letter from Divisional Commander to Winifred Carney, dated 26/3/21.

20 Winnie: Life in Northern Ireland

1 PRONI, Home Affairs File HA/5/2108, Raid Order 153.

2 *Ibid.*, Raid report, 25/7/22.

3 *Ibid.*, Report of Constable MacGregor, 25/7/22.

4 *Ibid.*, List of exhibits found on Winifred Carney, dated 25/7/22.

5 *Ibid.*, Letter from Winnie Carney to Major Leithes.

6 *Ibid.*, Particulars of persons arrested under regulation 23 of civil authorities (special powers) act, Winifred Carney.

7 *Ibid.*, Application for detention order for Miss Winifred Carney.

8 *Ibid.*, Reply to application for detention order.

9 *Ibid.*, File No. C.I.D. 1345/603, dated 28/7/22.

10 *Ibid.*, File 1345/603, dated 2/8/22 and 3/8/22.

11 *Ibid.*, Letter from Winnie Carney to Civil Authorities, dated 4/8/22, re being treated as an ordinary prisoner.

12 *Ibid.*, Letter from Winnie Carney to Civil Authorities, dated 4/8/22,

re. request for parole to attend the Irish Trades Union Congress in Dublin.

13 *Ibid.*, Minute sheets H1345/603, Poynting to Governor, Armagh Prison, dated 5/8/22.

14 *Ibid.*, Report on outcome of prosecution of Winifred Carney, SB 24/6359.

15 *Ibid.*, Letter to Commissioner's Office, dated 5/8/22.

21 Winnie and George

1 Woggon, *Silent Radical*, pp. 21–2, records this being recalled by George McBride.

2 PRONI, Home Affairs File HA/5/2108, Letter to the Minister for Home Affairs from Winifred Carney, dated 22/3/26.

3 *Ibid.*, Letter to Winifred Carney, dated 13/4/26.

4 *Ibid.*, Letter to the Minister for Home Affairs from Winifred Carney, dated 21/5/26.

5 *Ibid.*, Letter to Winifred Carney, dated 8/6/26.

23 Winnie and George: Married Life

1 Byrne, Patrick, 'The Irish Republican Congress Revisited', www.connollyassociation.org.uk/about/the-irish-republican-congress-revisited/

25 Goodbye Winnie

1 *The Torch*, 27 November 1943.

BIBLIOGRAPHY

Books:

Arthur, Max, *Forgotten Voices of the Great War* (Ebury Press, London, 2002)

Bardon, Jonathan, *A History of Ulster* (Blackstaff Press, Belfast, 1992)

Bardon, Jonathan, *Belfast: A Century* (Blackstaff Press, Belfast, 1999)

Bartlett, Thomas, *Ireland: A History* (Cambridge University Press, 2010)

Barton, Brian, *From Behind a Closed Door: Secret Court Martial Records of the 1916 Easter Rising* (Blackstaff Press, Belfast, 2002)

Brodie, Malcolm, *The Tele: A History of the Belfast Telegraph* (Blackstaff Press, Belfast, 1995)

Caulfield, Max, *The Easter Rebellion* (Gill & Macmillan, Dublin, 1963)

Collins, Peter (ed.), *Nationalism & Unionism: Conflict in Ireland 1885–1921* (Institute of Irish Studies, Queen's University, Belfast, 1994)

De Rosa, Peter, *Rebels: The Irish Rising of 1916* (Bantam Press, New York, 1990)

Edwards, Ruth Dudley, *James Connolly* (Gill & Macmillan, Dublin, 1981)

English, Richard, *Irish Freedom: The History of Nationalism in Ireland* (Pan Macmillan, London, 2006)

Falls, Cyril, *The History of the 36th (Ulster) Division* (Constable, London, 1922)

Fox, R.M., *Rebel Irishwomen* (The Talbot Press, Dublin, 1935)

Fox, R.M., *Green Banners: The Story of the Irish Struggle* (Martin, Secker & Warburgh Ltd, London, 1938)

Fox, R.M., *The History of the Irish Citizen Army* (James Duffy & Co. Ltd, Dublin, 1944)

Fox, R.M., *James Connolly – The Forerunner* (The Kerryman Ltd, Tralee, 1944)

Greaves, C. Desmond, *The Life and Times of James Connolly* (Lawrence & Wishard, London, 1961)

Kleinrichert, Denise, *Republican Internment and the Prison Ship 'Argenta',* *1922* (Irish Academic Press, Dublin, 2000)

Levenson, Samuel, *James Connolly: A Biography* (Quartet Books, London, 1977)

Lyons, F. S. L., *Ireland Since the Famine* (Fontana Press, London, 2009)

MacEntee, Seán, *Episode at Easter* (Gill & Son, Dublin, 1966)

Marreco, Anne, *The Rebel Countess: The Life and Times of Constance Markievicz* (Phoenix Press, London, 1967)

Matthews, Ann, *Renegades: Irish Republican Women 1900–1922* (Mercier Press, Cork, 2010)

McCoole, Sinead, *Easter Widows* (Doubleday Ireland, Dublin, 2014)

Moore, Steven, *The Irish on the Somme: A Battlefield Guide to the Irish Regiments in the Great War and the Monuments to their Memory* (Local Press Ltd, Belfast, 2005)

Murphy, Allison, *When Dublin was the Capital: Northern Life Remembered* (Belcouver Press, Belfast, 2000)

Nevin, Donal (ed.), *Between Comrades. James Connolly: Letters and Correspondence 1889–1916* (Gill & Macmillan, Dublin, 2007)

O'Casey, Sean, *The Story of the Irish Citizen Army* (Oriole Editions, New York, 1919)

O'Faolain, Seán, *Constance Markievicz* (Jonathan Cape, London, 1934)

O'Neill, Marie, *Grace Gifford Plunkett and Irish Freedom* (Irish Academic Press, Dublin, 2000)

Orr, Philip, *The Road to the Somme: Men of the Ulster Division Tell Their Story* (Blackstaff Press, Belfast, 1987)

Parker, Alan F., *Belfast's Unholy War* (Four Courts Press, Dublin, 2004)

Seaman, L. C. B., *Post-Victorian Britain 1902–1951* (revised edition, Routledge, London, 2003)

Shooter, Lt Col W. A., *Ulster's Part in the Battle of the Somme* (The Somme Association, Newtownards, 1996)

Taillon, Ruth, *When History was Made: The Women of 1916* (Beyond the Pale Publications, Belfast, 1999)

Various, *Dublin's Fighting Story 1916–21: Told by the Men Who Made It* (Mercier Press, Cork, 2010)

Ward, Margaret, *Unmanageable Revolutionaries: Women and Irish Nationalism* (Pluto Press, London, 1989)

Woggon, Helga, *Silent Radical: Winifred Carney, 1887–1943: A Reconstruction of her Biography,* Studies in Irish Labour 6 (SIPTU, Dublin, 2000)

Bureau of Military History Witness Statements
www.bureauofmilitaryhistory.ie:

Aoife de Burca, WS 359

Brighid, Bean Ui Fheadidh, WS 484

Brighid, Bean Ui Mhairtin, WS 398

Bulmer Hobson, WS 81; 'His Memories of Roger Casement', WS 1365

Catherine Rooney (Byrne), WS 648

Christopher Joseph Brady, WS 705

Denis McCullough, WS 916

Desmond Ryan, WS 724

Eamon O'Duibhir, WS 1474

Elizabeth Corr, WS 179

Frank Booth, WS 229

Frank Robbins, WS 585

Grace Plunkett, WS 257

Helena Molony, WS 391

Henry Corr, WS 227

James O'Shea, WS 733

Jeremiah Joseph O'Leary, WS 1108

John Joseph Scollan, WS 318

Joseph Good, WS 388

Kathleen O'Kelly (née Murphy), WS 180

Kevin O'Shiel, WS 1770

Michael Cremen, WS 903

Nora Connolly (O'Brien), WS 286

Seán MacEntee, WS 1052

Seán Nunan, WS 1744

Seán T. O'Kelly, WS 611

Very Rev. Fr T. O'Donoghue, WS 1666

William O'Brien, WS 1766

William Oman, WS 421

George's Statements:

'A Veteran Recalls', *Battlelines, the Journal of the Somme Association*, issue 17, 2000, pp. 9–11

Transcript from recording held at The Somme Association Archives

Journals, Articles and Booklets:

An Phoblacht

Battlelines: Journal of the Somme Association, Issues 14 (1998), 15 (1998), 16 (1999), 17 (2000)

Catholic Bulletin, 'Events of Easter Week, Miss Julia Grenan's Story of the Surrender', Vol. 7, pp. 396–8

Celebrating the Ulster Covenant 1912–2007, booklet, available on *http://quis. qub.ac.uk/ulster/Ulster_Covenant.pdf*

Fox, R. M. 'Typist with a Webley', *The Irish Press*, 9 March 1965

McMaster, Johnston in partnership with Maureen Hetherington, 'Remembering a Decade of Change and Violence in Ireland, 1921–1922', *Ethical and Shared Remembering: Commemoration in a New Context*, booklet (The Junction: Community Relations and Peace Building, 2011)

Steele, Seamus (ed.), *1916–1966: Belfast and Nineteen Sixteen, commemorative booklet* (National Graves Association, Belfast)

The Workers' Republic

Ulster Covenant Jubilee Committee, *Ulster Covenant Jubilee Souvenir 1912–1962*, booklet (Belfast, 1962)

Ulster-Scots Community Network, *For Valour – Ulster VCs of the Great War*, booklet (Belfast, n.d.)

Ulster-Scots Community Network, *Herstory III: profiles of a further eight Ulster-Scots women*, booklet (Belfast, n.d.)

Ulster-Scots Community Network, *Young Citizen Volunteers: 10th September 1912*, booklet (Belfast, n.d.)

Various, *Celebrating Belfast Women: A City Guide through Women's Eyes*, booklet (Women's Resource and Development Agency, Belfast, n.d.)

Newspapers:

Belfast News-Letter, The

Belfast Telegraph

Irish Independent

Irish News, The

Irish Press, The

Online Sources:

1901 & 1911 Census of Ireland, www.census.nationalarchives.ie

'1914 – Irish Volunteers during the Howth Gun Running', https://stairna heireann.net/2016/07/26/1914-irish-volunteers-during-the-howth-gun-running/

A Patriotic Socialist Republican: Winifred Carney, http://www.politics.ie/forum/history/18150-patriotic-socialist-republican-winifred-carney.html

An Phoblacht, www.anphoblacht.com

BBC – Voices 16 (Director and Series Producer Paul McGuigan) – contributions by historian and author, Margaret Ward, www.bbc.co.uk/programmes/articles/winifred-carney

Bunbury, Turtle, 'Death on Bachelor's Walk', http://www.turtlebunbury.com/history/history_irish/history_irish_bachelors_walk.htm

Byrne, Patrick, 'The Irish Republican Congress Revisited', www.connolly association.org.uk/about/the-irish-republican-congress-revisited/

Eddies Roll of Honour: Royal Irish Rifles – 15th Battalion, http://freepages. genealogy.rootsweb.ancestry.com/~econnolly/rohsdgw/royalirishrifles/ ririflesbat07.html

History of the Workers' Educational Association, James Connolly Society of Canada and the United States, www.marxists.org/archive/connolly

Labour History Review, online.liverpooluniversitypress.co.uk/loi/lhr

Milltown Cemetery, www.findagrave.com/cgi-bin/fg.cgi?page=dfl&GRid= 20142692

National Library of Ireland, http://www.nli.ie/1916/exhibition/en/content/ sevensignatories/

O'Shannon Snr, Cathal, 'The Man and his Work', www.siptu.ie/aboutsiptu/ history/jamesconnolly

South Belfast Friends of the Somme Association, www.belfastsomme.com

The Dictionary of Ulster Biography, www.newulsterbiography.co.uk

The Long, Long Trail – The British Army in the Great War, http://www. longlongtrail.co.uk

The National Archives of the UK, 'First World War and Army of Occupation Diaries', www.nationalarchives.gov.uk

The Wild Geese, www.thewildgeese.irish

UK, WWI, Service Medal and Award Rolls, www.forces-war-records.co.uk and www.ancestry.co.uk

Ulster History Circle, www.newulsterbiography.co.uk

Ulster-Scots Community Network, www.ulster-scots.com/publications

University of Limerick, Queen's University Belfast, and NUI Galway – joint website and commemoration app – 'Women in Ireland, 1912–22', www. ul.ie/wic

Walker, Lynda, 'Women and the 1916 Rising', http://www.communistparty ofireland.ie/unity/003war.html

'Winifred Carney – The Women of 1916', https://stairnaheireann.
net/2016/02/07/winifred-carney-typist-with-the-webley/

www.independent.ie/irish-news/1916/thinkers-talkers-doers/cathal-brugha-
a-very-complex-patriot-34267743.html

www.irelandsown.ie/

www.nidirect.gov.uk/proni/ulstercovenant/images

Winnie's Documents:

Letters of Winifred Carney to Miss O'Brien describing prison conditions
in England, 14 August and 16 October 1916, and a letter dated 6 November 1921: National Library of Ireland, William O'Brien Papers, MS
20766

PRONI, Military Archives, Winifred Carney, Home Affairs File HA/5/2108

James Connolly's letters to Winnie Carney are reproduced on pp. 529–42 of
Donal Nevin (ed.), *Between Comrades. James Connolly: Letters and Correspondence 1889–1916* (Gill & Macmillan, Dublin, 2007)

INDEX

MERCIER PRESS

IRISH PUBLISHER - IRISH STORY

We hope you enjoyed this book.

Since 1944, Mercier Press has published books that have been critically important to Irish life and culture. Books that dealt with subjects that informed readers about Irish scholars, Irish writers, Irish history and Ireland's rich heritage.

We believe in the importance of providing accessible histories and cultural books for all readers and all who are interested in Irish cultural life.

Our website is the best place to find out more information about Mercier, our books, authors, news and the best deals on a wide variety of books. Mercier tracks the best prices for our books online and we seek to offer the best value to our customers, offering free delivery within Ireland.

Sign up on our website to receive updates and special offers.

www.mercierpress.ie
www.facebook.com/mercier.press
www.twitter.com/irishpublisher

Mercier Press, Unit 3b, Oak House, Bessboro Rd, Blackrock, Cork, Ireland